Blücher

BLÜCHER

Blücher

The Uprising of Prussia Against Napoleon 1806-1815

ILLUSTRATED

Ernest F. Henderson

LEONAUR

Blücher
The Uprising of Prussia Against Napoleon 1806-1815
by Ernest F. Henderson

ILLUSTRATED

First published under the title
Blücher and the Uprising of Prussia Against Napoleon 1806-1815

Leonaur is an imprint of Oakpast Ltd

Copyright in this form © 2021 Oakpast Ltd

ISBN: 978-1-78282-984-3 (hardcover)
ISBN: 978-1-78282-985-0 (softcover)

http://www.leonaur.com

Publisher's Notes

Contents

To

His Excellency

Field-Marshal Von Xylander

This Life of Field-Marshal Von Blücher is Respectfully

Dedicated by the Author

Preface

Blücher is chiefly known to English readers as the man who came to Wellington's aid at Waterloo. The object of the present volume is to show that he had a separate existence of his own and performed other great deeds in the cause that are equally deserving of praise. Strange that he has never been made the subject of an English biography and that of his German lives none have been translated into English! The present work cannot pretend altogether to fill the gap, as the plan of the series, if I have understood it rightly, is to treat the movement as fully as the man.

I shall feel a certain satisfaction if I can succeed in establishing Blücher in his rightful position, as the peer of Wellington in all that concerns the overthrow of Napoleon. "You forget Wellington's Spanish campaigns," I shall be told. "You in turn forget," I shall answer, "that Blücher was the one progressive, inspiring element among the leaders of the allied armies from the year 1813 on." Without Blücher's decision to cross the Elbe at Wartenburg there would have been no Battle of Leipzig; without his cutting loose from Schwarzenberg in March, 1814, there would have been no closing in of the allies on Paris; without his brave endurance at Ligny in spite of the non-arrival of the promised reinforcements, Wellington would have been overwhelmed at Quatre Bras and there would have been no Waterloo.

No time could be more favourable than the present for writing a work on Blücher, seeing that it is the centenary of the great events in which he played a part. This fact has given the impetus to a whole new literature on the subject based very largely on new material from the war archives. In a splendid series of works all the campaigns have been treated objectively and critically and in such detail that we can follow the movements of each army literally from day to day.

I owe much to Binder von Kriegelstein's two volumes on the war with Austria in 1809; to von Caemmerer's and von Holleben's volumes on the spring campaign of 1813; to Friederich's three volumes on the fall campaign of 1813; to von Janson's two volumes on the campaign of 1814 in France, and to von Lettow-Vorbeck's two volumes on the campaign of 1815. All of these writers are high officers in the German or Austrian Armies, and their judgments have formed my last court of appeal in military matters. Purely literary works like those of Houssaye, for instance, who is an academician and not a military man, seem very puny in comparison.

Of great use to me has been a new life of Blücher in two volumes by von Unger; but the earlier lives by Blasendorf and by von Wigger are not altogether superseded. Von Unger gives a good working bibliography, which can be supplemented from the lists and the reviews that appear at intervals in the *Forschungen zur Brandenburg Preussischen Geschichte* and in the historical magazines.

I have consulted altogether many hundreds of books and articles that it would be useless to mention here without explaining just what I have gained from them and what I have discarded. Nothing is more misleading than such a bare list of authorities.

A winter in Munich enabled me to consult a great number of purely military journals that would not have been readily accessible elsewhere. It was the same with memoirs and contemporary correspondences; while the criticisms of books given in such journals were also often of value. I may mention especially; Streffleur's *Österreichische miitärische Zeitschrift*; the *Jahrbücher für die Armee und Marine*; the *Militärische Wochenblatt*; the *Allgemeine Militärzeitung*; not to speak of the regular *Zeitschriften* such as the *Preussische Jahrbücher*, the *Zeitschrift für Geschichtswissenschaft*, Westermann's *Monatshefte*, *Velhagen und Klasing's Monatshefte*, and the *Deutsche Rundschau*, all of which, and many more, have been made to contribute to this narrative. The dissertations, too, written for the attainment of the Doctor's degree at the different universities have frequently been of assistance.

The biographies of the great men of the time have furnished me with many details. Lehmann's *Scharnhorst* and his *Stein* supersede everything that has previously been written on either of those men; while Delbrück's *Gneisenau* is a perfect model of clearness and succinctness and has frequently been my guide when I began to get lost amid the mass of detail furnished by the larger works. Droysen's *Yorck* has not impressed me so favourably.

It will be seen that in these pages I have avoided controversy almost entirely. A latter opportunity seemed to be before me—to give a rounded account of a great hero and his work.

In conclusion I should like to say a word of thanks to Professor Horatio White of Harvard for drawing my attention to the folk-songs about Blücher and for most kindly looking up material on the subject.

E. F. H.

Boston, March 28, 1911.

CHAPTER 1

Prussia's Downfall

The history of Blücher is inseparably bound up with one cause: the liberation of Germany by the overthrow of Napoleon's colossal power. The limits of our narrative, accordingly, are the years 1806 and 1815, in the first of which Napoleon won the Battle of Jena over the Prussians; while in the last-named year Blücher brought about the decision at Waterloo.

Descended from noble ancestors, more than one of whom had followed arms as his profession, Blücher was born in December, 1742. It was the year which saw the end of Frederick the Great's first war with Maria Theresa. Blücher's father was of the branch of the family that had taken up its abode in Mecklenburg. He was scantily endowed with wealth but had sufficient influence to obtain for his six sons positions in almost as many different armies.

Gebhard Leberecht von Blücher, the subject of our present study, began his military career in the Swedish service at the age of sixteen, Sweden being at the moment one of Frederick the Great's many enemies in the Seven Years' War. Blücher's connection with the Swedish Army, however, terminated very suddenly; for he was captured in a skirmish, brought before the Prussian Colonel Belling, made a very favourable impression on that fiery officer, and, apparently without the least struggle of conscience, allowed himself to be given a post in Belling's own regiment. Blücher always, in later life, spoke of the episode with amusement and declared that the thought of it refreshed him whenever he was sad.

Belling proved a good friend to Blücher and exerted a strong influence over him. He helped the boy to procure the equipment necessary to a young hussar officer of that day—the fur-lined cloak, the gleaming sabre, the lace and fringes. He seems to have taught him, fur-

COLONEL BELLING

ther, his own strange mixture of piety and ferocity; for Belling would pray for his delinquent officers, would fall on his knees before every engagement, and would ride to battle with a hymn on his lips. But war he must have, and he was quoted as uttering the following prayer:

Thou seest, dear Heavenly Father, the sad plight of thy servant Belling. Grant him soon a nice little war that he may better his condition and continue to praise Thy name, Amen.

The final campaigns of the Seven Years' War were so defensive in their nature that Blücher had no opportunity greatly to distinguish himself, although he rapidly rose to the rank of first lieutenant. In the years that followed on the Peace of Hubertsburg he was stationed in various small garrison towns where we hear of him chiefly in connection with various matters that too often, even today, (1911), occupy the idle moments of gay young officers: drinking-bouts, duels, love affairs, and gambling. This would be scarcely worth mentioning but for the fact that even here he showed some of the characteristics that were to stand him in such good stead in later life. We involuntarily think of the campaign in France or of the Battle of Ligny when we read that losing a game never ruffled his calmness. A cotemporary writes:

He did not know the worth of money, losing it at play did not in the least affect his merry humour.

Blücher—he was then captain—saw active service again at the time when Frederick the Great was scheming to partition Poland, Prussian troops under one pretext or another being massed on the border of the doomed territory and even advanced into the interior. It was not open, honest warfare. The embittered inhabitants killed Prussians whenever they could do so undetected; and Blücher, for his part, here as throughout his whole military career, insisted on an eye for an eye and a tooth for a tooth. He went further in one case than his superiors approved and with consequences to himself that were to be very serious. It was a matter, practically, of torturing, in the hope of extorting a confession, a priest who was suspected of crime. But Fredrick the Great's policy at that special moment was to conciliate the Poles and make them consider him their benefactor.

Having been reported for misconduct Blücher was passed over at the next promotion and a first lieutenant, von Jägersfeld, given the place that he coveted; which so angered Blücher that he sent in his resignation to the king. The latter expressed his bad opinion of the whole regiment, and Blücher was cashiered and told that he might "go to the devil!"

A request for an investigation into the whole affair having been refused, Blücher, although passionately devoted to the military career saw himself debarred, apparently forever, from pursuing it, and was obliged at the age of almost thirty to seek another occupation. But a man with will and determination can succeed in very opposite pursuits. Blücher became a farmer. He married the daughter of Herr von Mehling, a landed proprietor of East Prussia, and received such valuable advice and aid from his father-in-law that, beginning in a small way with rented farms he was soon able to purchase his own estate in Pomerania.

Frederick the Great's anger against Blücher did not continue long, for we find him subsidising from a public fund, to the extent of ten thousand *thalers*, the improvement of the Gross Radow estate. But the king honestly considered that Blücher did not possess the qualities of which good officers are made. Again, and again Blücher applied for reinstatement in the army; he wrote to Frederick that it was not a matter of pecuniary advantage:

> But a most fiery longing to consecrate the best years of his life to His Majesty's service.

The old king was obdurate and remained obdurate to the time of his death, in 1786. It was many months later before Frederick William II. was moved by Blücher's pleadings to atone for what the latter considered a great injustice.

For sixteen years Blücher had now lived the life of a country gentleman; he was forty-five years old, and had been playing no inconsiderable part in the social and public life around him. One sees how strong was the vocation that made him eager to change this life of ease for one of strenuous effort.

The atonement made by Frederick William II. was very complete. Blücher was reinstated in his own former regiment and was given the same rank that he would naturally have held had he continued all the while in active service. It must have given him particular satisfaction now to find himself, once more, higher in rank than that same von Jägersfeld whose promotion had caused the original trouble.

Save for the bloodless campaign of 1787, in Holland, Blücher saw no active service until the coalition wars against the French Revolution. In the meantime, his duties were often of a most sordid and trivial kind. It was later counted among the great abuses in the Prussian Army that the head of a regiment or of a squadron was obliged to eke out his salary by mixing in matters of a purely commercial nature: to provide shirts, collars, hair-ribbons, and shoes for his men and reap what profit he could from the transaction; to draw emolument, too, from the cleaning of weapons and repairing of uniforms, from the fodder and physic of the horses, from the hiring of recruits and the granting of leave of absence to the soldiers. Another age was to invent the word "graft" for such dealings; as yet they were perfectly and openly permissible.

In 1793, Blücher was ordered to join with his squadron of which he was now colonel, the forces of Duke Ferdinand of Brunswick. He took part in a number of sieges and skirmishes which, though not of great importance in themselves afforded excellent training to the future opponent of Napoleon. In May, 1794, he achieved what he himself called the "goal of his desires," being advanced to the rank of major-general. He was already gaining a reputation for boldness and was likened to the famous General Ziethen of Frederick the Great's army. He was praised for the swiftness of his decisions, the energy of his actions, his indefatigability. We are told by a cotemporary that:

> From drilling his squadron, which was quartered at a distance, he would proceed to a hare hunt or a gay dinner and that same night, perhaps, to a surprise attack on the enemy, or to the laying of an ambush for the next morning. Having temporarily silenced the enemy he would enjoy himself at Frankfort gambling or going to the theatre.

The games Blücher played were, some of them, forbidden by law; and we have it on good authority that he "indulged in them to a truly immoderate degree." What Blücher really craved was excitement; and, when, later, he was afforded a sufficiency of that in the Napoleonic wars we find him able altogether to renounce his gambling for many months at a time.

Fate meanwhile had in store for him occupations other than military. The Peace of Basel, concluded in 1795, banned Prussia behind a line of demarcation and the result for her was ten years of ignominious neutrality and inactivity, during which Napoleon was allowed to act as though all the rest of Germany belonged to him. Three times during this period he vented his wrath on Austria, chastising her each time more severely and forcing her, at Campo Formio, at Luneville, and at Pressburg, to cede more and more territory. With the consent both of Prussia and of Austria he annexed to France the possessions of German princes on the left bank of the Rhine, promising indemnity, indeed, but at Germany's expense! This well-known transaction forms one of the most sordid pages in history. Prussia—it was in 1802—graciously accepted a slice of the German bishopric of Münster which was five times as great in extent as her own lost portion of Cleves. The inhabitants were bitterly opposed to the change.

Blücher, since 1795, had been in command of a part of the so-called Army of Observation designed to protect Prussia's neutrality. To him, now, was entrusted the task of occupying the new province. On August 3, 1802, he marched in with his troops and took possession of the city of Münster. At the same time Baron Stein was made president of the organisation commission; and the two men, who in the larger affairs of Prussia were destined to bear the same relation of political reformer and military executive, lived together under one roof.

Blücher's position as head of the armed force in a land where the Prussians were regarded as usurpers—as a matter of fact the diet of Ratisbon had thrown a shimmer of legality over the transaction—was a difficult one; but he acquitted himself of his task with great skill and success, exerting authority here and pacifying there, until after six months the so-called estates joined with the ecclesiastical authorities in asking the Prussian king to make Blücher their governor on the ground of his knowledge of local affairs, his honesty and uprightness, his amiability and charitableness, his cleverness and penetration, and his ability to keep the peace between soldiers and civilians. As Blücher never again occupied such a position—the request of course was granted—it is interesting to have this testimony as to his good qualities, and it may serve to correct the impression that he was nothing but a dashing soldier.

He was now head of the armed forces not only of Westphalia and East Friesland but also of Prussian Cleves. It was a good vantage ground from which to observe the designs of the French, which filled him with the greatest alarm. When the French General Mortier, in 1803, occupied Hanover, Blücher was so outraged that he hastened to Berlin only to find to his great astonishment that Mortier's move was looked upon with indifference. Blücher himself declared later:

All the misfortunes of Germany and of the Prussian monarchy are traceable to this event at the moment so insignificant.

Eager to embroil Prussia with England, Napoleon offered to cede to her Hanover; and the Prussian court weakly accepted the proposal and allied itself with France even after the troops of the latter power had deliberately violated Prussian territory. While the matter was pending, war was so imminent that the order to mobilise the Westphalian troops had actually been issued, and Blücher had declared that the moment of meeting the French as enemies would be the happiest of his life.

Prussia had sold her soul for Hanover and, as a direct result, became involved in a war with England which caused great harm to her own commerce. One can imagine the general rage and indignation, now, when it was learned that, after all, Napoleon contemplated restoring Hanover to England. Beside himself with indignation, Blücher in July, 1806, took it upon himself to write to Frederick William:

France means honestly by no power, least of all by Your Royal Majesty, who forms the sole remaining obstacle to her policy of conquest and subjugation in Germany.... All faithful subjects of Your Royal Majesty, all true Prussians, and especially the army, have felt and still feel the indignity of these French proceedings; and all wish soon, right soon, to avenge with blood the nation's injured honour. Whoever represents France's conduct to Your Royal Majesty in any other light, whoever advises Your Royal Majesty to continue making concessions, and remaining at peace with this nation is either very indolent, very short sighted, or else has been bought with French gold.

Here we find Blücher urging and counselling the very war that was to be the beginning of all Prussia's troubles. Was he entirely in the wrong? Not at all. His advice was for war instantly and not for war a month or two later. He wrote:

Each day gained in declaring war against France, is of the greatest advantage to Your Royal Majesty; for from hour to hour the French emperor strengthens his prestige, his influence, his usurped power, improves the organisation of his army, procures more tributary kings and princes, by means of oppression extorts new resources. One successful battle and allies, money and supplies, are ours from every corner of Europe.

Boyen wrote in his memoirs:

If Cato once had his unvarying formula for the destruction

PRUSSIAN OFFICERS AND SOLDIERS IN 1786

of Cartilage just so the expression 'We must fight France' had become a praiseworthy habit with old Blücher.

In August the king mobilised his troops, but in a half-hearted way. He never could boldly face a situation. He wrote now to Blücher, who would have to bear the first brunt of the war:

> To be sure I do not yet believe that there is any intention on the part of the French to undertake hostilities against us.

Blücher is told to be on the alert but without letting the French in his neighbourhood note the least unfriendliness in his conduct or giving them the slightest cause for suspicion—recommendations utterly imposable of fulfilment if the mobilisation was to be carried on with any energy. Blücher's answer to the king was dutiful; but to the Duke of Brunswick he vehemently expressed his hope that steps, offensive in their character, should at once be taken. Otherwise he saw no prospect of anything but shame and disgrace.

War was declared in the last days of September, 1806; but there was no thought of conducting an offensive campaign. Then came the downfall! On the 14th of October, the Prussians were defeated simultaneously at Jena and at Auerstädt, but so crushingly, so completely, that by the very next day Napoleon could levy an enormous fine on the Prussian provinces. Within exactly a week Berlin was in his hands.

Never had a whole situation of affairs been more completely misunderstood! Never had self-confidence been more misplaced. Countess Schwerin, the wife of the king's adjutant writes:

> Unconscious of danger, the army in all the glory and order of a grand parade, went to meet its destruction. Unconscious, too, did the leaders seem; for the enemy encircled us round about and no one had any news of him. In Naumberg when already outflanked by the French the court continued to lead the careless life of Charlottenburg and Potsdam.

In both of the battles at Jena and at Auerstädt, the same mistakes were made; the field was badly chosen, the reserves were held back too long. Both defeats were regular routs. Countess Schwerin writes, of Jena:

> As night fell, the *gardes du corps* came on to the heights. . . . The first glance across the plain showed all the horrors of a defeat in progress. Everywhere wavering, yielding battalions—retreating,

disorganised squadrons.

Gneisenau writes of that mad midnight rush for Magdeburg when the two beaten armies came upon each other in their flight:

Those were horrors! Rather death a thousand times than live through it again. . . . Never did army sink into such disruption.

Auerstädt was the more galling of the two defeats, because here the Prussians actually outnumbered the French. Boyen writes:

It was a regular achievement to lose the battle, everything there was in our favour.

Napoleon announced in his famous 22nd bulletin that the fine large Prussian Army had vanished like an autumn mist before the rising of the sun; and he notified his friend and ally the *Sultan* that Prussia had ceased to exist. A cotemporary, (Scheffner), writes:

I still am uncertain whether I am awake or dreaming; that we should have been beaten does not surprise me, but that in one single day we should have been struck so utterly dead goes beyond my powers of comprehension.

Gneisenau, whose future services to the state were to show that he was no mere idle complainer, writes bitterly at this juncture:

It may still be possible under certain conditions to save the monarchy; but the shame of the army annihilated through misfortunes due to its own fault can never be wiped away. Scarcely a trace of spirit is left in our officers. Some have purposely allowed themselves to be taken prisoners and numbers offered to surrender when they still might have escaped.

Among those who thus surrendered, deceived indeed by false asseverations of the French, was Hohenlohe, who commanded the largest remnant of the troops from Auerstädt. Blücher, in the last-named battle, had commanded but a few squadrons of cavalry. After his men had been seized with the general panic, he was doing his best to rally them when his horse was shot under him. Having managed to extricate himself he made his way to the king and implored him to let him lead the *Gendarmes*, one of the *élite* regiments, into the thick of the fight. Permission had already been given; but just as Blücher was about to sound the signal for attack there came a peremptory message that he was to withdraw the regiment and employ it to cover the retreat of Hohenlohe.

This, Blücher successfully did; successfully, too, he accomplished an independent detour around the Harz Mountains for the purpose of saving some artillery. At the time of Hohenlohe's surrender at Prenzlau he was a few marches in the rear awaiting reinforcements.

It was then that for the first time his name became known throughout Germany; for his brave retreat, if we except Gneisenau's defence of Colberg, was the brightest episode of the campaign. Even the knowledge that after Hohenlohe's surrender his own tiny force was alone, hemmed in between two French armies, did not daunt him, and he fought his way through to Lübeck, which was a fortified town. It was a free Hansa town and opened its gates to him most unwillingly; but the walls were hastily manned and the gates guarded.

By a fatal error of the young Duke of Brunswick, however, the enemy gained admittance, and here in Lübeck was played the last act in the little tragedy. The French commands, Bernadotte—whom we shall meet again, not as a French commander and not as Bernadotte but as His Royal Highness the Crown Prince of Sweden, fighting on the German side—writes that "every square, every street was a field of battle." Scharnhorst, who had been Blücher's mainstay during the retreat was taken prisoner.

Blücher himself, with a few cavalry men, escaped from the city and turned at bay in the open country to the north. Here at last he surrendered—but honourably, even proudly—making conditions under threat of fighting to the bitter end, such as are not often accorded to one in his plight. He was allowed to write in the formal act of surrender that the reason for his ceasing to make resistance was that food and ammunition were gone, and also to stipulate that the captured Scharnhorst should be released. Of all the blame that was thrown broadcast in those dark days none fell upon Blücher. He had even accomplished some good, for while the French were occupied with him the *Tsar* was busy preparing to make resistance in East Prussia. Napoleon himself wrote angrily:

These damned fugitives hold back nearly half of my army!

Blücher was exchanged for the French General Victor, but by an unfortunate decision of the king was placed in command of the forces that were reorganising in Pomerania and thus removed from what subsequently proved to be the only scene of activity, East Prussia.

In order to appreciate the intensity of the hatred inspired by Na-

SCHULENBURG

poleon and the depths of demoralisation to which he reduced Prussia it is necessary to follow him to Berlin. As his vanguard under Davoust entered the city the inhabitants behaved, according to Boyen, as one would expect only those unfortunates to act who had been deprived of their manliness. The proclamation of the governor, Schulenburg, who acted on his own responsibility without even having been ordered to capitulate, has become a classic:

> The king has lost a battle; the first duty of the citizens is to keep quiet!

Schulenburg's own memoirs have but recently, (1911), been published and one passage from them characterises him only too well:

> I have already said that I have firmness and decision; but strangely enough I show a certain weakness towards my household and my servants . . . a contradiction I can only explain by longing for peace and quiet and my desire to avoid unpleasant sensations.

Unfortunately, the same longing for peace and quiet possessed the commanders of all the chief fortresses of Prussia. As one after the other, with practically no resistance, they surrendered in rapid succession, the land found itself absolutely naked and defenceless, although according to all calculations the enemy should have been kept at bay for years. Gneisenau wrote:

> Oh, oh, our generals and commanders, these will be strange lines in history!

And then the humiliation of Napoleon's reception in Berlin! It has only been surpassed in our own day by the manner in which a deposed Chinese emperor *kowtowed* to the dowager who supplanted him. When Napoleon reached Prussia's capital the chief magistrates as well as the king's ministers received him obsequiously at the Brandenburg gate and placed their services at his disposal. The royal family, with the queen in a raging fever, had fled to Königsberg. As the conqueror entered with his marshals the bells of the city were rung and the cannon fired a salute. Many actually greeted him as a saviour and benefactor.

In the palace of the Prussian kings a special throne was set up for him and the Prussian officials took a formal oath to "execute all the orders of the French and neither to correspond nor to have any other intercourse with their enemies." Reflect that the chief enemy of the French was their own king whom they were now denying! In order to placate Napoleon busts of Frederick William as well as of the *Tsar* were removed from places where he would be likely to see them, while the very postmen tore their badges from their arms to spare the conqueror the sight of the Prussian eagle!

Napoleon at once assumed control of the Berlin press. The *Preussische Hausfreund* and the *Freimüthige* were suppressed because of their general tone; the *Telegraph* was taken over bodily and even went so far as to publish scandalous calumnies against Queen Louise.

The Prussian people and their royal house were not merely to be punished, they were to be utterly humiliated, to be shown that the conqueror had set his foot upon their neck. On the top of the Brandenburg Gate, visible the whole length of the noble Unter den Linden, was a figure of Victory with four great horses to her chariot. This group Napoleon had lowered and sent off to Paris; and a great bare projecting iron stake was left as a daily reminder to the Berliners of how all their glory had departed from them. The sword of Frederick the Great was appropriated; while, at Rossbach, the monument erected in memory of Frederic's great victory over the French was overthrown.

Is it any wonder that in many hearts, Blücher's among them, hatred of Napoleon became a holy passion, a new religion? The poet Kleist voiced this sentiment more eloquently, though not more sincerely, than many another. He calls the Corsican:

> The most to be abominated man; the beginning of all evil and the end of all good; a sinner whom human speech is too mild properly to accuse and who at the day of Judgment will take away the breath of the angels; a parricide risen from hell, creeping round in the temple of nature, and shaking at all her foundation columns!

Napoleon had proclaimed:

> Prussia shall learn, that while it is easy to win lands and peoples through the great nation's, friendship, her enmity is more terrible than the storms of ocean.

This was now to prove literally true. At Tilsit Frederick William was not merely stripped of more than half of his provinces but Napoleon insisted on inserting in the peace treaty that he owed what was left to the intercession of the *Tsar*. The districts west of the Elbe went to form the kingdom of Westphalia for Jerome Bonaparte; the Polish provinces to form the duchy of Warsaw for Frederick Augustus, King of Saxony. Even the Tsar Alexander who had been Frederick William's ally until after Friedland consented to take a convenient little slice, the district of Bialystock.

Frederick William's address to his lost provinces reaches the heights of pathos;

> That which centuries and worthy forefathers, that which treaties, love, and confidence once bound together must now be severed. Fate commands, the father parts from his children; no fate, no power can tear your memory from the hearts of me and mine.

And the peasants of Mark wrote back:

> Our hearts almost broke when we read your message of farewell; so truly as we are alive, it is not your fault!

Not only Prussia but the German nation had become utterly disrupted. The rulers of Württemberg, Bavaria, and Saxony had accepted royal crowns from Napoleon's hands and were grateful for his permission to despoil their neighbours on all sides. Bavarian newspapers hailed him as the greatest benefactor of all Germans. When he came through Saxony the walls of the towns were placarded with greetings to the first man of his century, to the hero of heroes, to the immortal one. The University of Leipzig when he went there after his Erfurt Congress in 1808, formally presented him with a chart of the skies to show that it had for all time named the stars in Orion's belt "stars of Napoleon!" The words of the Psalmist: "The Heavens declare Thy glory, O Lord!" were no longer to apply exclusively to the Creator.

NAPOLEON IN THE TOMB OF FREDERICK THE GREAT

CHAPTER 2

Prussia's Regeneration

What were the chief causes that had brought about the unprecedented catastrophe in Prussia? First and foremost, the weak character of the king. Frederick William began to reign at a crisis where it was a case of God help his subjects were the head of the state to show either want of firmness, or want of judgment. His personal kindliness of disposition, his morality, his good intentions, and his real desire for the happiness of all around him could never serve as a substitute. His faults were of the most fatal kind. Obstinate, easily led, and as easily offended, Frederick William's life was made up of doubts, scruples, and hesitations. He was always asking advice but had no discrimination as to who were the best advisers. Strong men intimidated him; he never for instance felt at home with Blücher.

A little book, *Vertraute Briefe*, published already in 1807, the year of Tilsit, praises Frederick William as one of the most humane kings that ever lived but declares that the endeavour to do everything through love prevents him from taking decisive measures. He is like a physician operating for cancer who throws away the knife because of the cries of the patient:

> Then the poison eats in and all at once the whole body is affected. So, with the Prussian state.

The same writer speaks of the king's "too moral" point of view, of his inability to decide quickly, of his wish always to hold consultations. Then follows a surprising conclusion:

> He is the direct opposite of a tyrant and ought to be King of England. Then there would be peace in the world!

At a critical moment in the campaign of 1806, Frederick William was warned by old Countess Voss that he really ought to know more about the movements of the enemy, and his answer was wholly characteristic: to gain such knowledge one would have to employ spies, and with such people he would have nothing to do; they were good enough for a Napoleon! In his own account of the Battle of Auerstädt (*Deutsche Rundschau*, vol. 101) the king declares that the enemy's numbers and whereabouts were unknown, but *naïvely* admits:

> Although probably the enemy had pretty correct previous information of our approach and of our strength.

Lombard, the cabinet councillor who was accused of having inspired Frederick William's timid polity in 1805, wrote in exculpation of himself:

> Do you know the king? My whole justification lies in this question. How would you have set to work to induce a monarch to make war who abominated the very thought of it and who, which is even worse, doubted his own capacity to lead? That is the great secret of our indecision and of all our perplexities. The Prussian monarchy differs in its organisation from other states: with us in war-time all branches of the administration centre in the army. The king therefore may not entrust the command to another; it would be the end of him were he not to appear at the head of his troops. Yet this king, whom no one reveres and respects more than I, was unfortunately not a born general. He has long known as well as any one that he would have to draw his sword whether he liked it or no; but always he has given in to himself, always he has flattered himself that some catastrophe independent of his own decisions would solve the difficulty. At last, as the troubles rolled up and the whole land with one voice demanded a change. . . . . he yielded, but quite against his will, of that I can assure you."(*Die Grenzboten*, 1906, 4.)

It is pitiful to see how a man like Napoleon could turn Frederick William around his finger. A kind word from Paris would make him shun his warlike advisers and even demobilise his forces. It is now known (*Militärwochenblatt*, 1907), that there was a moment in the Battle of Auerstädt when the calling up of reserves that were close at hand might have meant victory, but that a letter from Napoleon delivered on the field threw Frederick William into one of his old agonies of indecision.

FREDERICK WILLIAM III.

Why shed so much blood? to what end? I have been your friend these six years. . . . Why let our subjects be slaughtered? . . . Your Majesty will be vanquished, will have risked the repose of your days and the existence of your subjects without the shadow of a pretext. (R, von Lilienstern, *Bericht eines Augenzeugen, Tübingen,* 1809, ii.)

The favourable moment for calling up the reserves was allowed to pass; the battle was lost. After the battle Frederick William still cherished hopes of Napoleon's clemency and foolishly revealed the whole weakness of Prussia in a letter to him. (*Anon.: Preussen in den Jahren, 1806-7.*)

Apart from the weak character of the king there were inherent defects in the army itself. A cotemporary writes in 1805:

Outwardly, much shimmer, glitter and polish—behind it, worm-eaten wood! (*Die Grenzboten,* 1906.)

The manner of recruiting was wrong, the material bad, and the system of discipline one of intimidation, constraint, and suspicion. Every night officers had to stand ready to pursue those who might attempt to desert; camion stood loaded so as instantly to give the signal for the chase, while even in the barracks the more trusted soldiers had to spy on the new recruits and, if the latter had been acting suspiciously, were empowered to lock up their boots.

The punishments were degrading to the last degree. Scharnhorst, who was to do more than any other man to remedy the evils, tells us that any sixteen-year-old ensign might flog an old soldier half to death for carelessness in drill. For more serious offences there was the running of the gauntlet of two hundred men armed with salted whips. The culprit's hands were bound, his feet fettered, and a ball of lead was placed in his mouth lest he should bite his tongue off in his agony. The sight at times was too horrible for description. Boyen complained that such public putting to shame forever placed the hall-mark of a rogue upon the offender.

The armies that fought at Jena and Auerstädt were composed of men who did not respect themselves because no respect was shown to them. The officers were often proud, arrogant, and incapable, and many of them far too old to be capable of fulfilling the duties of their positions. After the Duke of Brunswick's death, the one who should have seized the command, Möllendorf, was eighty-one years of age! Frederick the Great was indirectly to blame for this; in his will he had urged that none of his faithful old officers should be dismissed. Instead they were placed in command of the fortresses and were given to understand that their posts were sinecures.

Everything about the Prussian Army was complicated and cumbersome. Each officer was in the habit of taking with him on the march from one to five extra horses loaded with articles for his comfort: not only a tent but a bed, a table, and a chair. There were 32,000 extra horses with the army that marched out to Jena. Blücher had already handed in a report "on lessening the baggage of the army and removing other hindrances to the mobility of the troops." But the military authorities, the "Upper War Bureau," had answered pedantically that "it was better to have the march combined with a little more fatigue and then beat the enemy more surely than to march more easily and be defeated."

Schulenburg, the man who was so anxious that the Berliners should keep quiet, had formed a special argument against the lessening of the number of horses. The nobility, he declared would be offended and humiliated by any change; the well-to-do would quit the service and those who remained would lose a part of their self-respect. The whole body of officers would fall in the estimation of the common man "and thus the finest ornament and greatest advantage of our army would be lost." The strong feeling of caste is exemplified in the remark of another officer: "A Prussian noble does not go on foot!"

This lightening of the baggage was only one of the reforms that Blücher had vainly tried to effect. In a report drawn up in 1805, he had recommended making military service compulsory for all, shortening the length of time the soldiers should be obliged to remain with the army, giving better pay and better treatment to each individual. Prussia after the Peace of Tilsit was indeed a stricken state; but the germs that were fermenting within her were germs of progress, not of dissolution, and her rise within eight years to a proud and commanding position seems almost magical.

It reminds us of how Frederick the Great, surprised and all but overwhelmed at Chotusitz, managed to form his troops in line of battle while actually under the fire of the enemy, marched them up the hill on which the Austrians had entrenched themselves, and gained a splendid victory. Just so Prussia, maimed and mutilated, with all the rottenness of her old institutions suddenly laid bare and her faith shaken in all her old divinities, with 150,000 Frenchmen quartered on her territory and more ready, if need be, to fall upon her, saddled with an indemnity that only grew larger the more of it was paid, rose from the very depths, shook herself free from the slime that adhered to her, created for herself a new form of government and a new army, and not only won back what she had lost but paved the way to undreamed of glory both for herself and for a united Germany.

The first step was to induce the king to rid himself of the advisers who had helped to bring things to such a pass. Baron Stein, the head of the reformers, did not hesitate to brand publicly the king's favourites Lombard, Haugwitz, and Beyme as shameless and inefficient, as liars and *roués*. Himself made prime minister and virtual dictator as the one man who could still save the state, Stein practically put an end to the old cabinet *régime*.

The next step was to pay enough of the war indemnity to make the French consent to leave Prussian territory. Napoleon seemed insatiable. His original demand of 73,000,000 *francs* soon rose to 154,000,000 and, by a sort of jugglery, after 140,000,000 had been paid and revenues to the amount of 60,000,000 had been seized, the amount due was still placed at 140,000,000! Napoleon declared himself in 1809, that he had drawn a full billion from Prussia, which included of course the support of his troops. We must remember that the whole population of Prussia at this time was but about four and a half million people.

The economies practised would have seemed impossible a little earlier. The burden fell on one and all and the hardships endured, as may well be imagined, gave nourishment to the ever-growing hatred of Napoleon. Salaries and pensions were cut to the lowest figure; and even charitable institutions like the deaf and dumb asylum and the school for the blind had their funds withdrawn. All the innocent pleasures that add so much to the German's enjoyment of life—the opera, the royal orchestra, and the like—were abandoned.

Into the financial and legislative measures which made it possible for Prussia to hold her head above water we cannot be expected to enter here. The results were wonderful considering all the difficulties. The reforms, too, had an object greater than the mere momentary release from a burden of debt—the elevation of the people. The work was taken up all along the line.

From the pulpit and the lecture-desk Schleiermacher and Fichte thundered their denunciations and pleaded for a change of heart. They had to choose their words cautiously, for they were surrounded by French spies. Fichte, especially, must have laughed in his sleeve at the

ON THE RAFT AT TILSIT

censors who were unable to penetrate the philosophical crust with which he concealed his patriotic utterances. He hammered into his hearers the idea of personal responsibility:

> That no man and no God can help us, but that we alone must help ourselves if, indeed, help be still possible.

He scourged those who refused to fight for the national cause, or to give freely for the national defence, or to perform their other duties to their communities. He gave them positive recommendations: to read German history, especially of the time when Germany was great and powerful, to educate their children in republican principles and also in such manual occupations as would make them useful citizens.

What Fichte did for the mind, Jahn, the inventor of gymnastics, did for the body, training a race of young patriots to resist oppression.

Meanwhile Stein's celebrated edicts had gone forth. Serfdom was abolished, land-tenure and feudalism divorced, class distinctions prohibited:

> From the date of this decree, (October, 1807), there can arise no further relation of subjection, neither through birth nor through marriage nor through the voluntary acceptance of a condition of servitude, nor through contract.

And again:

> After St. Martin's day, 1810, there are none but free people.

Stein reorganised the whole system of state administration. The king was induced to give up a part of his prerogative and appoint a prime minister to whom the other ministers were to report. The eight departments were overhauled, the greatest changes being made in the war department.

Stein's fall from power is familiar to all who read history. Had he not committed an act of incomprehensible imprudence he might have gone much farther and even achieved a parliament. But an intercepted letter, not even written in cipher, spoke of nourishing the feeling of hostility to Napoleon, of spreading the news of the Spanish insurrection, and of joining with the patriots in Westphalia and Hesse-Cassel. The letter was published by Napoleon in the *Moniteur* and the French emperor did not rest until Stein was an exile with a price set on his head.

Meanwhile the reform was under way that was to have the most immediate and tangible results: the reorganisation of the army. Blücher, still commanding on the shore of the Baltic, took the liveliest interest in the proceedings, and his voice even had some influence on the deliberations. For Gneisenau, who had been appointed a member of the reorganisation commission, came to visit him and to learn his views as to what should be done.

The end and aim of the reform was to raise the self-respect of the soldier and make the army, above all, one of patriots. Strange to say more blindness, more stubborn attachment to the old order of things was met with here than in any of the other reforms. The organisation commission, although headed by Scharnhorst, one of the most single-minded and ardent of all the patriots, contained members like Massenbach, Lottum, and Bronikowski who were still steeped in the old conservatism.

It is strange to see men of the nineteenth century still clinging to the old idea that members of the nobility possessed a higher sense of honour than members of the common herd and should therefore have an exclusive right to be officers; still maintaining that the only way to keep soldiers in order was to make them afraid. Outside of the commission, too, there was much opposition to the reform. Yorck, who later commanded under Blücher and was one of his bravest generals, could never forget that he himself was a nobleman and that the reformers wished to take away his privileges. He once said to Prince William of Prussia:

If Your Royal Highness take away my rights and those of my children, on what do your own rest?

Yorck was jubilant when he heard that Stein had been disgraced, and he spoke of Scharnhorst and his adherents as a viper brood that would one day dissolve in their own poison.

Scharnhorst was a quiet man but he was possessed of immense force and determination; and he proceeded to get rid of those members of the reorganisation commission who were out of sympathy with its objects and to fill their places with strong, progressive men. It was now that Gneisenau was called in; there were also Grolman of whom Niebuhr said in 1813: "Such a man I have never yet seen; he would be the proper commander for Germany;" Götzen, who had done wonders in organising defence in Silesia, and Boyen who was eventually to succeed Scharnhorst as Minister of War. The reorganisation committee became so powerful a body that the king himself rarely ventured to oppose its decisions.

Frederick William had been forced by his latest convention with Napoleon to promise that his army should not exceed the number of 42,000 men—a galling engagement to have to make but one that, at all events, made speedy reform more possible. A higher standard was at once established both for officers and men, and the old system of recruiting, that amounted to the hiring of mercenaries who had no loyalty whatever to the cause, was abolished.

One of the prime necessities was to discover and punish those who had been chiefly responsible for the recent disasters. Every surrender, whether of a fortress or of a troop was subjected to a rigid investigation; every officer who had been captured was to show under what circumstances this had occurred and to bring his witnesses; every general—and even Blücher was included—was to send in his defence in writing. In Blücher's case the special investigating committee reported literally:

> No proof of neglect of duty can be found against the commanding general; consequently, this surrender belongs to the small number of those that were justifiable.

Those whom the investigating committee did not exonerate were regularly court-martialled; and punishment was meted out to all who had shown want of courage, who had surrendered when they might have escaped, who had returned to their homes when they should have rallied to what was left of the army or who had pretended to be ill in order that they might fall into the hands of the enemy. It was counted as an extenuation if one who had been guilty of faults in the first part of the campaign had conducted himself well during the operations in East Prussia.

A burdensome provision was that any officer who sought reinstatement in the army should first prove that he had previously done his duty. All felt that for the commanders who had so hastily surrendered Prussia's strong fortresses to the enemy no punishment could be too severe. When no recent law could be found to cover their case it was determined to go back to a law of the Great Elector which provided very clearly that surrendering, except in case of extreme need, should be considered a capital crime. Seven high officers were then condemned to death; one escaped and, for the rest, the punishment was changed to life imprisonment. Even this penalty was a mere concession to public opinion.

The king in his heart must have known that the ultimate blame rested with himself. He had failed to repair or to provision the fortresses, although his attention had been drawn to the matter; he had installed as commanders worn out old men; he had intended that the positions should be sinecures. Of this, in one case at least, most positive proof was furnished. One of those convicted, Romberg, produced a note in which the king told him he would be given the governorship of Stettin because, as his strength was declining, it would "undoubtedly be agreeable to him to come into quieter circumstances."

The statistics of the work of the investigating committee show one remarkable result. A large proportion of the lower officers cleared themselves entirely and lived to cover themselves with glory in the War of Liberation; but of 143 generals which the army counted in 1806, only two, Blücher and Tauentzien, commanded in 1813.

Under the new *régime* the whole conception of the officer's duty changed. He was appointed because of merit, not because of high birth; he was to be an example to the soldiers in the matter of patiently bearing the fatigues of the march; he was to go on foot and carry his knapsack on his back; he was always to remember his "honourable calling, that of leader and educator of an estimable part of the nation."

The commanders are to see that their subordinates "neither treat their soldiers roughly nor permit the insults that are still occasionally the custom." The cruellest of the penalties were entirely abolished. Gneisenau had been strong on that point and had published in a Königsberg newspaper an article entitled "Freedom of the Back." Boyen, too, had declared publicly that the best disciplined army would be the one that had the most humane laws and regulations. Detention in a fortress now took the place of running the gauntlet and there began to be talk of rewards as well as of punishments.

Grolman wished it introduced as a custom in the churches that the names of all who had fallen in war or had died of their wounds should be written up in gold letters; that their wives should be placed in the front seats; that the seating of the soldiers should be according to the degree of their bravery in the field and that those who had shown any cowardice should be given "the lowest place in the church, far back against the wall." The idea was extravagant of course but that a man like Grolman could cherish it shows how the whole conception of what the army was and what it might be expected to accomplish had changed.

Of what use, one may ask, was all this enthusiasm for military reform when by the terms of the convention concluded with Napoleon in September, 1808, the army might not, for ten years to come, number more than 42,000 men? What could such a handful accomplish against Napoleon's hundreds of thousands? Scharnhorst, especially, who had become an expert in ruses, had laboured with this problem and had found the solution. While outwardly conforming to Napoleon's conditions he nevertheless long eluded the vigilance of the French. The numbers were always the same, but not the men!

A considerable portion of the youth of the land gained at least the rudiments of military training by spending a month in camp while those already trained were given leave of absence. Those who came for this short time worked doubly hard at the simple tasks assigned them: to move at command, to load quickly, and to fire straight. It meant a great deal to them, this training, for every one of them had come with the grim determination to hasten the day of reckoning with the oppressor!

CHAPTER 3

Austria's Struggle for Liberty

Napoleon could never have acquired such supremacy in Germany had Austria and Prussia worked in harmony. The fault, it must be confessed, was chiefly Prussia's; for from 1795, to 1806, she had maintained a selfish and undignified neutrality that had brought her some commercial prosperity to be sure, but that finally left her friendless and alone at Napoleon's mercy. She had, during those eleven years, renounced all voice in German affairs. Without a murmur of opposition, she had allowed the head of the House of Hapsburg to proclaim himself Emperor of Austria and the Rhenish states to form a confederation under the open protectorate of Napoleon—which last step had brought about the dissolution of the thousand-year-old Holy Roman Empire.

She had not retaliated even at the outrageous violation of German territory involved in the seizure of the Duke of Enghien, taken from his own house, at Ettenheim in Baden, by a band of French soldiers, who approached under cover of the night. The duke, Napoleon maintained, had headed a conspiracy; he was dragged to Vincennes, tried before a court-martial, sentenced, and shot at the side of his own open grave. The incident had, it is true, saddened the sensitive heart of Frederick William III. and made him a little less eager for the projected alliance with Napoleon, but the bait of Hanover had finally overcome his scruples.

Indignation at Enghien's death was one of the causes that had induced the Tsar Alexander of Russia to join the third coalition against Napoleon. The war that followed had been more than humiliating to Austria which was in no condition to fight. Those "gentlemen in Vienna," as Pitt once complained, were always "one year, one army, and one idea behindhand." After the surrender of Mack at Ulm an

Austrian officer himself had written:

> The shame that oppresses us, the filth that covers us can never be wiped away.

The outcome of the Battle of Austerlitz, finally, and the joining of Napoleon by Prussia had driven Austria into concluding the Peace of Pressburg, (Dec. 26, 1805), by which she divested herself in France's favour of thousands of square miles of territory, of 3,500,000 inhabitants and a yearly revenues to the amount of 14,000,000 *guldens*.

Austria had stood this curtailment of her power for nearly four years and, under Stadion and Prince Charles, had been busy with internal political and military reforms not unlike those which in Prussia were undertaken by Stein and Scharnhorst. Then the cup of wrath ran over. Grief for the lost territory, vexation at having no voice in European affairs, anger at the way in which Napoleon deposed legitimate kings—the King of Spain was the emperor's brother—horror at the indignities shown to the Pope: all this had driven Austria to desperation. If only she could have waited until Prussia's reorganisation was complete!

Austria's decision had been hastened by Napoleon's Oriental policy, by the danger that the powers under France's immediate influence would completely surround the domains of the Hapsburgs and isolate them from the rest of Europe. Was the fear merely illusory? Did not Napoleon's plan to divide Turkey between France and Russia, his promise of Moldavia and Wallachia to the *Tsar*, his demand of a French right of way to Dalmatia all point in that direction?

There were indeed different ways of reading the signs of the times and there was a peace party as well as a war party at Vienna. Both were headed by persons of great influence. The empress herself was in favour of war and laboured for it unceasingly until success at last crowned her efforts. There was much truth in the complaint made by the Frankfort *Journal* that women and coxcombs had drawn up the plans of campaign and that all that remained for the authorities was to sanction measures passed at some levee.

The moment for war, the spring of 1809, seemed well chosen. As a result of her reforms Austria was better equipped than ever before; Napoleon on the other hand was finding the revolt in Spain more serious than he had anticipated and had felt obliged to withdraw some of his forces from Germany and to replace others by regiments formed of raw recruits. It was one of the chief arguments of the war party that

EMPEROR FRANCIS II.

nothing could be more unwelcome to Napoleon at this moment than a war with Austria. All had confidence in Prince Charles the royal military reformer; great hopes were based too on the new institution the *Landwehr*, which was established here in Austria even earlier than in Prussia. The example of Spain had shown the value of popular forces.

Prince Charles, although he possessed some good military qualities, was opposed to this war on principle and once declared that he "washed his hands of it like Pilate." The great body of the people too were not very enthusiastic at the prospect, and it was necessary to stimulate artificially their excitement. Already in 1808, Austria's warlike preparations, described at the time as "feverish," had set Europe to talking and had been the cause of Napoleon's making his theatrical display of friendship for the *Tsar* at Erfurt where, it will be remembered, Talma played to a parquet of kings, and the drummers were silenced when the new ruler of Württemberg approached with, *Taisez-vous! Ce n'est qu'un roi!* His language to Austria, proudest of the monarchies, had been no more respectful.

He had written to Emperor Francis denouncing the faction that was precipitating the imperial cabinet "into violent measures which would be the origin of misfortunes greater than those which had gone before." He went so far as to tell Francis that had he pleased he might long since have dismembered Austria; and, lest there should be the slightest misunderstanding on the point, he repeated his assertion in another form: *ce qu'elle est, elle l'est de mon voeu.* He warned His Majesty against reopening a discussion that had been settled by fifteen years of war.

But Austria had gone too far to be influenced now by threats. She was convinced, too, that for all Alexander's display of friendship towards Napoleon the *Tsar* would be unwilling to join him in making war against herself. Then there was the hope of aid from Prussia as well as from the other German states; indeed, Austria claimed to have had positive assurances of support.

She issued a proclamation which, it was hoped, would fan the sparks of patriotism into a mighty flame:

> We take up arms to maintain the independence of the Austrian monarchy but also to regain for Prussia her freedom and national honour. The insolence that threatens us has already humiliated Germany. Our resistance is the last prop, our cause the German cause. With Austria, Germany was free and happy;

only with Austria's aid can she become so once more. . . . The present moment will not recur again in centuries. Seize it before it forever escapes you!

But Austria was doomed, as a cotemporary expresses it, "to fall from the clouds." Frederick William III. especially proved a broken reed. Early in 1809, the Prussian king and queen paid a visit to the Tsar Alexander at St. Petersburg. The virtuous pair who had suffered such mental agonies and such bodily privations revelled in luxury, and for three weeks life was one continual round of festivities. Queen Louise could once more adorn her beauty and trail silken robes through grand apartments., One ball, indeed, she could scarcely have enjoyed, though it would have been bad policy to refuse it when tendered. It was given her by Caulaincourt the ambassador of Napoleon!

But the real importance of the visit was that it determined Frederick William's policy as to the Austrian war. The *Tsar* warned him as positively as possible not to join Austria against Napoleon. The king was *glacé d'effroi*, we are told, and, on his return to Königsberg, refused to conclude a convention with the Austrian emissary sent for the purpose. In vain Stadion sent Prince Schwarzenberg' to St. Petersburg to work on the feelings of the *Tsar*. Alexander was obdurate; Austria was the aggressor and he, the *Tsar*, was Napoleon's friend. All that could be obtained was the intimation that Russia hoped not to have to strike any hard blows against Austria.

Seeing that war was really inevitable, Napoleon, in January, 1809, returned from Spain. He was very scornful of his enemy. He wrote:

Have the waters of the Danube acquired the same properties as those of the River Lethe?

He declared with ponderous playfulness that he was going to "slap Austria's face," for it was a "lazy, headless state." There was no formal declaration of war on either side; but Austria took the first decisive steps by issuing her manifesto and sending troops across the Inn. Word of this was brought to Napoleon by the heliograph to Paris and be travelled night and day to join his troops in Bavaria. Although he had nearly 800,000 men at the different scenes of war, only about 200,000 were immediately available; while Austria had 339,000.

With this war of 1809, there began, as Stein expressed it:

The fifth act of a great tragedy that was to end either with the consolidation of the kingdom of servitude and lies or with the

CARICATURE OF NAPOLEON WITH INSCRIPTION IN GERMAN, "THIS IS
MY BELOVED SON IN WHOM I AM WELL PLEASED"

return to a rational lawful state of things.

Stein had been in Austria since his proscription but with Blücher, Gneisenau, Scharnhorst, and others had carried on a violent literary campaign against Napoleon. Stein once likens the latter's pride to the pride of Satan, and it is doubtless at this time and from this group of men that there issued a pictorial representation designed to work upon the minds of the common people—it was a very usual weapon among the French revolutionists—showing Napoleon rocked in the devil's arms with the inscription underneath;

This is my beloved son, in whom I am well pleased.

The operations in Bavaria, in the neighbourhood of Ratisbon, are counted among Napoleon's supreme achievements. On his arrival he had found the position of his troops very unfavourable and that of the enemy very strong. He quickly changed all that. After a week of skirmishing Archduke Charles abandoned all thoughts of taking the offensive and limped off with his army to Vienna by the roundabout way of Bohemia.

His withdrawal was a terrible blow to the Prussian patriots, whose plans were nearly ripe for precipitating Prussia into the struggle. Stein's own plan was for a *lever en masse* under the colours of the old Holy Roman Empire and with the device on the banners of "Death and Destruction to Napoleon Bonaparte." The lukewarm were to be treated as traitors, and Stein went so far as to advocate that the king should be actually forced into the path of liberty should he seem disinclined to enter it of his own accord.

Gneisenau had similar and even more radical ideas. One imagines oneself back in the days when St. Just promulgated his laws against suspects, and imposed forced loans with a stroke of his pen. According to Gneisenau all authorities who did not show zeal in arming the nation's defenders were to be deposed from office, all nobility not consecrated by wounds or by sacrifices in the cause of freedom to be abolished. The property of the indifferent was to be seized and divided among those who had been wounded and those whose fathers had been slain; while kings who directed armies against the patriots were to be deposed and ministers who did not sympathise with the cause were to be declared outlaws.

What interests us more particularly in all this is that Blücher was the man unanimously fixed upon to lead the victorious armies. To be sure, he was going through a very serious illness at the time. Not only

BARON STEIN

was his body affected but his mind was a prey to the wildest delusions. Boyen writes:

> He actually believed that he was pregnant with an elephant; . . another time he imagined that his servants, bribed by France, had heated the floor of his room very hot so as to cause him to burn his feet. When he was sitting, therefore, he kept his legs raised from the ground, or else he would jump round on tiptoe!

One night the house was roused by sounds of a fearful struggle; it was Blücher fighting the phantom of an officer for whose dismissal from the service he had been responsible. Still again we hear of his imagining that his head was made of stone and asking those about him to smite it with a hammer.

Boyen attributes Blücher's troubles in great part to his grief at the condition of public affairs, but in part also to habits of dissipation. Scharnhorst, indeed, during the brave retreat with Blücher to Lübeck had discovered qualities in him that made him refuse to consider for a moment the idea of having any one else at the head of the army, he wrote:

> You are our leader and our hero, even should you have to be carried before or behind us on a litter.

And again:

> He must lead though he have a hundred elephants inside of him.

The Austrian War had set certain elements in Germany regularly seething with excitement; as is well known there were various isolated undertakings directly due to sympathy with it. Duke Frederick William of Brunswick raised a regiment of cavalry, chose a white death's-head for his device and, assisted by Austrian troops, fell upon Leipzig, Dresden, and Meissen. Driven back by the troops of King Jerome of Westphalia he was still fighting the French in Franconia when the Austrians concluded the truce of Znaim. Two other revolts were speedily quelled: one organised in Hesse, by the Prussian, Lieutenant Dörnberg, for the purpose of taking captive King Jerome; another under Lieutenant von Katte, who endeavoured to recapture the important fortress of Magdeburg. Both were overshadowed in importance by the undertaking of Schill.

Schill was a young officer who for his bravery during the siege of Colberg was well known in Berlin and was worshipped there. There had been a time when old soldiers of Frederick the Great had crowded round to kiss his stirrups and the scabbard of his sword. Schill now electrified Germany by riding out of Berlin with his regiment and declaring himself at war with Napoleon. At Dessau, Halle, and Bernburg he was joyfully received and reinforcements flocked to his standard.

Blücher went through hard inward struggles at this time He was burning to do just what Schill had done but was held back by a reverence for the king that was almost religious. He made every effort to obtain the latter's sanction. He wrote that Schill's step was an indication of the eagerness of the nation to join Austria in throwing off the burdensome yoke; there was danger that the Prussian people might defy all authority and the very throne be shaken:

> All this can only be avoided by Your Majesty's placing yourself at the head of your people, taking advantage of their present mood, and so strengthening your authority that they will at once stand by you in any cause. The longed-for moment has come to restore to your lands their former boundaries and regain the privileges of Your Royal House; should this moment not be seized, general disintegration is to be feared.

Schill's design had been to unite his forces to those of Dörnberg. He had left Berlin on April 28th but by May 4th he had learned that both Dörnberg and Katte had failed in their undertakings and also that Archduke Charles had been defeated in no less than five engagements near Ratisbon. Schill fought in two small skirmishes but was finally brought to bay in Stralsund by Danish and Dutch forces. There was fierce fighting in the narrow streets in the course of which Schill personally unhorsed the Danish general, Carteret, but the numbers were too unequal and Schill himself was killed.

Blücher, publicly at least, always spoke of Schill's deed with disapproval. Frederick William had pronounced it an act of unpardonable insubordination and refused to allow the erection of a stone to Schill's memory. Blücher declared that it was a device of his own enemies to compare him to Schill:

> Yes, doubtless they have told the king that I was going, like Schill, to cross the Elbe with the troops. But woe to these wretches! If I find the man who so shamefully misuses my name his life, even at the high altar, shall not be safe from my vengeance!

Schill became one of the great martyrs of the liberation movement.

Eleven of his officers were court-martialled and shot and of those who escaped Blücher took some nine hundred under his protection. A number were carried off to France where they were branded and sent to the galleys.

The Schill episode, and more especially the kindness that Blücher showed to Schill's former soldiers, not disarming them but preparing to form them into a separate troop, brought about strained relations between the old general and the king. Blücher was given a sharp reprimand for mobilising without permission; and a younger general, Stutterheim, was entrusted with powers that—so it seemed to Blücher—conflicted with his own.

Thereupon Blücher flared up in fiery anger. He wrote to the king that he had lived in the false delusion of enjoying the latter's favour and confidence: should this not be the case he begged to hand in a request for his discharge and would claim no pension; although, being poor, he would have to seek service elsewhere. There is reason to believe that he actually offered his sword to Archduke Charles. It was no mere fit of anger that guided him. In the letter to the king one notes the injured pride indeed, but even at such a moment he cannot refrain from exhorting Frederick William to seize the opportunity that may never recur and join in the great struggle.

How keenly he felt in the whole matter is evidenced by a letter that Blücher wrote to Gneisenau:

God knows with what grief I quit a state and an army in which I have been for fifty years. It breaks my heart to abandon a master for whom I would have given my life a thousand times. But all the same, by God in Heaven, I will stand no more slights! I will not be treated as a superannuated commander. Younger men shall not be placed ahead of me!

One sees, however, that his anger is directed as much against the king's general policy as against the injustice done to himself. He continues in this same letter:

If the king do not make up his mind, if we take no steps to break our chains—well, those who will may wear them, not I! I have sacrificed everything for the state; I leave it as one quits the world, poor, naked, and bare. But I shall go, wherever it be, with a quiet conscience and accompanied by many honest folk.

No one was more alarmed than the king at the storm that had been conjured up. He assured Blücher that he still felt the fullest confidence in him, and as a mark of his sincerity advanced him one step further in the military hierarchy making him "general of cavalry" instead of "general lieutenant." Blücher still held for a time to his plan of seeking service elsewhere but gradually his anger subsided. The thought of a "German fatherland," a new thought for those days, helped to sustain him and the expression occurs frequently in his letters.

We have spoken of the failure of the first operations undertaken by Archduke Charles against Napoleon and of the former's retirement to Bohemia. The archduke himself, who had started out with no enthusiasm for the cause, was thoroughly discouraged and wrote to Emperor Francis that nothing more was to be hoped for from such an army against such an enemy. The sentiment in Berlin was more hopeful, for the feeling prevailed that to have retreated in good order after losing five successive engagements was in itself something of an achievement. Blücher, as a general, had his own reasons for satisfaction. He considered that Napoleon by marching on Vienna before annihilating the Archduke's army was marching straight into a trap. And such might have proved to be the case had not Napoleon estimated the fundamental weaknesses of Charles and his forces better than did Blücher.

By May 11th, Napoleon was proceeding to bombard Vienna which, indeed, offered scarcely more resistance than Berlin had done three years before. The general sentiment of the citizens was in favour of cowardly submission.

At Aspern, on May 21st, and 22nd, the Austrians gained a victory and Archduke Charles showed that, whatever might be his shortcomings as a leader, want of personal heroism was not one of them. For, seizing a standard and bearing it in his own hand, he led a regiment against the enemy, inspiring by his example all the rest of the troops. All the same, Austrian writers themselves confess that though Aspern was a victory it was one of which the nation had little reason to be proud, for by all the rules of probability, it should have been much more decisive.

Napoleon had been surprisingly incautious, marching his troops by an unsafe bridge to the little Danube island called the Lobau and attacking, with only 20,000 men, a much superior force. The bridge collapsed and the French Army was cut off from its reserves; yet the Archduke proceeded as slowly and pedantically as if his one idea was not to expose his own forces to the least risk. A high military authority has summed up Charles's character as follows:

He lacked the inspiring and convincing power that springs from a passionate desire to stake everything.

We know from the military manual (*Grundsätze der höheren Kriegskunst für die Generäle des österreichischen Armee*; 1806), that Charles put into the hands of his officers that "staking everything" seemed to him the worst crime in the military calendar, the manual says:

> Never, shall a general take up a position or engage in the least undertaking without reserves to safeguard him from all possible happenings.

The Prussian General Müffling had pointed out in this connection that victory might well depend on simultaneously calling all the forces into action.

One can imagine how the news of the victory at Aspern delighted Blücher and the other German patriots. Blücher considered that the decisive moment had come and urged the king to give him 30,000 men and let him accomplish Prussia's liberation. He wrote playfully to a friend:

> Mr. Napoleon is in a fix, *in der Tinte*. . . . It seems as if light were breaking in upon us.

When the king refused his request Blücher was in despair. He and Gneisenau even planned to quit the Prussian service formally and raise troops of volunteers to serve under Archduke Charles. Blücher wished first, however, to have an interview with Frederick William, and asked Gneisenau and Scharnhorst to find a pretext for summoning him to Königsberg. Archduke Charles meanwhile had disappointed all the hopes placed in him. He failed to follow up the victory of Aspern although the French, on their little island of Lobau, were practically at his mercy.

For six weeks, incredible as it may seem, he remained inactive while the French built so many bridges that Napoleon's bulletin, *enfin il n'existe plus de Danube pour l'armée française*, was literally true. It has been seriously maintained that the archduke was so taken up with celebrating his victory and writing and printing a flowery report of it—"no longer will posterity call Napoleon the invincible darling of fortune, etc."—that he had no time to think of anything else.

On June 15th, Archduke John was defeated by Eugène Beauharnais at Raab. In his letter of congratulation to his stepson Napoleon spoke of the insignificant affair as the "granddaughter of Marengo and Friedland." The tide indeed was all in his favour. From the 26th to the 29th of June, his troops bombarded Pressburg and on the 5th and 6th of July, was fought the great Battle of Wagram. On the first day of the battle, the Austrians held their own; on the second they were signally defeated. The numbers engaged, 154,000 French against 135,000 Austrians, were greater than in any European battle hitherto recorded, if we except the vague accounts of the Saracen and Mongolian invasions.

Even after Wagram Blücher moved heaven and earth in his endeavour to induce Frederick William III, to make common cause with the Austrians. He wrote to the king that, according to all reports, the French Army was in a great state of demoralisation; that Napoleon's success would prove illusory, for by crossing the Danube he had come into territory more favourable for the operations of his enemies; that matters were going badly on France's other fields of war. Blücher wrote, from his very soul:

> Most gracious king, grant the request of a man who has grown grey in your service, who is as honest as he is devoted to you, who is ready to sacrifice himself for you, and whose most ardent wish is to make the last days of his life of benefit to you and to your glory. If Your Royal Majesty will permit me to cross the Elbe with a corps of your troops I will pledge my head to regain possession of our lost provinces. . . . What thanks you will reap from the whole German nation when it shall learn of your decision to free it from its unbearable yoke!

He begs the king not to be angry with him:

> At all events I shall have unburdened my heart and shown my honour of foreign fetters. I was born free and so must die!

Blücher's activity in the cause was so great that it had attracted the attention of Napoleon. "Who is supposed to be ruling in Prussia?" he had angrily asked Frederick William's envoy in Paris. "Is it that man in Silesia (Götzen), or is it Schill, or is it *Bluquaire?*"

Austria's struggle for liberty ended with the armistice of Znaim (July 12, 1809). Broken in reputation, covered with reproaches by his own imperial brother, Archduke Charles laid down his command. Prussia, indeed, fell into a panic. What if Napoleon, as he had done after the peace of Pressburg, should elect to turn northward, what if there should be a second Jena? Even Frederick William now went so far as to promise to join Austria should that power renew hostilities.

Blücher writes at this time expressing the hope that Emperor Francis may himself take command of the Austrian troops and end the armistice. He continues to urge and to fortify the king and speaks hopefully of the spirit of the troops. Then came the news, from Götzen in Silesia, that there was every prospect of the peace becoming final. Blücher answered:

Your letter overwhelms me. Thus, then are we to reap the reward of all our procrastinations!

And to the king he writes in a marvellously frank tone of reproach:

The fate in store for us is horrible. . . . Only a few months ago Your Majesty could have given the proper turn to what is the common cause of all nations. It pains me excessively that you, most gracious ruler, should have refused the urgent and respectful request that only true, unbounded devotion made me venture to proffer.

He goes on to paint the actual state of affairs in the darkest colours possible: France will undoubtedly re-occupy the greater part of Prussia's provinces; Napoleon will probably put an end to the monarchy; there is no longer anything to lose. But as an honourable death is better than a branded life the king is urged to try the last means of salvation and call his people to arms. Germany will realise that its freedom hangs by a thread and will, too, prefer death to shame. As a first decisive step Blücher advises driving the French garrison from Stettin.

Blücher knew that his language to the king was unusually bold, but he was now thoroughly aroused. He writes to Götzen that he is waiting to see how the king will take it and whether Frederick William will not at last awake from his slumber and tell those who prattle of safety and who fawn around him like lazy beasts to go to the devil.

Once more the thought of doing what Schill had done entered Blücher's mind. A later utterance of Gneisenau seems to establish this fact beyond a doubt. But with the peace of Schönbrunn the opportunity passed, and Prussia had to lie in the bed that she had made for herself. She was to endure humiliations worse than anything that had gone before.

As for Austria, she was out of the reckoning. She had played her last card and lost.

CHAPTER 4

Before and After the Russian Campaign

Bad as things had been in the days of Jena and Tilsit the kingdom of Prussia fell to actually lower depths in the period between the collapse of the Austrian and the banning of the Russian campaign. Napoleon's prestige had reached to a height where Prussia could never expect to assail it. The only German power with which she could hope to co-operate, Austria, was not only conquered but had been rendered completely submissive. Metternich, the incarnation of reaction, had taken the place of Stadion as Austrian Prime Minister; and one of his first acts was to bring about the marriage of Napoleon and the emperor's own daughter, Marie Louise.

The cold-blooded Hapsburg, who little deserved such praise, was likened by his courtiers to the God who had given His only-begotten Son for the good of His people.

Prussia's position was worse than in 1806, or 1807, because now she had to cajole and flatter the man under whose oppressions she was secretly groaning. In every diplomatic move, in every military measure that she inaugurated she had to try to avoid the Argus eyes of countless French informers. She owed Napoleon a debt impossible to pay and had continually to appeal to him for delay; her statesmen trembled in their boots for fear they should be obliged to sacrifice still more of the scanty territory that remained in order to satisfy his inexorable demands. We shall see presently how Prussia, like Austria, had to join forces with him to avoid being trodden under his iron heel.

An event in the royal family added immeasurably to the general gloom. It is impossible for us to appreciate all that Queen Louise stood for to the Prussian people. Her grace and beauty, her kindness and charitableness, her supposed good influence over the king were favourite themes in every household, and Napoleon's persecution of her, the indignities to which she had voluntarily subjected herself by going to plead with him at Tilsit—all this had endeared her still more to the people. And now at the darkest moment of all she was taken ill and died, (July 19, 1810). One intimately connected with the court (Countess Shwerin) writes that as Fredrick William stood at her bedside and realised that all was over he cried in agony; "She might have been saved, but she is my wife and therefore must needs die!"

Blücher felt her death as a personal sorrow and wrote a letter that shows a side of him rather different from the more familiar picture of the reckless gambler and rugged warrior and avenger;

> I am as if struck by lightning! The pride of womanhood has departed from the earth. God in Heaven, it must be that she was too good for us! ... How is it possible for such a succession of misfortunes to fall on a state! In my present mood I should be pleased to hear that the earth had caught fire at all four corners!

As to the personal charm of Queen Louise there seems to have been but one opinion among contemporary writers. Strictly speaking she was not beautiful for her features were irregular; but she had much sweetness and animation, a childlike, earnest gaze, a graceful bearing on all occasions.

With the death of Queen Louise, so one who knew her (Countess Shwerin), declares, there vanished the last shimmer of glory and of joy from the Prussian court which had lost its central figure;

> The lonely, joyless life of the king reacted on those around him. It grew ever stiller and less brilliant in the Berlin world. The age seemed to have grown more and more evil, more and more sad.

Later, as is well known, the king was to contract a morganatic marriage with Countess Liegnitz, but his grief for Louise was sincere, even if occasionally shown in a way that shocks our modern sensibilities. Boyen writes:

> For a long time, the king when he came to receive reports wore on his breast the handkerchief with which the queen had dried her last sweats and kissed it when he thought himself unobserved.

Prussia was, meanwhile, almost as solitary among nations as Fred-

QUEEN LOUISE

erick William was among kings. Russia had once been her friend, but the Tsar Alexander, after Tilsit, had become the devoted ally and admirer of Napoleon. In January, 1809, Alexander, as we have seen, had entertained the Prussian royal pair at St. Petersburg, but then for a time their relations had been cool.

In the summer of 1810, Alexander again became friendly to Frederick William, sending, in confidence, to warn him of Napoleon's evil intentions regarding Prussia and expressing his readiness, in case of certain eventualities, to furnish active support. The real explanation of his condescension was that he was growing alarmed for his own safety, that the once dreamed of plan of dividing Europe with Napoleon was not any nearer to realisation, and that in any transaction of the kind it was evident that Napoleon would claim the lion's share. And even in his own interests the *Tsar* could not permit such dismemberment of Prussia as Napoleon seemed to be contemplating.

Alexander's fears increased as Napoleon made more and more progress, sweeping the old legitimate rulers of the different European states from their thrones and replacing them by his own relatives and adherents. Hanover, Hamburg, and Bremen were to be annexed to France; the Grand Duchy of Frankfort was established ostensibly for the dispossessed Primate Dalberg, but in reality, for Eugène Beauharnais.

The *Tsar* was especially injured and offended when the Duke of Oldenburg, who was his own relative, was driven from his duchy. Holland, first given to the brother of Napoleon, was later declared part of the latter's family possessions; while in Sweden his General Bernadotte was elected crown prince. Where would it end, this gradual spread of the Napoleonic influence? Napoleon himself was now the son-in-law of the Emperor of Austria; and it is said to have been the greatest of all vexations to Alexander that the spoilt Corsican had not chosen a Russian princess. Napoleon, indeed, had made enquiries to that end and then had let the matter drop.

That an unfriendly spirit was developing between the *Tsar* and the French emperor was important; but there were grievances that more directly concerned the welfare of Russia. Napoleon's embargo on English wares, which the *Tsar* had agreed to assist him in maintaining, was causing great hindrance to Russian trade; while the establishment of the Grand Duchy of Warsaw promised to engender complications everywhere along the border.

Napoleon's tyranny over Prussia had meanwhile become more and more marked, more and more oppressive. The pecuniary demands were increased under every sort of pretext; new military roads or rights of way through Prussian territory were claimed on other grounds, but the real object was to render the eventual occupation of Prussia more easy; in those fortresses which were still occupied by French garrisons provisions and ammunition were accumulated. Boyen, who with Scharnhorst, was a member of the military commission that had to deal with Napoleon complains of the scornful tone in which new demands were made. No secret was made of what treatment Prussia had to expect.

Already, even more keenly than Russia, she felt the hardships of the European blockade. Some of the forbidden wares had come to be looked upon as necessaries of life; and although in the winter of 1810, and 1811, hundreds of sleighs forming long caravans brought coffee, sugar, and the like to Berlin the supply was immeasurably short of the demand. Boyen tells us of a curious state of affairs that resulted: how the Prussian Government, while officially prohibiting the entry of English and colonial wares, secretly bribed Napoleon's officials to permit of their being smuggled in.

Napoleon was a man not easy to outwit; but on the other hand, he could not be everywhere at once. In spite of all his efforts an army of considerable proportions was gradually being organised in Prussia. In the plan of campaign which Scharnhorst had drawn up for future emergencies the chief reliance was placed on certain fortresses like Pillau, Grandenz, Colberg, Spandau, Neisse, and Glatz. They had already been vacated by the French, and it was hoped and believed that they could repel an invasion until help could arrive from England or Russia.

It required superhuman efforts to raise the money sufficient to provision and repair these fortresses at a time when France was draining the land of such large sums. To aid in accomplishing this result Hardenberg, who had already once been Prussian minister, was now recalled and appointed chancellor of state—a new office and one that gave him very great powers. Judgments differ greatly as to the amount of benefit derived from his administration. He instituted reforms, in the spirit of the French Revolution, that were most welcome; he made the heavy taxes as little burdensome as possible, and he avoided a cession of territory that had seemed inevitable; so much must be placed to his credit. On the other hand, his general policy was weak and vacillating. We have a striking characterisation of him by a Prussian nobleman of the time, whose memoirs have only very recently been published in full:

Clear-sighted, of an agreeable personality but frivolous and dissipated he had carried with him into hoary old age the behaviour and the inexperience of a youth. Thus, while not lazy he was never quite up to his duties and always followed the impulse of the moment. I saw a great deal of him and knew him through and through. All his life he was untrue to women, marrying, seducing, abandoning this one or that one, while at the same time keeping in with ten others: just so he acted in his capacity as minister, grasping at everything, meddling with everything, but retaining and finishing nothing. (Von Marwitz.)

Boyen, who was more friendly on the whole, acknowledges that Hardenberg's general policy was reckless but consoles himself with the thought that fools rush in where angels fear to tread.

With two such men as Frederick William and Hardenberg at her head the policy of Prussia swayed back and forth between friendship for Napoleon and friendship for the *Tsar*. In the spring of 1811, on the occasion of the birth of the King of Rome, as Napoleon called his son, Prince Hatzfeld was sent to Paris to express Frederick William's inalterable sentiments of respect and affection for the emperor and his desire to convince the latter of his own sincerity. Napoleon answered with similar meaningless phrases but then acted in so haughty and disdainful a manner with regard to an alliance proposed by Hatzfeld that the king and Hardenberg were driven over into the camp of the patriots and consented to the plans of Scharnhorst and of Blücher with regard secretly to extending the armaments.

This undertaking Napoleon himself now furthered in a very surprising manner. Bent on increasing his own garrison in Danzig beyond the number stipulated in the treaty he invented the bogy of an expected invasion by an English fleet and instructed his ambassador to warn the Prussian authorities to increase their vigilance. Scharnhorst suggested drawing a cordon of troops along the shore of the Baltic, and the French ambassador could see no objection. But Blücher was thus enabled to concentrate his forces and take an advantageous position near Colberg where he threw up strong redoubts.

But for such extensive earthworks were not thousands of day-labourers necessary? And who would be the wiser if these were one and all "crimpers" or men who had enjoyed a month at least of military training? In order to allay suspicion these were chosen from distant points. They were organised and learned further military discipline while arms and equipment were secretly prepared for their use. By the end of August, the Prussian Army actually consisted of nearly double the number of soldiers permitted by the treaty, while weapons, and also artillery were at hand for 120,000 more!

Napoleon could not, of course, be kept in entire ignorance of what was going on. He made preparations for a possible siege of Colberg, Spandau, and Neisse and directed Davoust who commanded what still remained of the French forces in North Germany, to march on Berlin and *tous prendre et désarmer* without manifesto or previous warning so soon as the French ambassador should have been ordered to leave his post.

In order to placate Napoleon Scharnhorst was ostensibly removed from the post of Minister of War, but was secretly ordered to retain the direction of all the more important matters pertaining to the office. Naturally the most simple and straightforward of men, Scharnhorst for the good of the cause, became a perfect master in dissimulation. He even wrote to Napoleon in terms of abject flattery and by his whole bearing and manner brought it about that the French spies ceased to regard him with suspicion. Yet he was more than ever the centre and soul of the opposition, ceaselessly occupied in bettering and increasing the army, in strengthening the fortresses, and in going on important missions. We find him travelling in every disguise: as a wounded Russian colonel returning from Turkey, as a petty official from Magdeburg, as Boyen's servant, as a day-labourer, as an invalid seeking relief at a watering-place in Bohemia or Silesia. In order the better to deceive the French as to his whereabouts he would date his letters incorrectly.

Blücher, Scharnhorst, Gneisenau, and Boyen had set themselves the task of keeping the king from any further alliance with Napoleon. Scharnhorst pointed out to Frederick William how little confidence could really be placed in the emperor; he showed him that Prussia by her very position, in communication by sea with that England which he was making such efforts to isolate, would always be a stumbling-block in Napoleon's way. Frederick William would listen to no such reasoning but kept reverting to what had become with him a fixed idea: that the fault lay with the Prussian Army and with the Prussian people and that no trust could be placed in either one or the other. Where were the generals, he would ask scornfully, who were fit for more than to wear embroidered collars and plumed hats? He knew of none!

Scharnhorst had never wavered in his belief that Blücher was the man to command the army that should fight Napoleon. After a visit to him at Treptow in July, 1810, he paid him the most glowing tribute one man could well pay to another. Never had he known, he declared, such an honest, straightforward, high-minded, and patriotic nature, so free from selfish aims, so ready to make every sacrifice, even the sacrifice of life itself.

As the year 1811 wore on, the political developments struck a chill as of death to the hearts of the patriots. Boyen speaks of Prussia's *mastless* policy; the ship of state veered with every wind and ran first on one sand bank and then on another. At a moment when the wind was blowing towards Russia Scharnhorst was despatched to conclude a military convention with the *Tsar*. Alexander met him more than half way, promising to consider any occupation of Prussian territory by the French as a *casus belli* against the latter power. Scharnhorst returned with a document all ready for the king's ratification.

But it was too late, the wind had already changed; honeyed words from Napoleon, coupled with apprehensive, even terrifying, reports from his own councillors had completely won Frederick William for a renewal of the old subserviency to France. Blücher was more immediately affected than anyone else; for the work of fortifying Colberg and training extra soldiers, with which he had so long been occupied, was now deliberately abandoned—ordered to cease at once.

Worse still, as a scapegoat was needed, a victim to propitiate the wrathful Napoleon, Blücher was chosen as that victim. He had finally been caught red-handed with 7,000 "crimpers" by the French consul sent from Stettin to spy upon him. The French ambassador formally demanded his dismissal from the army.

The king wrote to Blücher on November 11th, 1811, in an extremely friendly tone but intimating that he was under the necessity of sending him into a sort of banishment:

> Inasmuch as the present circumstances do not admit of your being given another sphere of activity and because, in consequence of those same circumstances, it seems desirable to me myself that you should seek another place of residence until something else is determined upon, I feel prompted to inform you of this and to leave entirely to you the chance of your future habitation.

In a second note, written on the same day, Frederick William explains more fully under what compulsion he is acting and declares that he trusts to Blücher's patriotism to show a willing submission. The king does justice to Blücher's zeal and to the services performed in the past, informs him that he is sending him 2,000 *thalers* for travelling expenses, requests him to keep the contents of the letter secret, and finally adds words that must have done much to cheer the old general cast adrift at the age of 69:

> I have it in mind to place you in a position to renew your activity so soon as there shall be an opportunity.

Blücher answered that, much as he regretted renouncing his activity, he saw the necessity for it, and would carry with him the conscious satisfaction of having faithfully served his king and his country throughout a number of years. He chose Stargard for his residence and remained there during the winter of 1811-1812.

It was a period of upheaval through which the Prussian state was now passing, and the new policy meant estrangement not from one but from many of the king's patriotic subjects whose places were taken by men much inferior in ability. Boyen who, as a member of the military reorganisation commission had done so much to put the nation in a state of defence and in whom the king had reposed the greatest confidence, now felt that he too had become superfluous. Frederick William no longer consulted him on important matters and even ceased to invite him to table; the more shallow of the courtiers already treated him as one who had fallen into disgrace.

It is Boyen who gives us the most dramatic account of the culmination of the negotiations with Prance. Suddenly and unexpectedly he was summoned to the palace, (March, 1813), where he found the assembled ministers and generals with "*faces an ell long*" because French troops had marched from Mecklenburg into Prussian territory and were, so the informant had reported, marching straight on Berlin. A council of war was about to be held. There was talk of evacuating Berlin and Potsdam, but it was declared that for such a step it was now too late; that all one could hope for was to save the royal family and that even then the king would no longer be regarded as a respected ally by Russia, as had always hitherto been the case, but would be a mere fugitive in his eastern provinces. Boyen writes:

> I stood at the window, in the usual council chamber of the palace, and was endeavouring to weigh all these considerations, that I might form a final judgment for the approaching conference, when I was roused from my train of thought in a manner

worthy of a romance. A post chaise drew up hastily before the balustrade of the palace, an adjutant stepped out and, perceiving me at the window, waved to me joyfully and pointed to his despatch-case. I called him in and learned in the course of the long speech, which our ambassador in Paris had doubtless taught him, that he was bringing the much longed-for and most advantageous treaty of alliance already ratified by Napoleon. . . . The momentary anxiety about the advance of the French was dissipated; I went back to my interrupted affairs in a most singular frame of mind.

As the reader must have perceived, Boyen is highly sarcastic and bitter; for this seemed the final blow to all the work of the patriots. Napoleon had bullied Frederick William's envoy in Paris, Krusemark, into signing a treaty most disadvantageous to Prussia. Krusemark had been loftily shown the consequences of a refusal by the Duc de Bassano and had been given but twenty-four hours to make up his mind.

The treaty, which Napoleon was certain Frederick William would ratify rather than give his capital over to Davoust's tender mercies, was one of subjection rather than alliance. It was more humiliating, even, than anything that had gone before. Prussia was to send a contingent of 20,000 men which might be employed by Napoleon anywhere save in Spain, Italy, and Turkey.

Of course the clause had in reality but one meaning; for Russia, hitherto Prussia's friend, was the one enemy Napoleon now had in view. Another contingent of 20,000 Prussians was to garrison fortresses to be designated by Napoleon while, in addition, practically the whole Prussian territory was to be thrown open to the emperor's troops and to be subject to their requisitions. In addition to the fortresses still in French hands, Spandau, the key to Berlin, was to be delivered over. The only two alleviations were that Potsdam, where the king had his different palaces, was to be spared from quartering soldiers and that the southern portion of Silesia was to be considered neutral. On the whole the children of Israel were not in worse bondage than were the Prussians by the terms of this treaty of alliance.

On hearing of its conclusion, the *Tsar* wrote to Frederick William in a tone more of sorrow and reproach than of anger—and indeed had he himself shown a willingness to begin hostilities on Prussia's western frontier the treaty would probably never have been ratified. He wrote now:

And so, we are enemies, Sire! . . . But how can you think. Sire, that even should Russia be subjugated your safety will be assured by France, or that even during the actual continuance of the war Napoleon will ever really look on you as a trusted ally? No, Sire! Great were the dangers you would have incurred by joining Russia; but will it not now be the same?

And he proceeds to hold out the pleasant prospect of complete subjugation to France.

Nothing could have been more complete than the despair of the patriots at the signing of this treaty. The king's friendly attitude to Napoleon had been bad enough; now he was his abject slave. A few days earlier, even before the worst was known Blücher had written to Gneisenau:

> After his unfortunate battle, (Kolin), Frederick II. wrote "All is lost save honour"; now one must write, "All is lost and honour too" . . . It almost seems as if they wished to show the nation that they are tired of ruling it. *O tempora! O Mores!* . . . I have briefly written my anxiety to the king but am inclined to think no attention will be paid to it.
> We awakened (writes Marwitz) as from a deep slumber. To this, then, it had come, that we were to be obliged to count ourselves among those Germans so utterly despised who lent themselves to be used as the tool of tyranny against the liberties of others. The last shimmer of hope in our own eventual salvation was gone. We too had sold our future to the conqueror for a share in the booty of world-conquest. A weight as of lead crushed down our spirits.

The king himself was not spared frank utterances. Von Keith, once the friend and intimate of Frederick the Great but now tottering on the brink of the grave wrote with trembling hand that he, Frederick William, was divesting himself of his sovereignty to become Napoleon's servant. Boyen comments:

> It seemed as though in this writing the voice of the immortal monarch spoke wrathfully to his grand-nephew.

Gneisenau inveighed in his usual virile language against the cowardice, the shame, and the defilement of handing over the blood and the property of the people to the will of the foreigner and declares that the king has delivered himself bound hand and foot to his worst

RUSSIAN OFFICERS

enemy; while Scharnhorst complained bitterly that those in high places had lost all love of glory, all chivalrous sentiments, and had become mere slaves to enjoyment.

Meanwhile the clash between France and Russia became more and more imminent. Soon the largest army that had been mustered since Xerxes rolled on its way to the Russian frontier, almost engulfing Prussia. It has been reckoned that the quartering and feeding of these 650,000 men cost the latter power something like a billion francs. Into the details of the gigantic expedition we need not enter. In Prussia, of course, the news of the initial successes, of the Battle of Borodino, of the entry into Moscow, of the burning of the city, of the ghastly retreat, of the slaughter at the Beresina, of Napoleon's return to Paris, were followed with the most intense excitement.

On the 14th of December, Napoleon had written to his ally, Frederick William, that he would like the Prussian contingent increased from 20,000 to 30,000 men; on the 16th appeared the emperor's famous bulletin in the *Moniteur*. It was the first acknowledgment of disaster and was coupled with the news, intended to alleviate the sorrow of his faithful subjects, that *la santé de sa majesté n'a jamais été meilleure!*

On December 21st, the first Russians crossed the Prussian boundaries in pursuit of the French, and Tettenborn with six hundred Cossacks entered Tilsit. The tattered remnants of the *Grande Armée* were herded together in Königsberg like so many sheep, and it was noted that the number of officers who had managed to save themselves was out of all proportion to that of the common soldiers, a favourable circumstance for Napoleon since—if the Prussians allowed them to escape, which they never should have done—he would have here the nucleus for a new army.

But Prussia was still France's ally in spite of all the pressure that was brought to bear on the king. There was a certain chivalrousness in not deserting an ally in misfortune; but that was not the ground that Frederick William took. He still trembled in his boots at the thought of Napoleon.

Blücher had gone to Silesia where the king had given him a castle and an estate. Breslau, indeed, which now became the rallying point for the patriots, attracted him more than did his rural solitude. He wrote to Scharnhorst early in January:

I am itching in every filler to grasp the sword. If His Majesty, our King, if all the other German princes, if the nation as a whole do not now rise and sweep from off German territory the entire rascally French brood together with Napoleon and his whole following, then it seems to me no German man is any longer worthy of the name. It is now the moment for doing what I advised already in the year 1809: namely, for calling the whole nation to arms and for driving out those of the princes who refuse and who place themselves in opposition even as we do Bonaparte. For it is a question not of Prussia alone but of reuniting the whole German fatherland, of reconstructing the nation.

We are on the threshold of the most stirring time in German history, the time that was to be marked by the greatest number of heroic deeds and by the prevalence of the most heroic sentiments. It was in these days that the great bard of liberty, Ernst Moritz Arndt, uttered his most heart-stirring words calling on his people to rise at the flaming signal and go to meet the dawn that is breaking;

The harvest awaits the cutter, the moment has come for plunging the steel into the enemy's breast:

A path for freedom! Purify the soil!
The German soil, oh cleanse it with thy blood!

The longings of Blücher and of Arndt were no longer vain dreams, they were in a fair way to be realised. The full extent of Napoleon's disaster became more and more apparent as the bands of disorganised fugitives, hollow-eyed, frost-bitten, clad literally in rags, passed through the German towns. They were not molested, but a great step forward was taken when on December 30, 1812, General Yorck commanding the Prussian contingent, after inward struggles which only those familiar with the man's soldierly character can appreciate, determined on his own responsibility to throw the treaty with Napoleon to the winds and sign a convention of neutrality with the Russians. That convention of Tauroggen has well been called the point of departure for the whole war of liberation.

We shall have much to do with Yorck in our subsequent narrative, and it is worth dwelling here on the steps that led up to his great decision.

The Prussian auxiliaries, unlike the contingents from the South German states had not followed Napoleon to Moscow. Together with the French corps of Marshal Macdonald they had remained as a reserve in the neighbourhood of Riga. Yorck was not their original com-

YORCK VON WARTENBURG

mander but had succeeded Grawert. At the first news of Napoleon's difficulties Yorck had been approached by the *commandant* of Riga, Essen, and urged to turn on Macdonald, arrest him, and shut him up in the fortress, a suggestion to which Yorck had not even deigned an answer, although he had sent the letter to Frederick William. Essen was soon replaced by Paulucci who was still more urgent, sending bulletins to Yorck of Napoleon's successive disasters and representing to him how easily now Prussia might become the arbiter of Europe and Yorck himself the liberator of his fatherland.

When Macdonald on December 18th began a retreat to the Niemen the Russians managed to segregate Yorck's column and kept renewing their efforts to win him. He sent an emissary to the king to ask for instructions but received no satisfactory answer. The golden moments were flying. Had he remained on the side of the French he might possibly have kept the Russians in check for a while, but they would have been sure then to take vengeance on Prussia before the popular uprising which Stein and Scharnhorst were planning could come into effect.

Yorck finally yielded. He sent a message to the Russian general, Diebitsch, to the effect that he was ready to abandon the French and their cause and appointed a meeting with the general for the next day. An attempt was later made to prove that Yorck had acted according to secret orders from the king and a man, Major Wrangel, came forward with the assertion that he personally had brought those orders. But Wrangel's narrative will not bear criticism, and Yorck undoubtedly acted on his own responsibility. He notified the king of what he had done and expressed his own willingness to die should he have failed in his duty as a subject and a true Prussian. He is awaiting the king's decision, he writes:

> Whether I shall march against the real enemy, or whether the political situation requires that Your Royal Majesty condemn me.

From Königsberg, where in the absence of the governor-general, von Bülow, he assumed command, Yorck wrote, indeed, to von Bülow to ask if men have sunk so low in Berlin as not to venture the attempt to break the chains of slavery so humbly borne for five years:

> Now or never is the time for regaining liberty and honour.

Here in East Prussia Yorck was kept in countenance by Baron Stein who had become the trusted adviser of the *Tsar* and who believed

71

that the moment had come for defying Napoleon's ban and inaugurating a general uprising. Blücher himself wrote joyfully:

> Stein, my honest old friend is there; now, I hope, there will be some real progress.

Early in February the Estates of East Prussia voted to raise 20,000 men for the newly instituted *Landwehr* and 13,000 for the reserves.

What was passing in the mind of King Frederick William all this time is difficult to fathom. His natural impulse, as usual, was to do nothing and to await events. He did not ratify the convention of Tauroggen and as late as January 24th, Napoleon wrote confidently to Eugène Beauharnais that he was expecting Frederick William to furnish him with cavalry. It has become a *fable convenue* in Prussian court circles, influenced, one fears, by the subsequent course of events, that the king all this time was merely cleverly dissimulating for the ultimate good of his country. His son, who later, as is well known, became the first emperor of a united Germany, wrote in 1869, how, fifty-six years before, he had been standing near when Frederick William received the news of Yorck's signing the convention and how the king, after absenting himself for half an hour:

> Came back with an expression of satisfaction such as we had not seen him wear for a long time but which seemed to contradict what he said to us and to the adjutants and tutors who were standing near.

It was very filial and very politic for William I. to offer himself as a witness of the "expression of satisfaction" on his father's face; that was the expression his subjects, both then and later, would like to have seen him wear. But we know positively that at this time Frederick William was still hoping for peace with France on the basis, as he himself expressed it, of "live and let live"; that was "the chief aim of all." So Yorck's conduct could not have been anything but distasteful to him. Hardenberg, too, confided to von Marwitz that Napoleon's resources were at an end and that the Prussian Government hoped to achieve its aims by negotiation. Marwitz writes:

> I was paralysed with amazement, so the lesson had not yet been learned, the trend of events not comprehended. Napoleon not yet seen through!

Boyen, finally, writes that the king's treatment of Yorck, who learned from the newspapers that he had been dismissed from the army but refused to believe it until he should have received a personal announcement from the king (the Russians saw to it that no such communication came through their lines), was not merely a measure to placate Napoleon but was seriously meant and that Frederick William's anger was real:

> The king, whose peculiarity it was to demand mechanical obedience even when mental processes were concerned and who never enquired into the grounds or the results of an action or paid any regard to difference of circumstances, saw here, from his own standpoint, nothing but a direct rebellion against his authority on General Yorck's part.

We all know that Frederick William did eventually put himself at the head of the patriotic movement; but he did so in such a way that no credit whatever is due to him for his decision. The fact that he left Berlin and took up his abode in Breslau, which was the centre of the anti-French activity, was greeted with indescribable joy by the Prussian people; but he went there, it is to be feared, because he had been made to believe that his own life and liberty were no longer safe in Berlin. In vain Hardenberg, who had suddenly veered once more to the patriotic side, had urged him to strike, had gone down on his knees to him at Potsdam and had wetted his hand with his tears.

But at last one day—it was January 17th—Hardenberg drove in the greatest haste in his coach and six to the king's palace to announce a plot of the French against the safety of the royal family. The information, he said, had come from the secret police, though one is tempted to imagine it might have originated in Hardenberg's own fertile brain. The result was immediate. The king called in every available guard and, in Berlin, men hastened to the church towers ready to sound the alarm the moment the French resorted to violence. Without difficulty Hardenberg then persuaded the king to go to Breslau.

Even here the hesitations did not cease; and Blücher, for one, chafed bitterly at the delays. As the weeks went on the fiery old general grew desperate with impatience. Once more he urged that he be given 30,000 men with which to sweep the French from German soil; he longed to be up and at them *wie das heilige Donnerwetter*—like an avenging thunderbolt.

At last the king agreed—but grudgingly, unwillingly—to issue a call to arms. He still distrusted his people; he believed there would not be any considerable response to the appeal. An Austrian envoy writes on February 25th:

> The day before yesterday, General von Scharnhorst assured me that the king, after a long internal struggle, had finally acquiesced in his view. Scharnhorst would not say what had decided him but gave me his word that the king was now determined to break with France and that once this prince had come to a decision one could count on his carrying it into execution.

Three days after the envoy wrote this report—and here, too, Scharnhorst's influence was decisive—Blücher received the following formal communication from the king:

> I have determined to place you in command of those troops that are to be the first to take the field. I order you accordingly to mobilise here as speedily as possible. The importance of the commission thus entrusted to you will convince you of what confidence I feel in your military experience and in your patriotism.

Napoleon must speedily have learned of Prussia's change of front, for already on March 1st, he said to the Austrian ambassador:

> The Prussians are no nation; they have no national pride. They are the Gascons of Germany; we have always despised them!

Berlin was no longer a safe place for a French garrison. Week after week the tone against them and against the fugitives from Russia had been growing more and more bitter. The street urchins jeered at these cavalrymen who had lost their mounts, at these barefooted infantry, offering derisively to hold the horses of the former and black the boots of the latter. The Cossacks on the other hand were covered with kisses and showered with gifts.

On March 4th, the French evacuated the city and when, that same night, the Russian general, Czernitcheff, together with his officers, appeared in the royal theatre, they were greeted with applause that seemed as if it would never end. What was a sham spectacle compared to this actual putting to flight of the oppressor, what a false hero to these real liberators? Four days later Blücher was informed by a despatch from the king that not only was he to command all the troops assembled in Silesia—his army all through the war was to be called the Silesian Army—but also the army-corps of the Russian general,

Wintzingerode. Yorck's corps, on the other hand, and the brigade of General von Bülow were to be under the Russian commander Wittgenstein, while two other Prussian corps were to receive their orders from the Russian general-in-chief, Prince Kutusoff.

On March 13th, war was officially declared against France and a treaty with Russia, concluded more than a fortnight earlier, was made public. On the 17th, Frederick William, from Breslau, where he had been joined on the previous day by the Tsar Alexander, issued a stirring manifesto prepared for him by the patriots in which he summoned to arms all able-bodied men between the ages of seventeen and twenty-four. The summons, or rather the invitation applied not only to Prussians but to all Germans.

On the 19th, it was decreed that there should at once be established a threefold division into army of the line, *Landwehr* and *Landsturm*. The *Landwehr*, which was eventually to consist of nearly 150,000, was to contain men up to the age of forty and to perform active service in the field, while the *Landsturm* was to offer a last desperate resistance on the part of all who had strength to brandish any kind of a weapon, even axes, pitchforks, and scythes, against an invading enemy. Should the worse come to the worst, should they be obliged to abandon their towns or farms, they were to destroy their grain, pour out their wine, burn their mills, choke their wells with rubbish, and shake the fruit from their trees.

Frederick William to the last had expected but small results from his call to arms. According to Marwitz he had said; "Call out volunteers? A very good idea; but none will come." They did come, not by hundreds but by thousands. A wave of enthusiasm such as had not been known since the time of the crusades swept over Northern Germany. Classes from the universities, even youths from, the schools, sought and obtained permission to enlist. No less than nine of the boys from the famous Gray Cloister school in Berlin were to find death on the field of battle. Fichte, who had done so much by his stirring "talks to the German nation" to rouse the spirit of patriotism drilled in the same company of the *Landsturm* as Schleiermacher, and when they offered to make him an officer declined with, "Here I am only fit for a private."

The women were as zealous as the men. They hastened to turn their husbands' blue Sunday coats into uniforms and otherwise equip them for the campaign. They sent their jewellery and silver plate to the mint, and it was considered a high mark of honour to wear the simple iron ring with the inscription "gold I gave for iron." It has been calculated that as many as 150,000 wedding-rings must thus have been exchanged. Gneisenau wrote that he could scarcely refrain from tears at the sight of so much true nobility of soul, so much patriotism as was everywhere shown.

Was there so much merit then in raising an army against Napoleon, who had just lost nearly half a million of his best troops? Yes, because in comparison with the little state of Prussia whose whole population could have found shelter within the walls of one of our great cities, France's resources were inexhaustible. By the 1st of April, decrees of the French Senate had called out no less than 660,000 men. The new troops, indeed, were largely composed of mere infants, two-thirds of them being under twenty years of age. But there were veterans who could be withdrawn from Spain, Portugal, and Italy.

The way in which Napoleon formed his raw material into regiments, officering them, equipping them, and supplying them with artillery and ammunition, was one of the achievements that few other men could have accomplished. There was something almost superhuman in the fierceness with which he drove and spurred on his subordinates, assuming the while such a tone of assurance towards even his allies in Germany that they hastened to obey his commands. And he saw to it that everywhere reports of his rapid progress should be spread. His envoys were instructed to announce each circumstance and each detail of the approach of his different armies. One of his despatches concludes:

> Let it be everywhere known that in a very short time we shall drive back the Russians behind the Niemen.

And indeed it was a marvellous achievement that already by the end of April, 1813, he had succeeded in massing on the Elbe, Weser, and Saale more than 226,000 men and 457 cannon, while from every direction reinforcements were on the way. He was like a gladiator who for one moment has been prostrated by a terrible blow but who, the next, is in a fair way to become master of the situation.

CHAPTER 5

The Spring Campaign of 1813

The general plan of campaign of the allies in the spring of 1813, was to mass three armies along the River Elbe so as to block Napoleon's, advance. The most northerly one, under the Prussian general, Yorck, and the Russian general, Wittgenstein, was to advance to a point almost due west of Berlin; Blücher and Wintzingerode were to march from Silesia direct to Dresden, while the route of the main Russian Army under the command of Kutusoff was to be in the middle, between the other two, so that in case the one or the other should be attacked and hard pressed he could readily go to its assistance.

The plan unfortunately was but imperfectly carried out. The Russians were always deliberate and slow to move; and in this case Kutusoff's army was exhausted by its long marches across the *steppes* in pursuit of the French. As a matter of fact, it did not even start from the Russian headquarters at Kalisch until long after Blücher had reached the Elbe, so that the latter, whose whole forces numbered but 40,000, could not follow his natural inclination and boldly take the offensive. The viceroy of Italy, Eugène Beauharnais, was already at hand with more than 80,000 men, and reinforcements were reaching him in a steady stream. The Rhine Confederation had remained faithful to Napoleon, still believing in his lucky star; and Bavaria, Württemberg, and other states had already sent their contingents.

There was much to disquiet Blücher. It Is true, on the 5th of April, his forces attacked and dislodged French outposts that had already crossed the Elbe and established themselves at Möckern, driving them back across the river with considerable loss. Blücher then himself crossed the Elbe and made his headquarters in Dresden, whence he pressed on to the River Mulde. But the intentions of the enemy, which greatly outnumbered him, as we have said, were by no means clear. It was learned that Eugène Beauharnais was massing his troops on the lower Saale, but it was impossible to tell whether this was for the purpose of remaining on the defensive or whether the viceroy intended to attack.

Napoleon's own whereabouts, too, was a mystery. Might he not make a sudden attempt to wedge his way into the gap caused by Kutusoff's delay and separate Blücher's army from that of Wittgenstein? And Blücher was in a country, Saxony, which had not yet declared which side it would espouse, that of the hero in whose honour its chief university had christened the stars or that of its own German kith and kin. The Tsar Alexander and King Frederick William were already in negotiation with King Frederick Augustus, and Blücher ordered his troops to spare the Saxon population in every way and not to fire on Saxon troops unless in actual self-defence. He might have reflected indeed that since the wars of the Reformation Saxony had always preferred alliance with the foreigner and had not the least vestige of German feeling.

Gneisenau, in Blücher's name, now issued a stirring manifesto:

Saxons, we Prussians enter your territory stretching out to you a fraternal hand. A terrible judgment has been held in Eastern Europe by the Lord God of hosts; and, through the sword, through hunger and through cold, the angel of death has swept out of existence thrice a hundred thousand of those foreigners who in the pride and arrogance of their good fortune endeavoured to subject the land to their yoke. Guided and directed by the finger of providence we are marching forth to fight for the security of time-honoured thrones and for the independence of our nation. We are in the company of a brave people that has bravely thrown off foreign oppression and that in the full consciousness of its own victory, promises victory to the enslaved nations. . . . . The friend of German liberty we shall regard as a brother; the erring weak one we shall gently lead back to the right path; but the dishonoured pander to foreign tyranny we shall mercilessly pursue as a traitor to the common fatherland.

This eloquence, which was slightly hollow, was borrowed from the most violent days of the French Revolution; and the whole idea of a general issuing such a proclamation at a time when negotiations were in progress was so displeasing to an autocrat like Frederick William that Blücher received a rebuke almost amounting to a reprimand. We shall see frequently in the course of our narrative how the gentle king resented strong language or anything like a threat of violence.

Of even more serious consequence than the question whether or not His Majesty of Saxony would throw his weight on the side of the allies was that regarding the intentions of Austria. Napoleon was the emperor's son-in-law; Austria's recent chastisement still burned in her memory. She had every reason to be jealous of Prussia and of Russia as well; if they, combined, were to prove victorious over France she would have as much to dread from them as from the more distant Napoleon. The guider of Austria's destinies was now Metternich, the most thorough of utilitarians.

Of the different courses open to him Metternich for the moment chose a middle one. It was his wish that neither the French nor the allies should gain a complete predominance. His great longing was for such a peace as should keep them in equilibrium and give the minor German states, of which he posed as the protector, time to develop and strengthen themselves. This, however, was not the role that Napoleon desired Austria to play. It was he who by his acts and by his language made her veer towards the camp of his enemies. On April 11th, matters had gone so far that Metternich declared to his *chargé d'affaires* in Kalisch, who must have repeated it to the *Tsar* that "the role of ally of France is almost at an end; Austria is preparing to appear on the stage as a principal power."

The report of Schwarzenberg who had been sent as special envoy to Paris that "the Emperor Napoleon fears nothing so much as a breach with Austria" only served to make Metternich more independent and to strengthen him in the view that Austria was destined to play a great part in European affairs. He estimated at this time that, if given a few weeks for preparation, Austria could put 120,000 men into the field. The Saxon and the Austrian questions showed signs of merging, for Saxony made it plain that she would be more or less governed by Austria's decision; and, indeed, on April 20th, concluded with her a treaty of "armed neutrality for the attainment of the healthful goal of peace." That was only twelve days before the first great battle with Napoleon!

Two days earlier, on the eighteenth, news had reached Blücher's headquarters of the approach of the great emperor in person. On April 15th, Napoleon left St. Cloud; late in the night of the 16th, he reached Mainz. His original plan had been to unite all his forces and begin his campaign on the Vistula; but he found himself blocked on the Elbe, and it was evident that the first clash would come in Saxony whose frightened king now fled to the Königstein taking with him the contents of his famous green vault and the rarest pictures from the Dresden Gallery.

By the evening of April 25th, Napoleon had reached Erfurt, and on that same day Gneisenau wrote to Hardenberg:

> The enemy are crossing the Saale, still in small detachments; but yet they are to be seen at every traversable point. I believe that we are on the eve of great events and that bravery will decide where intelligence is lacking.

The "intelligence that was lacking," it is safe to infer, was on the part of King Frederick William and of the Tsar Alexander who, realising the importance of the encounter that was to take place, had now come to the scene of war in person and who were not as welcome there as they themselves possibly imagined. It was already difficult enough to discern who was the real commander-in-chief of the army. That position had originally been destined for Kutusoff, but the Russian general who had at last set his army in motion from Kalisch had been taken ill on the march, and indeed he died on the 28th of April. The *Tsar*, with Frederick William's consent, then gave the chief command to General Wittgenstein, but not to its former full extent—which fact, at such a critical moment, already produced considerable confusion.

It was specified that the armies of Blücher and of Wintzingerode should be subordinated to Wittgenstein, but no mention was made of two other corps, one under Tormassov and the other under Milora-dowitsch. These received their orders directly from the *Tsar* and the *Tsar* himself had in each case to seek the advice either of Scharnhorst or of his own general, Toll. There was less disharmony than might have been expected, but one sees the cumbrousness, and awkwardness of the whole arrangement, which rendered necessary frequent consultations and the proposal and rejection of many plans.

Wittgenstein's position was humiliating in the extreme. Raised suddenly to a command for which he was not in the least fitted, he soon found plans being put into operation with regard to which he had not even been consulted; and the plan that he did draw up—for a battle to be fought at a point east of Leipzig—was rejected at head-quarters in favour of one by Toll. This plan of Toll's, which was then followed, was to unite the whole army between Leipzig and Alten-burg, then to cross the River Elster in the direction of Lützen and

THE
SCENE of WAR
IN SAXONY
1813

strike for the enemy's flank as their army approached from the south along the Leipzig road.

If conditions at headquarters were not all that could be desired, the spirit and disposition of the soldiers were beyond praise. It was to this attitude of the troops to which Gneisenau alluded when he declared that bravery would decide the campaign. We have tributes from all sides. Blücher himself speaks of their good discipline, though more particularly with reference to their good treatment of the Saxon inhabitants; while Boyen, who was very critical in such matters, relates of the men that their warlike appearance and their respectable behaviour excited much comment.

Never, did I see troops which inspired more confidence.

The secret lay in the quiet revolution that Scharnhorst, Boyen himself, and the other members of the Military Reorganisation Commission had so patiently brought about. These were no longer the criminals, the drunken victims of the press-gangs, the cowed peasants who had fought and run in 1806. They were all free men imbued with a sense of honour and of their own importance and aflame with the desire to wipe out the shame that had been inflicted on their country.

The crisis drew nearer and nearer. Napoleon's forces greatly outnumbered those before him, but in one respect, because of the haste with which he had made his armament, he was outclassed—the allies had 670 cannon, as against only 457 of his own. This accounts for the wholly disproportionate losses even where the French won the victory. Napoleon was far from being fully aware of the changed spirit that had come over his old adversaries; but that he expected hard fighting is shown by the fact that along his line of communication—in Erfurt, Frankfort, Münster, and half a dozen other towns he had established hospitals calculated to care in all for 20,000 sick and wounded.

On the evening of May 1st, it was made known to the Prussian Army that Wittgenstein had determined to give battle the following day, and Blücher was ordered to make a night march to Pegau, on the right bank of the Elster. The incompetence of Wittgenstein was brought home to him when, towards morning, Yorck's corps came directly in his own path having received orders to cross the Elster by a bridge farther up the stream when another, lower down, was available. This one faulty command alone occasioned a delay of several hours, and while not of great consequence, as might easily have been the case, nevertheless kept Blücher's tired troops from their needed rest on the very morning of a battle. A modern critic declares that Wittgenstein's plan as a whole "shows in a truly astounding manner how far behind the Russians were at that time in the matter of leading an army."

The forces that met in battle at Lützen on May 2nd, were very unequal, amounting with due deduction for the troops stationed at a distance to 145,000 French against 88,000 of the allies. Blücher's troops, under cover of a low hill, were facing the village of Grossgörschen, which was to be many times lost and won before the day was over. It was nearly midday when Blücher himself, flourishing his sword, galloped up to Wittgenstein and asked permission to open fire. Wittgenstein's object, briefly stated, was to pass by the villages of Grossgörschen, Klein Görschen, Caja, and Rahna and gain the level fields around Lützen, where his cavalry would have had a chance to show its superiority over that of the French.

To that end, the cavalry, commanded by Wintzingerode, had been grouped on the left wing all ready to rush forward the moment the villages should have been taken. But the taking, or rather the holding, of those villages proved an impossible task. The quadrangle formed by them became a perfect inferno; indeed, to it was confined the whole fighting of the day, now one side, now the other gaining an advantage.

One is grateful for a glimpse of Blücher, in this battle, given by a member of his own staff:

> Blücher, with the most absolute imperturbability, remained, for the most part at points of more or less danger, indefatigably smoking bis pipe. When it was smoked to the end, he would hold it out behind him and call "Schmidt!" whereupon his orderly would hand him one freshly filled and the old gentleman smoked away at his ease. Once, for a time, we halted quite near to a Russian battery and a bomb fell directly in front of us. Everyone shouted, "Your excellency, a bomb!"
>
> "Well, let the hellish thing alone!" said Blücher calmly. He stood by until it burst and then, and not until then, changed his position.

But he was not to remain altogether immune. It was approaching four o'clock in the afternoon when, together with Yorck, he drove the two corps commanded by Ney and Marmont back past Klein Görschen and Rahna; but in the desperate struggle that followed his horse was shot under him and a bullet inflicted a wound in his own side. He sent a member of his staff to Yorck ordering him to assume command, then rode back to the reserves where his wound was investigated. For a moment he feared the worst; but when the surgeon assured him that the injury was not serious, he could scarcely wait to be bandaged before mounting his horse and rushing once more into the thick of the fight.

The French superiority in numbers was by this time beginning to tell; and Wittgenstein learned that still further reinforcements of the enemy were making ready to outflank him on either side. All the same, Yorck led a fresh attack on one of the four villages, Caja, where Napoleon himself was stationed. Such carnage resulted now that, as we are told in the sober, official account of the battle:

> The whole quadrangle was so thickly sown with dead and wounded that it seemed as if several battalions had bivouacked there.

One final event of the battle, between six and seven in the evening, proved decisive. It was an attack of Mortier, at the head of the imperial guards, on the very centre of the allies. One after another three of the four villages were lost; at Grossgörschen alone was a successful resistance offered.

As darkness descended the *Tsar* and the King of Prussia left the field, but with the hope of renewing the battle on the following day. In a hasty council of war, however, held by Wittgenstein it was decided that the troops had become too dispersed and were too exhausted to think of reorganising during the night. Blücher had practically no voice in the matter, for Wittgenstein was commander-in-chief. How the old general grieved over the news that the day was to be counted as lost may well be imagined. Although he had been in the saddle since two o'clock in the morning and had been slightly wounded, as we have seen, he now demanded in fiery words to be allowed to dash through the darkness with what cavalry he could muster and make one last attack. The permission was accorded.

A Frenchman who was standing near to Napoleon's own person relates what subsequently happened:

> The burning villages lighted up the horizon when suddenly on the right flank of the French Army a line of cavalry dashed by with a muffled roar, coming right up to the square (formed by his body-guards) behind which was the emperor. I believe that had they advanced quickly two hundred paces further Napo-

leon and his whole suite would have been captured.

As it was, Blücher's little force retreated, having lost a number of men. But his undertaking was not in vain. Napoleon was very apt to overrate the weakness and disorganisation of armies that he had defeated; we shall see him doing so again find again. But here was proof positive that the Prussians and Russians were not intimidated, for they had bearded him in his very den. It may doubtless be ascribed to the respect inspired by this attack that the allies were allowed to retire from the field at their leisure and almost unmolested. By Gneisenau's advice the retreat took place, not in the darkness of the night but in broad daylight and in full view of the enemy.

And indeed, it was an unusual defeat. Though technically beaten and forced from their position the allies had not the least feeling of having been vanquished, but rather an immense pride in their achievement. Napoleon's losses had nearly been double their own—22,000 to 11,500—and he had captured practically none of their guns. Blücher wrote later in very inelegant but expressive language:

> The French may *Wind macken*, (which we may translate with 'blow,') as much as they please; they are not likely to forget the 2nd of May!

Nor was Blücher himself likely to forget it, for praises and honour were showered upon him from all sides and the *Tsar* sent him the cross of St. George with the following personal letter:

> The bravery which you displayed in the encounter of May 2nd, the services which you performed on that great day, your devotion, your zeal, and your splendid habit of always being present at the point of greatest danger, your persistency, even when wounded, in not quitting the field of honour: in a word your whole conduct throughout the battle has filled me with admiration and with gratitude.

Still, a defeat is a defeat, and is not usually followed by all the agreeable consequences of a victory. The disadvantage in the present case was that the allies abandoned to Napoleon the whole line of the Elbe which became his base of operations; while by choosing the direction which they did in their retreat they left the defence of Berlin to the small army of General Bülow. Napoleon had a predilection for capitals and was to make several attempts in that direction. Gneisenau, indeed, declared that he failed to understand why Wittgenstein should have abandoned the line of the Elbe before actually being forced by the enemy to take that step.

The Prussian headquarters were altogether very critical of Wittgenstein's leadership. Blücher in a report to the king speaks of one of the Russian general's commands as "absolutely impossible to carry out," while Gneisenau writes to Hardenberg;

> The chief evil from which we suffer is the leadership of the army. Count Wittgenstein is not equal to it himself and the confidence he formerly placed in General Diebitsch has vanished.

Gneisenau writes on another occasion of his attempt to obtain an interview with Wittgenstein, Diebitsch, and d'Auvray—the latter was the Russian chief of staff. It was on the very day before the Battle of Lützen.

> I went to see these men three times in Borna, and all three times I found them in bed—afternoon, evening, and morning.

The line of retreat chosen by the armies of the allies was towards Silesia where there were strong fortresses like Glatz, Neisse, and Silberberg-Wartha under cover of which it would be possible to rest and to await the mustering and drilling of the new volunteer regiments that were in process of formation. There was another reason, too, for choosing so southerly a line of retreat. Austria was on the very point of coming to a decision, and it was believed that the vicinity of the Russian and Prussian troops might encourage her. It would be much easier to fix upon a common plan of campaign. There was little fear that the fact of the allies being in retreat would help deter Austria from joining them; only three days before the battle Metternich had assured the *Tsar* that a temporary reverse would make no difference in his government's calculations.

Napoleon, viewing the matter in the light of past experiences and unaware of the regenerate spirit in the camp of the allies, had expected that the defeat of Lützen would shake the friendship of the *Tsar* and Frederick William and that the Prussians would separate from the Russians and hurry to protect their own capital. Accordingly, he divided his own forces, ordering the larger part under Eugène Beauharnais to continue the pursuit of the Russians, the smaller part under Ney to march against Berlin.

It was now that, in order to leave no enemy in the rear, he sent an ultimatum to the hesitating King of Saxony, ordering him to sign a declaration that he still considered himself a member of the Rhine Confederation, that he would conclude no treaty with any power not sympathising with the fundamental ideas of that organisation, and that he would fulfil the duties which his membership imposed. The king submitted the very same day and ordered the fortress of Torgau to be opened to the French.

Napoleon's march in pursuit of the allies tardily begun—it was three days after the Battle of Lützen before he was near enough to skirmish with their rear-guard—was to prove most fatiguing and to be accompanied by great loss. Good military critics blame Napoleon for the faulty arrangements made for provisioning his army. His commissariat department was badly organised at best, and as the enemy succeeded more than once in temporarily cutting his communications the result was lamentable. Young and inexperienced as his soldiers were, this was all the harder to bear with equanimity, and two great evils resulted; lawlessness and plundering on the one hand, and, on the other, wholesale desertion.

We hear of Macdonald having to delay the march that had been ordered because so many of his men were marauding; while again even the newly arrived Saxon auxiliaries had to be detailed off to gather in the stragglers. The unwillingness to fight was so great that many mutilated themselves so as to be classed among the wounded, and the hospitals had an unusual number of cut and broken fingers to treat. Altogether it was estimated that in the fortnight between the 2nd and the 16th of May, no less than 15,000 men had left the ranks without sufficient cause.

Almost immediately after the Battle of Lützen Wittgenstein had made the announcement—not taken very seriously at the Prussian headquarters—that he intended shortly to give battle once more to Napoleon. He kept his word, however, and chose Bautzen, which was an important point strategically because on the line of the Russian communication with Kalisch. The choice was not a bad one, but Blücher as well as Gneisenau blamed the manner in which Wittgenstein drew up his army and the long delay which allowed Eugène to bring up his forces and concentrate them at leisure in a very strong position. Had he, Wittgenstein, stationed his army above Bautzen, it was believed, and attacked the French on any one of the three days between May 14th, and May 17th, victory might have been practically assured. On the 19th, Napoleon himself arrived and took command.

The two-day Battle of Bautzen was in many ways a repetition of Lützen. The *Tsar* and Frederick William were once more in evidence and the evils of the divided command were more apparent than ever. Advice was freely asked and then unheeded. Blücher felt indignant with Wittgenstein for interfering in matters that he considered belonged to his own province, while Wittgenstein for his part felt more than ever slighted by having measures adopted without his advice being asked. Gneisenau, for his part, was opposed to Wittgenstein's plan of remaining on the defensive and his disposition of his troops was so faulty that, as a modern critic expresses it, he sacrificed from the beginning every possibility of a real victory. At the end of the first day the French had made a distinct gain, having fought their way across the Spree, which runs through Bautzen.

The next day, the 21st, Ney succeeded in fighting his way round into the very rear of Blücher's corps. Because of a difference of opinion between the *Tsar* and Wittgenstein insufficient forces, were despatched against Ney and the final result, reached at four in the afternoon, was that the allies determined once more to retreat. Frederick William had learned wisdom by the Russian campaign and declared in these days:

Endurance is the watchword for this war; only through endurance will the annihilation of the enemy be possible.

Once more the losses were to the disadvantage of the French, 22,500 as compared with 10,850. Napoleon is reported to have cried:

What, no result, no trophies, no prisoners, and such butchery!

Once more the retreat was orderly and successful; once more Napoleon found that he had been mistaken in his estimate of his adversaries. "These beasts have learned something!" he is said to have remarked. There were skirmishes on the ensuing days which almost assumed the proportions of battles—one at Reichenbach on May 22nd, one at Haynau on the 26th. If we count those who perished by sickness, which carried off more than did the enemy's bullets, the awful death toll of the French in ten days was nearly 20,000

The conditions with the allies were much more favourable. The provisioning arrangements were much better, and reinforcements were at hand in ever-increasing numbers. Gneisenau was in favour of turning and giving battle again, this time on one of the old battlefields rendered immortal by Frederick the Great—at Burkersdorf, at Schweidnitz, or at Bunzelwitz. But conditions at headquarters were such that no decisive action could be taken. It is true even the *Tsar* had been brought to see the incapacity of Wittgenstein, and the latter had been relieved of the chief command, though still acting in a responsible position—equivalent in fact to Blücher's.

But the new commander-in-chief, Barclay de Tolly, whose official title now was "leader of army affairs in general" was very little better. Gneisenau, whose opinion is worthy of consideration if for no other reason than that he himself was to play such an important part in the later operations against Napoleon, complains of Barclay's pedantry and his too great attention to petty detail and declares that he is "absolutely lacking in ideas." Barclay's unnecessarily gloomy way of looking at the situation, his insistence that the Russians should at once have at least six weeks of complete rest, his blindness to the actual advantages and his false estimate of the strength of the French, who seemed to him too formidable when in reality the allies outnumbered them by 10,000—all this made him refuse to consider plans for an encounter that would very likely have proved decisive. Gneisenau writes:

> We are burdened with heavy chains, and have little hope that things will improve because there is no one to seize and combine the elements of victory.

A skirmish with the enemy did take place, at Gross Rosen, on May 31st, and it ended to the advantage of the allies; but within a single day's march were troops to the number of 96,000, which if called into action might have routed the whole French Army. While this great force remained practically unemployed Napoleon was allowed at the eleventh hour to occupy the fortress of Breslau!

On the very day that this happened representatives of Prussia, Russia, and France agreed to a temporary truce, which four days later, at Poischwitz, was transformed into one that was to last six weeks. It eventually was prolonged still more—to the 10th of August. Who first proposed this truce is not clear. At the moment it was looked upon by the Prussian patriots as the greatest of calamities, so many of the efforts of the past had concluded in a similar manner! Gneisenau pronounced it unnecessary and detrimental from every point of view, even from the psychological. Napoleon himself, however, later designated it as the greatest mistake of his life. But his double object at the moment was to strengthen his cavalry by withdrawing troops from Italy and to come to an understanding with Austria.

Austria's ideal, as we have seen, was not a war but a peace, a peace of which she should dictate the terms. Napoleon's designs on Prussia and on Poland had filled her with alarm for her own safety. There was none of the holy zeal for liberation that by this time had inspired even the *Tsar* himself. She would have joined the party that offered her the greatest inducements. Napoleon did offer her two-fifths of the spoils after he should have dismembered Prussia; but that could not balance the loss of independence should a Napoleonic kingdom be formed to the north of her and a duchy of Warsaw to the east.

Metternich, on June 26th, held an interview with Napoleon at Dresden that lasted for nine long hours. It was the stormiest interview that can be imagined. The French emperor allowed himself to be carried away by passion to the extent of declaring to his father-in-law's representative that he regretted his whole connection with Austria, including the marriage with Marie Louise! He would not listen for a moment to Austria's proposal for a peace contingent on the abandonment of a good part of France's conquests in Europe and the dissolution of the Grand Duchy of Warsaw.

All the same at Reichenbach on the following day these terms were definitively formulated and Austria agreed, should they not have been accepted by Napoleon on July 20th, at the latest, to join the allies and declare war against France.

This treaty of Reichenbach of July 27th, did not, indeed, go nearly as far as Prussia could have desired; for it did not require the dissolution of the Rhine Confederation or the return to Prussia of all, or of even nearly all, of the land she had lost. But it was a step towards the final goal. Austria would take part in the war, that was the main thing achieved. Even should Austria subsequently make peace on the basis she had laid down, Prussia would be free to continue the struggle until she should have obtained her own terms.

Napoleon not only did not accede to Austria's demands but disdained for a long time even to send a representative to Prague where Prussian, Austrian, and Russian emissaries were holding a conference. Caulaincourt did at length appear there but had no counter propositions to bring forward. The emperor himself had meanwhile made a flying visit to Mainz where, it is said, the sight of his fine troops all ready for action inspired him with courage to renew the war. The truce was to run out on August 10th; on the 8th, an ultimatum was sent to Napoleon; on the 9th, the latter wrote to his brother Jerome that he meant to punish Austria well for her senseless arrogance; on

METTERNICH

the 11th, Austria declared war.

Contrary to all their expectations Prussia and Russia had benefited marvellously by the truce of ten weeks with Napoleon. Besides drawing over Austria to their side, and making her promise to put a large force in the field immediately, they had increased their own numbers to a far greater extent than had their adversaries. Those were golden hours for the drilling of the newly organised *Landwehr*, whose chief fault, as it proved later, was that they had not been hardened by years of service and that they were too ready a prey for death and disease.

It was largely due now to the *Landwehr* that the Prussian field-army, which at the beginning of the truce on June 4th, had numbered but 60,000 numbered at the end of it, on August 10th, 160,000. All in all, the army of the allies, if we include the Prussian, Russian, Austrian, Swedish, and Mecklenburg contingents, the English-German troops, the reserves, the, blockading corps, the garrisons, and the armies of observation, reached the total of 860,000 men. The French, on their different scenes of war, numbered 70,000 less.

These are figures so enormous as to be scarcely comprehensible. No such armies had been heard of in civilised times and they show the Titanic nature of the struggle that was engaging. More men were to fall on the battlefield of Leipzig than had ever been killed and wounded in one battle since history began to be written; nor can one readily recall a subsequent battle in which the numbers were exceeded.

Blücher during the truce had been chafing and champing his bit like a chained war-horse. But his anxiety was now relieved; there would be no peace. And he himself was to find his sphere of influence greatly enlarged. He was no longer to be general of a few divisions but to be commander-in-chief of an independent army. Under him were to be the Prussian general, Yorck, and the Russian generals, Langeron and Sacken. Yorck himself had been proposed for the chief command but had been rejected because of his tactlessness, and of qualities that made it almost certain that he could never live in harmony with his Russian officers.

Blücher had made a great impression by his bravery at Lützen, Bautzen, and Haynau; and the force of his personality outweighed the arguments that had been brought against his appointment: he was too old, he had been mentally unsound, his military methods were antiquated, he had no experience in commanding large forces; he had little real knowledge either of strategy or of tactics; he was illiterate to a great extent and would not be able to confer with his Russian subordinates either in their own language or in French; he was addicted to drink and to gambling. These charges were true either in whole or in part; yet Blücher had qualities that compensated for everything. He had an indomitable will and an unfailing courage and hopefulness; friendly and free with his men, he inspired them with absolute devotion and knew how to spur them on to almost impossible efforts; like Frederick the Great he himself was at his best in moments of the greatest need; his presence of mind and the quickness of his decisions were marvellous; if he knew little of planning a battle and abhorred maps he had the wisdom to commit such matters to those who were competent and then to put their's vigorously into execution. *"Gneisenau lenkt und ich gehe vorwärts,"* he once wrote; which may be freely translated with:

> Gneisenau, being my chief of staff and very reliable, reports to me on the manoeuvres that are to be executed and the marches that are to be performed. Once convinced that he is right I drive my troops through hell towards the goal and never stop until the desired end has been accomplished—yes, though the officers trained in the old school may pout and complain and all but mutiny!

We must add to Blücher's other qualifications a hatred of Napoleon that made the latter's overthrow the ruling passion of his life. He had seen him now at close quarters and the result had been to inspire him with contempt, he said of the world-conqueror after Bautzen:

> Let him do his worst, he is really nothing but a stupid fellow!

CHAPTER 6

On the Katzbach and at Wartenburg

Austria's accession to the coalition, throwing as she did eventually not less than 130,000 men into the scale, altogether changed the general military and political situation. To be sure Napoleon had always despised this particular enemy; he had shortly before said to Metternich:

> If you wish war you shall have it, *au revoir* in Vienna!

Schwarzenberg, who was now appointed commanderitn-chief of the Austrian forces had led the Austrian contingent during the fatal expedition to Moscow. He had done this by special request of Napoleon, so that in reputation at least he must have stood very high. In the following pages, indeed, we shall find him playing a very sorry role which may be explained in part by the fact that the war, all along, was merely a political move on the part of Austria and that her generals were held in leading-strings by her ministers, and also by the presence at headquarters of the *Tsar*, of Frederick William, and occasionally of the Austrian emperor himself. If Schwarzenberg can be granted a certain amount of tact and patience in dealing with the sovereigns, who were constantly interfering in purely military matters, it must be said, on the other hand, that an energetic commander, unhampered by considerations other than military, might have brought the war to a conclusion much sooner than was the actual case.

The very plan of campaign itself, drawn up under the immediate influence of the sovereigns at Trachenberg and amended at Reichenbach, has been described by competent critics as a blow in the face at all the progress that had been made in military science since the beginning of the French Revolution. There was no clear main object laid down. The allies were merely to harass the enemy; the generals

SCHWARZENBERG

were all to play a role like that of *Fabius Cunctator*, occasionally attacking the flanks of Napoleon's army and, if possible, cutting his lines of communication; but avoiding decisive actions and only engaging in battle if the forces opposing them were numerically very inferior. So faulty was the plan in every way that what successes the allies eventually gained may be ascribed to Blücher's conscious disregard of its whole spirit.

At the conclusion of the period of truce the allies had three main armies in the field: Blücher's, Bernadotte's, and Schwarzenberg's. Bernadotte, Napoleon's own former marshal, had been elected Crown Prince of Sweden and commanded a force of no less than 150,000 men, made up of Swedes, Russians, and Prussians. Bernadotte was a cold, calculating politician who had sold himself to the allies for a very high price. It has been written of him:

> When he landed in Stralsund on May 18th, he had in his pocket five treaties that would have aroused the envy of a Gustavus Adolphus. Three great powers had guaranteed him the acquisition of Norway; England had consented to the cession of Guadaloupe and the payment of a million pounds sterling; while Russia and Prussia had also promised him respectively 35,000 and 27,000 men to reinforce his 30,000 Swedes, and had prescribed no conditions as to how these troops were to be employed. He had indeed made the very most of the nimbus that his own cleverness and the superstition of others had thrown around him, ruler as he was of but a small, impoverished land. (Quoted by Friederich, i., 18.)

It cannot be said that Bernadotte had ever shown any marked military ability, his rapid advancement having been due more to his self-assertiveness and his powers of persuasion than to anything else. He had done well at Austerlitz, indeed, but in a subordinate position; on the day of Auerstädt he had remained so inactive that Napoleon later all but court-martialled him. In the campaign against Austria, in 1809, Bernadotte had still further lowered himself in the French emperor's eyes and, after Wagram, had been sent back to Paris in disgrace. "*Il ne fera que piaffer*" Napoleon once said of him scornfully.

At the moment when the truce of Poischwitz lapsed Blücher's army numbered 200,000 men, but on August 11th, in consequence of orders from the main headquarters, he had despatched 120,000 men to join the Austrians in Bohemia. Schwarzenberg, against whom it was expected that Napoleon would turn the brunt of his attack, could thus dispose in all of an army of 250,000, while reinforcements brought Blücher's own depleted numbers up to more than 105,000. An estimate made by the most careful and satisfactory of all modern military writers (Friederich), places the total numbers available for actual service in the field at 512,113 for the allies and 442,810 for the French. England had sent no troops to the German seat of war, but by treaties concluded during the truce had granted a subsidy to Prussia of 666,666 pounds sterling and another to Russia of nearly double that amount.

The weakening of Blücher's army for the benefit of Schwarzenberg had one unexpected good result. The change took place after Napoleon had already laid his plans and it upset his carefully made calculations. He had fixed his heart on striking as of old for the enemy's capital and detaching a force of 75,000 men to form the army which should capture Berlin. Against the other armies he would meanwhile remain on the defensive. Marshal Marmont now vehemently opposed this plan. He would have preferred a direct attack on the great Bohemian Army. Marmont grew not only eloquent but prophetic; for he foretold the two defeats—the one at Dennewitz at the hands of Bülow, the other on the Katzbach at the hands of Blücher—that the French arms were soon to experience almost simultaneously with their victory at Dresden:

> In short I must repeat to Your Majesty that by drawing up three detached and widely separated armies you renounce the advantage assured to you by your own presence on the battlefield, and I very much fear that on the day when you think to have fought and won a decisive action you will hear that you have lost two battles.

Blücher on August 9th, had been summoned to the headquarters of the sovereigns at Reichenbach to receive his instructions for the conduct of his army. We know already the general tendency of the plan of campaign, and it is not surprising that Blücher's disgust so got the better of him that he immediately asked to be relieved of his command. He declared that he was totally unfit for such work, that the arts of a Fabius had always been foreign to him, and that a straight dash at the enemy was much more in his line.

Blücher's interview was not directly with the sovereigns, but with Barclay de Tolly acting in their behalf. It ended in a compromise.

Barclay declared that Blücher need not take his instructions, which forbade him to engage in battle unless against forces greatly inferior to his own, too literally, but might well make an attack whenever a favourable opportunity should offer. This was reassuring enough; but Barclay, as we have already seen, was not one to take upon himself heavy responsibilities, and when asked to put into writing this interpretation of the instructions, refused. Unwilling to let matters come to extremes Blücher did not insist, but contented himself with sending, through Barclay, a message to the sovereigns that if they did not approve of his attitude in the matter they would kindly, in their wisdom, give him another post. As no answer was returned to his message he assumed—fortunately for Germany—that he was to be allowed considerable latitude.

During the truce of Poischwitz the hostile armies had, by agreement, remained widely separated by a strip of neutral territory. Two imaginary lines, only one of which need concern us here, had been traced as the limits beyond which neither army should pass. The line nearest to the French ran in a general north-easterly direction from Kemnitz through Bethelsdorf, then along the River Bober as far as Lähn, crossing from there to the Katzbach which river the line then followed all the way to its junction with the River Oder.

The truce had stipulated that six days should elapse after its formal termination, August 10th, before actual hostilities should be resumed; but Blücher regarded it as an excuse for hastening operations that the French themselves had disregarded one of the clauses of the agreement. Already on August 13th, he began his advance through the neutral territory and, on the 16th, wrote to Hardenberg.

Today, still, I advance with the army to the Katzbach and tomorrow, should the enemy beat a retreat, shall be after him quick enough.

He had already heard of Napoleon's intention to send an army against Berlin and had warned Bernadotte to be on his guard.

Almost daily now there were skirmishes with the French. The Prussians and Russians were near enough to them for the enthusiastic cheers which greeted Napoleon, when on the 21st of August, he rejoined his army, to be distinctly heard although the River Bober ran between. The skirmishes cost Blücher many men but no more than did the forced marches he had been obliged to make, often at night. It was a new theory of warfare that the importance of the object to be gained might justify breaking the old rules with regard to the welfare of the soldier. Blücher was inexorable; he made unheard-of demands on his men.

The fight that he was forced to wage with Langeron and Yorck in this matter of not sparing the soldiers was as fierce almost as that against the French. Langeron, it will be remembered, was the general in command of one of the Russian corps that formed part of Blücher's army, and Yorck was the hero of Tauroggen.

Langeron's character was the opposite of Blücher's in every way. He was full of theories and he was overcautious by nature. Into his dealings with Blücher there entered a very curious element indeed. Although distinctly and definitely subordinated to the commander-in-chief, Langeron felt that he had been placed where he was for the purpose of safeguarding Russia's interests. Barclay de Tolly had shown him the original plan drawn up at headquarters for Blücher's army, a plan which as we know, Blücher had tacitly been allowed to modify.

Of this latter fact Langeron was ignorant; he saw in every energetic move of Blücher's an overstepping of the bounds of his authority, and felt justified in quietly placing what difficulties he could in the way of carrying out commands of which he felt sure his own imperial master would disapprove; and Blücher had not the least inkling of what was the cause of this passive resistance. The worst of it was that Langeron had much influence with the officers under him and had their moral support even when committing acts that went to the verge of open insubordination. When ordered on a night march he would declare that his troops were exhausted, that the necessary ammunition had not arrived or would give some other excuse.

Blücher, for his part, knew that a breach with Longeron might endanger the whole Russian alliance, and that without Russia, Prussia could never accomplish her liberation from Napoleon. So, he bore with Langeron as patiently as possible, and, on one occasion, at least, chose to consider as mere misunderstanding what was in reality a direct disobedience to orders.

It would seem as though Blücher had more than a fair amount of annoyances and difficulties to cope with, when we consider that with Yorck his relations were as strained as with Langeron. One would be tempted to throw some of the blame on Blücher himself, were it not utterly out of place in an army for a subordinate to criticise his commander-in-chief so continually and so publicly as did Yorck in this case. Blücher would probably not have endured it at all but for Yorck's so recent and so remarkable services to his country. Yorck's want of self-restraint fully justified the action of headquarters in not entrusting him with an independent command; but the fact that Blücher had been preferred to him must at times have embittered him, although on occasion their relations were really affectionate.

The main difficulty was a difference of theory as to the principles on which war, and especially this war should be conducted, Yorck maintaining that care for the comfort of the soldier and for bringing him to the greatest degree of efficiency was absolutely essential if the best results were to be achieved. Blücher, on the other hand, was more of an opportunist; there were times when he would have been willing to sacrifice almost the last man and the last horse rather than allow the enemy time to rest and recuperate. This was the attitude, too, of Gneisenau so that Blücher was not without strong support in his views.

Yorck had come to consider Blücher as an unsound enthusiast whose capacity had been overrated, whose popularity was undeserved. It is safe to say that at the present juncture Yorck was himself worn out with fatigue and more irritable than usual. He attributed the sacrifice of men on these awful night marches not to the pursuance of a serious and consistent plan but rather to mere blind ignorance and folly. So finally, his patience gave way entirely. He burst into the room at Jauer where Blücher and Gneisenau were dining with their officers and cried out:

You are destroying the troops, you are marching them to no purpose!

It is quite true Yorck's own corps had had particularly heavy losses; and it is also true that after a long series of deadly marches and counter-marches between the Rivers Katzbach and Bober, the army found itself almost exactly at the point from which it had started at the termination of the truce. Yorck in consequence denounced Blücher vehemently to the king, and at the same time handed in his own resignation with the sarcastic addition:

Perhaps my own imaginative powers are too feeble to comprehend the doubtless talented aims that inspire the command of General von Blücher!

But the very day on which this painful scene with Yorck occurred Blücher was brilliantly vindicated. He had had powerful reasons for clinging on to the skirts of Napoleon and at the same time not letting it come to a decisive engagement. He had skirmished with him, dallied with him, pursued him, and in turn tempted him to pursue: while all the time the great Austrian Army was advancing on Dresden where Napoleon had set up his headquarters. If Napoleon were kept busy, too, he might delay despatching reinforcements to the army under Oudinot that had been sent against Berlin. Now, at last, news reached the French emperor that Dresden was in immediate peril; he decided immediately to turn back and to take with him some of his best troops. This was the moment for which Blücher had been waiting.

On August 25th, Blücher wrote to his wife:

> The page has been turned. For three days Napoleon with his whole army has been attacking me and has done his best to force me to give battle. Happily, I have frustrated all his plans. Yesterday evening he turned back. I am following fast in his tracks and hope that Silesia is now saved. I have made Berlin secure by enticing the French emperor here and holding him fast for seven days..... I am well and much rejoiced to have put the great man's nose out of joint. He is said to be furious at his inability to make me give battle.

We see now the aims that Yorck's imaginative powers had been too feeble to comprehend. He must have seen his own error for he joined with great heartiness in the battle of the ensuing day. But the rubs with Blücher were to continue at intervals throughout this and the next campaign.

The French forces that remained to face Blücher were, even now, equal in number to his own; but they were under the command of Macdonald of whom Napoleon himself once said:

> He is good, he is brave but he has no luck.

On August 26th, Blücher had already given directions for an attack when he found that the French of their own accord were advancing across the Katzbach. On its way to the Oder the last-named river flows past Goldberg and Liegnitz and is joined, between these two towns, by another stream called the "raging Neisse." In the two angles formed by this intersection, in other words on both sides of the "raging Neisse" and on the south bank of the Katzbach, took place the great battle that takes its name from the larger stream. It was the first decisive victory the Prussians had won not only in this war but for more than half a century.

The corps of Langeron was stationed to the west of the "raging

Neisse," that of Yorck and that of Sacken to the east; and each of these generals showed his special characteristics that day. The Russian general, Sacken, was devoted to Blücher and we scarcely ever hear of so much as a difference of opinion between them. Sacken now received his orders to begin the attack on the French with a loud "hurrah!" and he displayed the same spirit throughout the whole day. By his fiery onslaught and by finally outflanking the enemy, Sacken did as much as one man could to win the battle; and Blücher, after all was over, paid him the highest of compliments, sending word to him as follows:

> I intend to call the battle 'on the Katzbach' in honour of Your Excellency, because the brave Russian troops under your command advanced to that stream fighting without interruption.

Yorck, for his part, grumbled and fumed as he received his orders, consumed unnecessary time in bringing his troops into exact formation, and then, forgetting everything but his immediate duty, threw himself heart and soul into the task and fought like a very god of war. It was his infantry that finally swept the enemy from off the plateau on which they stood, driving them headlong and in awful confusion down the precipitous banks of the "raging Neisse" and into the swollen waters of the stream. Blücher always expected something of this kind from Yorck. He once said of the old grumbler:

> He is a venomous fellow, he does nothing but make objections. Once under way, however, he bites harder than any of them!

The third of the generals, Langeron, finally, was as true to himself at this crisis as Sacken or Yorck. He was still possessed of the idea that he himself was the best judge of what risks should be run; and without sufficient cause left the fine position assigned to him near Seichau, was driven from a second position near Hennersdorf, and would have been utterly lost but for the vigilance of headquarters which, seeing his plight, sent a detachment to engage the enemy in his rear. Gneisenau reproached him afterwards in very plain language, accusing him of clumsiness and indecision.

Battles in which artillery plays a great part are apt to be much more deadly in their results; all the same there is something peculiarly horrible in an encounter like this on the Katzbach which was fought in great part with swords, bayonets, and the butt ends of muskets, and with the precipitous banks and rushing waters to complete the deadly work. Gneisenau wrote a few days later:

It was exactly like a battle of antiquity. Towards the end of the day there was a time when the firing ceased entirely until more cannon could be dragged up over the drenched ground. Only the cries of the combatants filled the air, while the decision was left to the bared weapons.

Blücher himself spurred on his men in person.

Macdonald's proverbial bad luck was with him. It was greatly to the disadvantage of his army when it had to retreat hastily that the raging Neisse and the Katzbach were both unusually full; in fact, during the battle itself the rain fell in such torrents that both became impassable save at one or two points. For that reason, the losses by drowning were actually greater than those from wounds, even though the fugitives who crowded the banks offered an ample target for the artillery. Some turned back and wandered among the woods, but Gneisenau ordered the alarm bell to be rung that the peasants might come together and kill or capture them. The insensate horrors of war are still further brought home to us by a letter of Gneisenau's:

> The roads between the Katzbach and the Bober are evidence of the terror that descended on the enemy. Corpses that have been run over are still sticking everywhere in the mud.

We have no correct statement, no plausible estimate even, of the numbers of the dead. Blücher declares that there was an enormous disparity between his own losses and those of the French and maintains that the Prussian total would be less than 1,000. How great the disaster was for the French, indeed, may be gathered from the fact that in the course of the battle and of the pursuit, no less than 18,000 prisoners fell into the hands of the Prussians. To this we must add the respective gain and loss of prestige: the French were defeated as never before, all the Prussian sacrifices, all the weary work of regeneration and reorganisation had fully justified themselves. A woman, a friend of Gneisenau's, wrote to the latter:

> Years of shame and of suffering are obliterated and we stand out in fresh lustre no longer unworthy of our great forefathers.

Blücher was determined that the pursuit should be relentless and unremitting. He urged his men on furiously through rain and blood and darkness. The enemy were to be prevented from resting even for a single day.

No wonder that Yorck was well-nigh discouraged. He wrote that the *Landwehr,* not only from exhaustion but from ill-will as well, were deserting by hundreds; he declared that it was a sheer impossibility to carry out all the commands. To this Blücher answered, praising the general spirit of the troops and their readiness to bear hardships, but declaring that in this particular case he could not find that their exertions had been pushed to the limit. He was undoubtedly a hard taskmaster, but he was bound to do thoroughly what he attempted.

Six days after the battle on the Katzbach he allowed himself to unbend and declared himself satisfied with the results achieved, proclaiming joyfully to his army that the enemy had been swept from Silesian soil:

> To your bravery, . . . to your exertions and steadfastness, to your patient endurance of hardships and want I owe the good fortune of having snatched a fine province from the hands of a greedy foe. We have struggled with cold, wet, and privations, and some of you have been insufficiently dad; yet without a murmur you exerted yourselves to pursue your defeated enemy. I thank you for such meritorious conduct. . . . You have seen the roads between the Katzbach and the Sober: they bear the marks of the panic and confusion of your enemies.

The remainder of the proclamation is somewhat in the spirit of Blücher's own old commander Belling who prayed God, it will be remembered, to send him a nice little war that he might the better praise Him:

> Let us sing praises to the Lord God of hosts by whose aid you have overcome the enemy, and let us publicly, in Divine Service, thank Him for the glorious victory. A three-fold salvo of artillery will conclude the hour which you consecrate to prayer. And then, once again, up and at your enemy!

Only three days before the battle on the Katzbach General Bülow, with a part of the so-called Northern Army, had won the Battle of Grossbeeren. Bülow, it will be remembered, was subordinated to Bernadotte, but he had won his battle in spite of rather than with the assistance of the latter. Many explanations have been offered for the Crown Prince of Sweden's extraordinary conduct both in this and in the next campaign: that he wished for political reasons to spare his Swedish troops, that he hoped to become Napoleon's successor on the throne of France or again that he did not really wish Napoleon's downfall; but the real fault seems to lie with his own egotistical character, his narrow-mindedness, perhaps also his incapacity. Some few of his sins have been exaggerated. It is not true that he deliberately tried to prevent Bülow from fighting the battle of Grossbeeren, or that Bülow flung at him the oft-quoted words:

Our bones shall bleach in front of, not behind, Berlin!

The pursuit, indeed, after the victory, was carried on in an amazingly half-hearted way. But we shall find problems enough in Bernadotte's later conduct.

We left the main army of the allies—the so-called Bohemian Army under the command of Schwarzenberg—advancing on Dresden; which move, as we know, compelled Napoleon to return from facing Blücher and thus enabled the latter to win the battle on the Katzbach. On the events of the Battle of Dresden, except as they cast a light on the exasperating condition of affairs at the headquarters of the allies and show what need there was of a commanding spirit like Blücher's, we need not dwell. In the wake of the Bohemian Army, it will be remembered, marched the Tsar Alexander and Frederick William of Prussia, and their one solution of every difficulty was to hold a council of war and talk things over.

The march had been begun without any clear goal or plan of operations, and not until, on August 22nd, it was learned that Napoleon and his guards were away fighting Blücher in Silesia, was it decided to attack Dresden. Even then the proceedings were most calm and leisurely. Napoleon's presence, we are told, usually had the effect of the head of the Gorgon Medusa; but certainly, his absence conduced to carelessness and procrastination. Schwarzenberg, as we know, had enormous forces at his disposal, but their march was not hastened, and by August 25th, only eighty thousand men were at hand in the neighbourhood of Dresden.

Even so, had the attack, as first intended, taken place at once the allies would have had every chance of victory. To be sure the hour set for the attack, four o'clock in the afternoon, was extraordinarily late, but even when that hour struck the council of war was still deliberating. All the disadvantages of having kings in camp now became apparent. Their words were so weighty, to themselves at least, that they had to be listened to with respect; at all events Schwarzenberg was not the man to stem their tide of eloquence.

When four o'clock struck Alexander was still wondering whether

ALEXANDER I.

it really was wise to make any attack at all, and after still further delib-eration it was determined to postpone operations, not until daybreak as Blücher would have done under similar circumstances, but again until four o'clock in the afternoon!

And meanwhile Napoleon, having no one to consult but himself, was approaching nearer and nearer at the head of his invincible guards. That night his campfires could be seen from the city walls, though not apparently by the sleepy besiegers. By nine o'clock the next morning the dreaded emperor was actually in Dresden conducting operations and organising victory. It was the very same day of Blücher's battle on the Katzbach, although the Battle of Dresden was to last not one but two days.

Contrary to the intentions of the council of war the fighting began early in the morning. At twelve a new council was called for the pur-pose of determining whether or not it would be wise to retreat. Fred-erick William had spirit enough to declare that an army of 200,000 men ought not to be intimidated by the mere fact of Napoleon's re-turn, but Alexander and Schwarzenberg thought otherwise. Frederick William, more apt to be obstinate when in the wrong than firm when in the right, yielded and Schwarzenberg rode away to give the neces-sary orders for the cessation of the fighting. Why he never gave them is an unexplained mystery.

What leaders of an army who could not even enforce their own commands!

The first day of the Battle of Dresden was entirely without result for the allies, except that their losses had been terrific. Schwarzen-berg's whole plan has been severely criticised. It was not clear, even, what purpose he had in view: whether he intended to make a seri-ous attack on Dresden, in which case he should have provided means of crossing the moats and climbing the walls, or whether he meant merely to make a demonstration in order to find out the strength of the enemy. There was no unity in the operations, weak forces being advanced against strong points and the whole battle line being too long for efficiency. All this had destroyed the confidence of the troops, and utter dispiritedness seized upon them when during the night such a rain descended that no campfires could be kept burning.

A war council nevertheless had decided that the battle should be resumed on the following day, and the attack of the French began already at seven in the morning. Into the details of the fighting we cannot enter. From the time of the wounding of Moreau, about one o'clock, headquarters seemed utterly incapable of giving commands. Shortly after three came the announcement that the left wing had been entirely annihilated, and it was determined to break off the battle and begin a retreat.

In this the first serious operation attempted since the expiration of the truce, Schwarzenberg had signally failed. In the battle itself he had lost 20,000 men, in the next two days of retreat 5,000 more. It was in the direction of Bohemia that he retired, but the defiles of the Erzgebirge were first to be traversed and there was great danger that here some of the detachments sent by Napoleon would cut them off and inflict great damage.

It is necessary to dwell on this retreat even though Blücher is not immediately concerned, for the reason that one of its incidents forms a turning point in the campaign. Blücher's victory on the Katzbach, too, was not without its influence on Schwarzenberg's operations, for the news of it was one of the considerations that prevented Napoleon from heading in person the pursuit of the allies, or rather that made him turn back after he had already reached Pirna. It is probable also that he underrated the damage already done to his enemies, for he considered that Vandamme, who already blocked the way by which the division led by Ostermann was to pass, had ample forces at his command for the attainment of the object in view. Ostermann himself, in the night of August 28th, sent word to Teplitz where he presumed that the monarchs would have their headquarters:

I see myself obliged to yield the field to General Vandamme and retire behind the Eger.

It is a pleasure for once to have to chronicle a salutary interference on the part of Frederick William. He and the Emperor of Austria had reached Teplitz, but not Alexander. Frederick William sent and urged Ostermann at all costs to hold his position because otherwise total disruption of the army was to be feared and, what doubtless was a more effective argument with the Russian commander, the personal safety of the *Tsar* would be endangered. It was entirely Frederick William's work, then, that a stand was made at Priesten against Vandamme, and the king sent his adjutants in all directions to beat up reinforcements from the other retreating columns.

The *Tsar* distinguished himself in equal measure. He had reached Dux, whence he had a broad view of the Teplitz valley, after the fighting had already begun. Seeing how matters lay, and that Ostermann was in pressing need of reinforcements, he induced Mettemich, whom he found in Dux, to change a command already given by Schwarzenberg and despatch Colloredo to the rescue. The result was a victory for Ostermann, but one very dearly bought and not decisive. Of his force of 14,700 men more than 6,000 lay dead and wounded.

Meanwhile the columns of the allies that were retreating by roads other than the new Teplitz road where Ostermann's skirmish took place had been less energetically pursued but the physical discomforts had been great. We have an entry for August 29th, in the diary of the 9th Silesian *Landwehr* regiment:

> The lack of all the necessaries of life continues and has become very acute. The soldiers, up to their knees in the swampy ground, tortured by the unintermittent downpour of rain, without food to sustain them, with neither wood nor straw at hand, in great part without cloaks and in linen trousers, experience the greatest misery. The general retreat begins at dawn, but several hundred stiffened, almost starved, men of the regiment had to be left lying. A great number died; a part of them cannot work their way out of the mud on account of exhaustion and fall into the hands of the enemy.

It was calculated by Knesebeck, Frederick William's adjutant, that up to September 8th—including therefore those who fell at Priesten, in the Battle of Kulm and in different skirmishes—the fine Army of Schwarzenberg had lost no less than 50,000 men!

It was necessary, as was recognised at headquarters, once more to engage Vandamme in order to prevent him from reaching the open country and cutting off the other retreating columns as they debouched from the mountain defiles. The spirits of the monarchs and of Schwarzenberg were depressed to the last degree and Schwarzenberg sent his adjutant to Blücher's camp—it was early on the morning of August 30th—with a strongly worded request to send him 50,000 of the 80,000 men that still remained to him after his skirmishes and his great battle.

The Austrian commander-in-chief even expressed the hope that Blücher in person would come with the desired reinforcements. It was a great confession of weakness and it was doubtless known that Blücher would be bitterly disappointed at having his independence curtailed. It must be said on the other hand that more was at stake even than the safety of Schwarzenberg's soldiers for the Austrian alli-

FRENCH ✠ ALLIES

NOLLENDORF

to Dresden

KULM

Teplitz
PRIESTEN

Road from

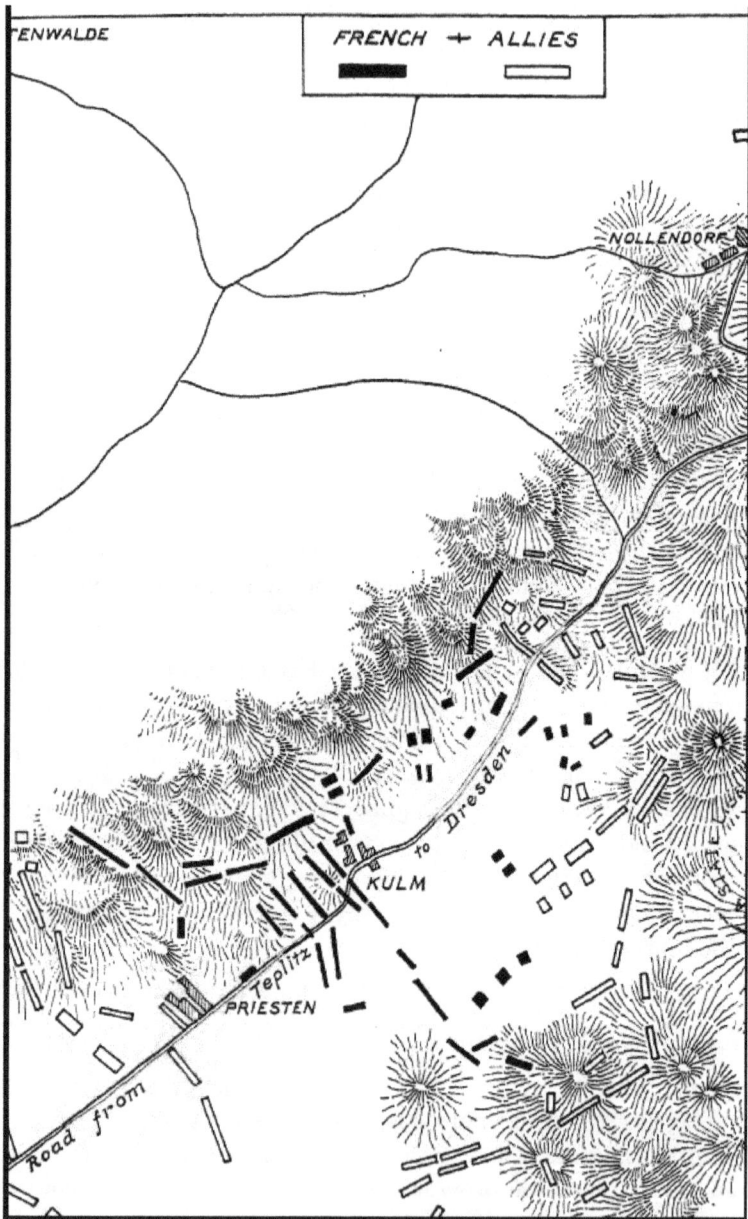

ROAD TO DRESDEN FROM TEPLITZ

ance might easily have been sundered.

But a turn of the tables, as sudden and complete as any during this whole war was at hand. At Fürstenwalde, across the hills from Priesten and Kulm was the corps of Kleist which had been hastily summoned to Ostermann's aid. Fortunately, as it proved, the nearest cross-roads, one by way of Graupen, the other over the Geiersberg, were so blocked with the debris of retreat—broken waggons, cannon, ammunition, and the like—that they would have been impassable for hours.

Circumstances therefore aided Kleist in forming the bold resolution to come across the hills from Streckenwalde to Nollendorf and following Vandamme along the so-called new Teplitz road to fall upon him in the rear. Well did Kleist earn that day the title that was later bestowed upon him of Kleist von Nollendorf! There was every danger of meeting other French columns on the march, or of having them come up from behind; but these were risks that had to be taken. He reached Kulm, where—not far from Priesten, the battlefield of the previous day—the combat was already in full progress, in time to combine with Ostermann in crushing the French as in a vise. Vandamme himself, who had shown throughout the greatest coolness and bravery, was captured and brought to Alexander. We are told:

> At the sight of the *Tsar*, Vandamme dismounted from his horse and kissed it; the *Tsar* received him solemnly and assured him that he would assuage his lot. (Quote from *After* by Friederich, i.)

The victory at Kulm was almost a complete compensation to the allies for their great defeat at Dresden. The French losses are estimated at 15,000, among them many generals and officers, not to speak of cannon, trophies and standards. Napoleon was struck as by a thunderbolt. One would like to know if he remembered Marmont's warning, that on the day when he thought to have won a great victory, he would receive news of two defeats. A serious student of this period, (Friederich), writes:

> With the Battle of Kulm, begins the chain of unceasing misfortunes that was to lead him through Leipzig to Elba, through Waterloo to St. Helena.

And another authority writes:

> Even the doubting Schwarzenberg began to believe now that the invincible one might after all be conquered, the hard struggle begun be brought to a good ending. So, it is not saying too

much to maintain that on the heights of Nollendorf broke the dawn of a better day. (Friederich i.)

The Battle of Dennewitz fought against the Northern Army on September 6th, brought a loss of 25,000 more to the French; while around Dresden itself provisions had become so scarce that it was impossible to provide sufficient nourishment for the soldiers. The weather, too, had turned cold, with much rain, and sickness became so prevalent that there were being cared for in the hospitals of Dresden, Leipzig, and Torgau, at the end of September, no less than 44,000 men.

But it is time to return to Blücher who was still in Silesia and, who as we have seen, had been urged by Schwarzenberg to come to his aid with 50,000 men. It was, more properly speaking, an order; for it is not to be supposed that Schwarzenberg would have taken such a step without the approval of the two monarchs over whose troops Blücher had command. But Prussia was now to experience the advantage of having a commander who could think and decide for himself. Even before the news of Kulm reached him Blücher had refused to co-operate with Schwarzenberg, clothing his refusal of course in respectful and diplomatic language and bringing to bear a whole battery of arguments.

He could do more service even to the stricken Bohemian Army, he maintained, by operations undertaken in the direction of the Elbe than he could by marching to join it over the mountain passes. As for his own army, the recent victorious engagements had inspired a feeling of mutual confidence among the men that it would be a grave error to dispel. There was a further consideration, too, and Blücher did not mince his words. It was not safe to leave the Swedish crown prince to his own devices; the presence of Blücher's army at not too great a distance might prove the salvation of Berlin.

On September 15th, headquarters formally acquiesced in Blücher's views; and there is no doubt but that, had he obeyed in the first instance, the results might have been fatal. Napoleon would doubtless have shifted the scene of war from the Saxon plains to the banks of the Spree and would never have been caught in the trap at Leipzig that Blücher and Gneisenau even now were preparing for him.

Already on September 5th, Blücher had written from Görlitz:

Since yesterday Napoleon is again ready to fall on me with all his forces. So long as he is in such numbers, he shall not tempt me to give battle. Should he turn aside and march to Bohemia he will find me a faithful companion and 'devil take the hindmost.'

Napoleon himself changed his plans almost daily: now actually starting for Bohemia and quickly returning to Dresden; now planning a new rush to Silesia, a fresh attack on Berlin; again, devoting his efforts to strengthening his line of retreat to France, and at the same time calling out fresh recruits not by the thousands but by hundreds of thousands. He declared in his decree that, if Prussia with five million inhabitants could raise an army of 200,000, the sacrifice now demanded of the French Empire with a population of sixty millions should not seem too great.

Blücher and Gneisenau meanwhile were becoming impatient. The commander of the allied forces in Bohemia did nothing but ruminate over their losses and forge plans for the future which have been described as "completely in the spirit of the dilatory strategy of the 18th century"; the Swedish crown prince, to the north, showed not the slightest inclination to take the initiative; Napoleon, too, was inactive, awaiting an opportunity to strike his opponents singly.

Blücher now showed his right to the designation of "Forward!" which was later universally to be applied to him. "Since the others will not do so," Gneisenau wrote on September 26th:

We shall open the play and shall assume the chief role.

Napoleon's forces still lay stretched along the Elbe from Königstein to Torgau, and the "play" consisted in making all three armies of the allies form an iron ring around him by which he must finally be strangled. The conception, doubtless, was Gneisenau's; which need not in the least detract from Blücher's credit. It was Gneisenau's special duty to draw up plans. Blücher assumed the responsibility and undertook the carrying out of the project. He himself was to join Bernadotte and fight his way across the Elbe further to the north and west, thus rounding Napoleon's army. Schwarzenberg's army, simultaneously was to advance from the south-east.

That the plan, that any energetic plan whatever, should meet with opposition was a foregone conclusion; and one is not surprised to find Blücher writing that he is having "the devil's own time," with the "committee of safety." Just whom he meant to designate by the "committee of safety" is not clear; but it might have meant almost any one from the king and the *Tsar* down to Yorck and Langeron. There was also Bernadotte, whose co-operation was absolutely essential.

Eventually the consent of all concerned was more readily won than might have been anticipated, and Blücher's troubles probably related more to details than to the general scheme, the possibilities of which must have been apparent even to the most obtuse. Bernadotte even seemed enthusiastic over the idea, declaring that although he had been promised command over all the different corps in his vicinity, he would waive this claim should Blücher join him. They would fight hand in hand, so he declared, "like good comrades." He even made suggestions for an advance on Leipzig and a battle against Napoleon.

In his negotiations with the Swedish crown prince, Blücher must have shown great patience, skill, and self-restraint to bring matters thus far; for he had a great personal antipathy to him. To those around him however he unbent and used language that he little thought history would perpetuate but that is worth recording as a specimen of what his real thoughts were and of what he could have said to Bernadotte had he wished: "If the dog of a gypsy don't come at once may *das heilige Kreutz-Granaten-Bomben-Donnerwetter* grind him to bits!"— an untranslatable oath which invites the strongest destructive agents known to wreak their will on the miscreant.

In justice to the Tsar Alexander it must be said that, before he learned of Blücher's plan but while the latter was preparing to put it into execution, he had suggested something very similar, with many exhortations to caution, indeed, and with a dozen alternative recommendations. It is also to the *Tsar's* credit that, when he did accept Blücher's plan, it was unreservedly and without the conditions that he had at first seen fit to attach.

On October 1st, realising that Dresden could no longer afford sustenance for his army. Napoleon directed the main body of his troops towards Leipzig, leaving but one army corps in his old position.

That Blücher was alive to the seriousness of his undertaking is clear from his instructions to Major von Rühle who was sent to choose a point for crossing the Elbe. The major was to make sure that on the further bank there was a position where an army of 50,000 men could hold at bay an enemy of three times that number. Rühle reported in favour of crossing at Elster, between Torgau and Wittenberg, and of choosing as a possible battlefield Wartenburg, around which the river makes a great curve so that both flanks of the army would be protected. Rühle's choice of Wartenburg, made after a superficial inspection from the further bank, was not in all respects a fortunate one; for the shrubbery concealed the real nature of the ground which was rough, broken, and swampy beyond description. Yet here was to take place, as the event proved, one of the most desperate struggles of the whole war.

Fortunately for the allies the French marshal Bertrand underrated the strength of his adversary, being under the impression that he had to do with the Crown Prince of Sweden alone, and indeed with but a fraction of the latter's army. Bertrand, accordingly, had left but a small force at what experience proved to be the one point passable for an army—the village of Bleddin. Even then, although Blücher had begun his crossing of the Elbe at dawn, it was two in the afternoon before Bleddin was taken and four before Wartenburg was entered.

The brunt of the day's fighting had fallen on the corps of General Yorck, who so distinguished himself by his personal courage and ability that the king later honoured him as he had done Kleist after Nollendorf, by bestowing upon him and on his family the title of Yorck von Wartenburg. His soldiers, too, in large part *Landwehr*, had covered themselves with glory. Yorck himself, full as he was of old military prejudices, had often grumbled at the new institution. But that evening, after all was over, he said of the *Landwehr* that it "had passed its examination with high honours"; and the next day he stood in the pouring rain with his head bared until the last man of the devoted troop had filed by.

Throughout the battle Blücher had remained at the head of the Elbe bridge despatching the troops as they reached the left bank to the points where they were most needed. It is told of him that he pointed to the smoke rising in the distance from the chimneys of Wartenburg and cried out:

Look, men, the accursed French are baking white bread for their breakfast; we'll take it from them while it is still hot!

He failed to carry out his boast in full but that evening he supped in the castle of Wartenburg and declared as he rose to speak at the banquet:

Thank God we have taken a great step forward towards the liberation of the Fatherland!

A sober professor of Breslau, (Steffens), who had won the admiration of Germany by throwing his academic calling to the winds and had followed the whole campaign, in great part as an honoured guest at headquarters, was with Blücher on this occasion. He calls the latter "this extraordinary man who will remain as unforgettable as the war itself." Blücher had a solemn tribute to pay that night. Scharnhorst, to whom he often declared that he owed everything in the world and without whose good offices he would very likely not have been chosen commander-in-chief, had been wounded in the Battle of Grossgörschen and had since died. Steffens writes:

> The whole solemn feast was transformed into a funeral celebration in memory of dead Scharnhorst. Blücher began to speak. Never did I hear a more stirring address, never an appreciation of the great warrior delivered more clearly, more brilliantly, more vividly. The almost involuntary outpouring of his eloquence was a wonderful product of poetic enthusiasm. As he ended, he called to him the son of the dead hero.

It is certain that had Scharnhorst been present in the flesh he would have rejoiced immeasurably in the turn affairs had taken. The links of the great iron chain that was to surround Napoleon were rapidly forging and Blücher was there to see that the ends joined.

SCHARNHORST

CHAPTER 7

The Battle of Leipzig

There is an element of comedy hitherto little noted in the great drama of the closing in of the allied forces on Napoleon at Leipzig, for Blücher has to resort to every possible expedient to make the leaders of the other two armies stand up and manfully meet their dreaded enemy.

The Bohemian Army, in consequence of the chastisement it had received at Dresden, advanced after the manner of a timid hare which cocks its ears at every sound. The instructions drawn up for the guidance of the subordinate commanders declared, indeed, that the object of the march was to draw the attention of the enemy from Blücher and the Swedish crown prince, who were occupied in crossing the Elbe; but then followed most characteristic and often self-contradictory orders. Decisive battles are to be avoided on principle, but single corps are to be "annihilated as far as possible." When the troops come into the neighbourhood of Chemnitz and Oederau "all too serious skirmishing is to be avoided because the Emperor Napoleon can and will reach there in not more than three marches from Dresden."

A critic, (Friederich), wonders if Murat who commanded Napoleon's outposts was likely to allow himself to be "annihilated as far as possible" without "serious skirmishing" and asks how long Napoleon could be drawn away from Blücher and Bernadotte by an army that remained passive. One sees throughout the document the awe in which Schwarzenberg stood of the man who could if he wished reach him in three days of marching.

Napoleon's own orders to Murat were to "keep the Austrians off to the limit of your power so that I can defeat Blücher and the Swedes before their junction with Schwarzenberg," which was no great task as the Austrians kept off of their own accord. Klenau, at Schillenberg, might have attacked and overcome Murat whose forces were inferior but did not venture to do so without orders from headquarters, which drew down upon Schwarzenberg the scathing criticism (from General Hake), that Murat had committed an impertinence *which a live man would have severely punished.*

When word finally came of Blücher's success at Wartenburg the Austrian-Russian council of war did decide unanimously that every effort ought to be made to reach Leipzig by forced marches; yet, singularly enough, in the next few days Schwarzenberg's marches were anything but forced. Sir Robert Wilson, who was with the army, gives as one reason for the cautious advance that a letter of Murat's had been intercepted which expressed joy on the part of Napoleon at the prospect of trying conclusions with Schwarzenberg!

It is easy to heap example upon example of the faulty leadership of this great army. Murat with an army but one fourth the size of Schwarzenberg's was allowed on October 10th, to bar the latter's way to Leipzig, the Austrians being so scattered as to be unable to take the offensive. On the 11th, headquarters was so ignorant of the whereabouts of the enemy that it expressed the hope of Wittgenstein's being able to intercept the corps of Augereau, when in reality Augereau was many miles distant on the Saale and Wittgenstein was on the Pleisse. The ignorance and indecision of those high in command naturally transmitted itself to their subordinates. Wittgenstein himself desisted from a carefully planned attack on Murat for no other reason, apparently, than that the enemy showed an intention of resisting. An Austrian staff-officer writes:

> We might have had the most brilliant day yesterday, but every effort to spur them on was in vain. They dream away the finest occasions, the most favourable moments.

Events now happened, indeed, which actually compelled the Bohemian Army to act. Murat, under a misapprehension, made a false move and retreated to Wachau; Bavaria, seeing the allies advancing from on all sides, fell away from Napoleon and, by the treaty of Ried, placed her forces at the disposal of the allies; and last, but not least, news came that Blücher was already at Halle, waiting to co-operate, and that Bernadotte was not far distant.

On October 14th, then, the Bohemian Army allowed itself to become involved in a desperate skirmish with Murat at Liebertwolkwitz, not far from Wachau. It was, almost exclusively, a cavalry fight, which lasted for seven hours; and although the losses in the end were about equal and the positions at the close of the day remained unchanged, the French could less easily repair their damage, for their cavalry was their weakest point.

Blücher, meanwhile, had again been having what he had called "the devil's own time" with Bernadotte. Quicksilver is not more elusive than the Swedish crown prince had proved himself. What his real purposes, what his secret motives were has been a matter of controversy from that day to this.

Bernadotte, as we know, had promised his cooperation to Blücher and had agreed to cross the Elbe. He did so, at Roslau and Aken, on the day after Blücher's struggle at Wartenburg, leaving a small detachment under Tauentzien and Thümmen to guard the line of retreat by the Elbe bridges. He himself camped on one side of the River Mulde near its confluence with the Elbe, while Blücher's army camped on the other. Napoleon on October 6th, left Dresden with 80,000 men intending to strike a blow either at Blücher or at Bernadotte, or at both, and then quickly turn against the Bohemian Army. It was on the 7th, that he wrote the order to Murat to keep back the Austrians as best he could until he, Napoleon, should have defeated Blücher and the Swedes. But he made one miscalculation; he believed Blücher and Bernadotte to be approaching Leipzig, when in reality they had remained quietly in their respective camps on the Mulde. There, having seen his error, he determined to seek them out.

The question what to do under the circumstances gave rise to great differences of opinion between Bernadotte and Blücher. The latter had been impatient to advance on Leipzig and to fight a battle with Napoleon wherever he could be found. Bernadotte had given a grudging consent to the advance on Leipzig but seems to have dreaded a battle with Napoleon as he would have dreaded the plague, proposing merely to cut the French emperor's communications and then postpone further operations until the junction with Schwarzenberg.

The news of the enemy's approach at the head of a large force changed the situation altogether. Blücher's army and that of Bernadotte, each on its own side of the Mulde, were still at some distance from each other; Napoleon could not be permitted to swallow up first one and then the other. Blücher, indeed, might have retired to the camp he had chosen at Wartenburg and here might have remained on the defensive, but against this idea his whole nature rebelled.

It was necessary above all things to come quickly to an understanding with Bernadotte, and Major von Rühle was despatched to the crown prince's camp at Zehbitz near Sorbig. The interview proved full of unpleasant surprises; for the crown prince showed no intention of joining in an attack on Napoleon but brought up an entirely new issue, the defence of Berlin, declaring that the only possible course now open to the two armies was to recross the Elbe, destroy the bridges, and make for the capital. Blücher's whole elaborate plan of surrounding and crushing Napoleon was thus quietly brushed aside.

Rühle answered with dignity that to the Prussian generals—why then should the Swedes insist upon it?—the defence of Berlin seemed of minor importance; and is said to have added: "if Moscow was burned Berlin too can be abandoned." To his certain knowledge, he declared, Blücher would never consent to recross the Elbe; but, if the worse came to the worst, would take his army behind the Saale and work round to the southward until he could effect a junction with Schwarzenberg. The Saale runs in a parallel direction to the Mulde, but further to the west.

Then came a further surprise. The mention of the Saale put Bernadotte on a new tack. The project, he declared, appealed to him; although in itself it was astonishingly bold, implying as it did the cutting of all lines of communication and the abandonment of the baggage and supplies that were still on the Elbe. Bernadotte's motives are incomprehensible, but it has been suggested that he never really believed that Blücher would consent to the plan. Blücher did at once consent and willingly assumed the entire responsibility.

So instead of Bernadotte's crossing to Blücher the latter prepared to cross the Mulde to Bernadotte, and the orders to this effect were given, as it proved not a single moment too soon; for scarcely had Blücher quitted Düben when the French entered that town. Langeron's corps and Sacken's corps both had narrow escapes from being cut off, while Gneisenau himself was on the point of being captured. As it ultimately turned out a few men engaged in foraging, a few of the wounded, and twenty waggon-loads of *Zwieback* were the extent of the enemy's booty. Blücher camped that night in safety on the further side of the Mulde next to the corps of Bülow who, it will be remembered, was one of the Prussian generals serving under Bernadotte.

But the troubles with the latter had only begun. When Blücher prepared to hasten across the Saale the sooner to effect his junction with Schwarzenberg it became evident that, after all, Bernadotte meant to remain in as close connection with his Elbe bridges as possible. In a personal interview between the two commanders the outward forms of politeness could scarcely any longer be maintained. Blücher was for making a stand near Halle and there accepting, if need be, a battle with Napoleon. Of this Bernadotte would not hear. He was so frightened by the vicinity of Napoleon, that like a child which seeks to interpose the mother's skirt between itself and danger, he insisted on Blücher's army taking up its position on his own right wing which, he imagined, would be the more exposed to attack. So entirely was he wrapped up in the thought of his own possible risk that he forgot, or at all events omitted to carry out, a formal promise to have his engineers, who were in advance, throw a bridge over the Saale near Wettin which would have enabled Blücher's troops to avoid a long detour in crossing the river.

Already before the bridge episode came to a climax Blücher had sent to General von Bülow to complain of Bernadotte's conduct and to ask if, in the event of the latter's refusing to take part in the battle that was imminent, he could count on his, Bülow's, assistance. Although this was, in a way, mutiny there came back a warm promise of adherence, which was renewed at a personal meeting. The conspirators, for such they were in fact, hoped also for the defection of another of Bernadotte's commanders, the Russian general, Wintzingerode.

When, the next day, which was October 11th, Blücher arrived with his army at Wettin and found no bridge by which to cross he curtly notified the Swedish crown prince that he had no alternative but to march to Halle, where he would concentrate his army. He presumed, he said, that his Royal Highness would advance towards Leipzig and co-operate with the Bohemian Army in a combined attack on Napoleon. To this Bernadotte answered in general, but it must be said in polite terms, deigning no answer however to the suggestion of advancing towards Leipzig.

The language that Blücher employed in private against Bernadotte at this juncture is not recorded, but even his powers of rhetoric and of expletive must have failed him in view of what subsequently happened. Bernadotte, hearing, what was true, that great damage had been inflicted on the corps of Tauentzien and Thümmen which he had left in reserve on the Elbe, but entirely wrong in his other assumptions, for Napoleon had at once returned to face Schwarzenberg at Leipzig, sent a letter to Blücher which showed him to be almost wild with terror. It declared that four French corps, headed in all probability by Napoleon himself, were marching on Wittenberg and that he, Bernadotte, had taken the resolution to recross the Elbe:

> I have not a single moment to lose! I am hastening the march of my troops in order, if possible, to make the crossing without disaster. The Tsar Alexander has informed me that you will execute my commands (my commands!) if you see the necessity. I beg you to regard the present writing as a summons to join me with as many of your forces as possible.

Blücher, with no means of knowing what truth there was in Bernadotte's statements, was outraged and surprised but at the same time in a quandary as never before. The moment of moments that he had longed for and worked for was at hand, and yet he was called upon to reverse all his plans and turn his back on Leipzig. If the information of which Bernadotte seemed so sure was true, if Napoleon was on the point of crossing the Elbe with his forces at Wittenberg, it might mean that the French emperor intended to march down the stream on the further bank, then to recross and come round in the rear of Blücher's own army. Or again it might mean that Napoleon was merely seeking to lure both Bernadotte and Blücher across the Elbe where he would leave them, out of harm's way, and then, destroying the bridges behind him, make for the Bohemian Army.

It was one of those cases where Blücher's ability to make quick decisions stood him in good stead. One can imagine to what interminable war councils such information would have led, had it descended suddenly on Schwarzenberg's headquarters. Blücher, on the contrary, at once and flatly, refused to be guided by Bernadotte's orders. In a letter to the latter he reminded him how often he, Blücher, had renounced his own plans, how the whole present situation, including the crossing of the Saale, was of the crown prince's own making; how without, hesitation, when he requested it, the latter had been given the more favourable position:

> Your Royal Highness now informs me that you intend to cross the Elbe at Aken. Through this movement I shall be cut off from the Elbe and nothing will remain for me but to join the main army.

Then follow words cleverly calculated to work upon the crown prince's fears:

> It is not yet clear to me how Your Royal Highness intends to effect your crossing of the Elbe and how, after the crossing, you

will maintain yourself *wedged in as you will be between the enemy, the Elbe, Magdeburg, and the Havel.*

Blücher goes on to say that he himself is that day sending out a reconnoitring expedition in the direction of Leipzig to find out the truth about the enemy's position and that also he has sent his first *aide de camp* to the *Tsar* to acquaint him with the position of his, Blücher's, own army and see what commands his Imperial Majesty may have to send. This last, of course, is an intimation that Bernadotte is not the person to give him orders. As a matter of fact, Alexander had given Bernadotte some such assurance as the latter claimed to have received but had done so without consulting Frederick William and without officially informing Blücher.

The Swedish crown prince was by this time in such a panic that he inspired pity in those who were about him. Krusemarck, the Prussian military *attaché*, wrote to Blücher:

> It would be a praiseworthy deed to raise the sunken courage of the *gnädiger Herr* for he already considers that all is lost. I beg Your Excellency most earnestly to inform him to the contrary.

Bernadotte had so confidently expected that Blücher would bow to his authority that he had given orders on his own responsibility to the latter's general, von Rauch, to lay a pontoon bridge over the Elbe at Aken. He had written to Rauch:

> General Blücher is approaching Aken by forced marches to join me. Together we shall give battle to the enemy in case he re-crosses to the left bank. Should he remain on the right bank we shall cross the Elbe in full force. To relieve you of all responsibility I inform you that I am authorised by a letter of the Tsar Alexander to issue commands to General Blücher in case of necessity. You will now see that success of the operations of the allied armies depends on your executing this command.

Blücher for his part wrote to Rauch:

> His Royal Highness did very wrong to disturb you after I had given you my directions, and you should have followed my orders. . . . That His Majesty the Tsar Alexander ever placed me under the commands of His Highness is as much news to me as is the fact that I am marching to Aken.

Bernadotte's panic was not without its lasting effects, for Tauentzien, whose nerves were doubtless already upset by the sharp rap Napoleon had administered to him, became as much alarmed as his commander-in-chief, destroyed one of the Elbe bridges, and ordered General Hirschfeld to follow him by the last remaining means of crossing and destroy that in turn. Hirschfeld answered Tauentzien much as Blücher had answered Bernadotte only with still less politeness. The order to follow, he declared, merely strengthened him in the determination to remain where he was and defend the only crossing by which help could be sent to Berlin in case a really strong enemy should seriously threaten it, an eventuality in which, in spite of the fears of Bernadotte and of Tauentzien, Hirschfeld evidently did not believe.

But the final result was that Tauentzien with a corps of 18,000 men made an incredibly swift march to the capital, reaching it in four days; that his men in consequence were in such a state of fatigue and demoralisation that they would have been of no possible use even had Napoleon been attacking Berlin, and that these 18,000 men were thus prevented from participating in the great encircling movement around Leipzig.

Bernadotte himself had, in the meanwhile, received more correct information about the position of Napoleon who, already on October 12th, had given up all idea of further operations along the Elbe. There was no reason for the Swedish crown prince, therefore, to cross to the right bank; and every member of the council of war that he finally called was opposed to the move. So, he came to his senses and wrote very politely to Blücher that he had abandoned his plan, would set out for Halle the following morning, and by evening would join him.

At Halle Bernadotte's troops could at least have served as a reserve for Blücher in the great battle that was to be fought. Bernadotte had not only assured Blücher that they would be there but, on October 15th, actually gave them their marching orders to that effect. What made him change these orders and concentrate his forces that night between Wettin and Petersberge is a problem too difficult for any historian. The marching orders themselves throw no light upon the matter but only involve it in more confusion:

> Since it is possible that a battle will take place in the neighbourhood of Leipzig the army must be in readiness either to support the main army or, in case that army should gain the victory, to inflict great damage on the enemy.

But the camp between Wettin and Petersberge was ten miles farther away from Leipzig than even Halle! Bernadotte in reality thus avoided every possibility of having his troops called into action. His own explanation, that he chose to make a shorter march because his troops were so much in need of rest, will not bear investigation. The troops had been resting all the previous day, and the march even to Halle would not have been an unusually long one.

There is an explanation that is at least plausible, though one must hesitate to state positively what went on in so complex and peculiar a mind as Bernadotte's. He had received news that troops under Ney stood between Dessau and Düben. The news was false; but he must have believed it true, and have feared an attack on his flank. In the habit of treating all happenings only with reference to himself he had preferred risking the whole success of the culminating action of the war to exposing his precious Swedes to a danger that in reality was only imaginary. So unnecessary did the change in the direction of the march and the early halt in Wettin seem to the military attachés in his army that they took the very unusual step of handing in a formal demand that he "should participate in an event that must decide the fate of Europe."

Blücher had allowed, indeed had requested, Schwarzenberg to assign him his place in the expected battle and to send him his marching orders. He was told to advance along the right bank of the Elster to Skeudnitz and then to approach Leipzig from a point farther to the south, passing through Lindenau. But, like all Schwarzenberg's plans of battle, this one for the great encounter at Leipzig had its weaknesses, and Blücher found that at Lindenau he would have to pass through a narrow defile where a handful of men could hold in check his entire army. This defect in the plan was remedied in time, but another faulty arrangement of Schwarzenberg's was to cause much needless effusion of blood.

The triangle between the Pleisse and the Elster which consisted of low, swampy land crisscrossed by streams and gullies was by its very nature a death-trap, and the bridge which crossed the Pleisse at Connewitz was so situated that a small force of the enemy concealed in the woods could rake it with their fire. Yet here in this triangle Schwarzenberg had determined to post a considerable part of his troops, among them a number of Russian regiments. Toll and other Russian generals protested vehemently against this plan and at last appealed to the *Tsar* who told Schwarzenberg peremptorily that his Russians should "cross to the right bank of the Pleisse where, and nowhere else, they belonged." Schwarzenberg was obliged to yield as far as the Russians were concerned, but he was infatuated with his plan and merely substituted Austrians for Russians in the fatal triangle. His chief of the staff, Langeron, believed that here was a chance to carry off all the honours in the great battle of the nations by outflanking the enemy.

The great battle began at last on October 16th, and resolved itself into four separate engagements: Wachau, Connewitz, Lindenau and Möckern. At Connewitz the criticisms made at the outset by the Russian generals amply justified themselves in practice. The bridge was soon barricaded and the concealed sharpshooters inflicted enormous damage on the Austrians, so that even as early as eleven in the meaning Schwarzenberg, who was watching the operations, expressed his fear that "after all we shall not get through by way of Connewitz." Merveldt, who was in command at this point, had already lost two generals and 4,000 men, while the advantage gained was purely nominal.

Schwarzenberg finally drew off a portion of the troops sending them back and around in the direction of Wachau, where they were much needed. No conception of hell could be worse than the spectacle which offered itself here at Connewitz three days later when the troops in pursuit of Napoleon were obliged to pass over the same ground. An officer writes:

> The road between the village and the bridge, was so thick with dead combatants sunk in the deep morass, that there was no use trying to move than *and the whole column marched over them!*"

Simultaneously with the fighting at Connewitz a combat that amounted to a regular battle in itself was going on at Wachau where, on the heights, Napoleon had drawn up the main body of his troops, 138,000 strong. It was in front of Wachau that Toll and the other Russian generals had urged Schwarzenberg to concentrate his forces rather than scatter than in positions like the swampy triangle between the Pleisse and the Elster, where they would be hampered by natural obstacles; now, as the event proved, the allies were in great numerical inferiority at the point where they were most needed and where Napoleon commanded in person.

The French emperor had seated himself at a table on the Galgenberg with maps and diagrams before him and a fire burning at his side. The enemy began the attack even before he had completed the disposition of his troops and the battle was soon in full swing. An eyewitness writes:

> Along the whole line there raged such a fearful cannonade as

the oldest veterans could not remember to have heard. Single discharges of cannon could no longer be differentiated, the earth literally trembled, and in far Leipzig itself the windows rattled incessantly.

By eleven o'clock some slight advantages had been gained by Napoleon and the latter sent word to his ally, the King of Saxony, who is said to have been found skulking in his cellar for safety, that "all was going well and the French had occupied the heights and the villages." At the same time Napoleon ordered that all the bells of Leipzig should be rung "to inform the army of the advantages gained." But when night fell and the deadly struggle ended the positions were not essentially different from what they had been in the beginning.

The scale inclined indeed in Napoleon's favour; but something more was needed than a half victory at one single point if he was to escape the net that was being woven around him. To be sure he had been more or less successful at Connewitz and at Lindenau too, but all this was outweighed by what he had lost through Blücher's attack on Möckern. Until the sound of the cannon from the latter direction reached him in the course of the afternoon on the Galgenberg he had not realised that Blücher was so near.

Already at nine that morning the distant smoke rising from the cannonading at Wachau had been pointed out to Blücher and his immediate response had been a "forward, march!" He calculated that, even though he should find himself unable to reach the main field of battle in time, he could at all events engage any French detachments that stood in the way and prevent them from lending aid to Napoleon. Between Möckern and Gross-Wiederitsch—to the northwest, therefore, of Leipzig—he came upon Marmont drawn up in force and with outposts at Lindental and Breitenfeld. These outposts were easily driven back.

In numbers Blücher had greatly the advantage, his army numbering 54,000 men as against only 27,000 of the enemy. But, not being seconded as he had expected to be by Bernadotte, Blücher feared an attack on his flank from the direction of the Mulde and, until very late in the day, had refrained from taking a personal part in the operations, holding a considerable portion of his troops in reserve.

As it was, by holding back Marmont's corps Blücher is believed by good critics, (Friederich, for instance), to have saved the day for Schwarzenberg's army; but the actual deeds of heroism were reserved for Yorck and his men. Seven times that brave commander renewed his attack on the village of Möckern, then proceeded to storm each house separately with terrible loss of life. Yorck lost that day one third of his entire corps. His last infantry reserves had advanced in vain over the corpses of their fallen comrades, when a dashing charge of cavalry finally decided the day. A report of the battle says:

> All who found themselves in the path of the attack, fell back, until such a snarl ensued that the horsemen could no longer penetrate it. The French fired only single shots and the Prussians gashed and stabbed, man to man.

The French were finally swept from the field and a conquered eagle, as a token of victory, was immediately sent to Schwarzenberg's camp.

Blücher was high-minded enough not to let his personal feelings towards Bernadotte interfere with his attempts to secure the latter's co-operation for the encounters that were still to come. He despatched to him the English military *attaché*, General Stewart, who was a personal friend of the crown prince. Stewart rode until exhausted, to Landsberg, and then sent on the following manly appeal:

> Royal Highness! I come from the battlefield of General Blücher and have the honour to send you a detailed account of this battle. I venture most humbly to beg Your Royal Highness to set out with your army for Taucha the instant you receive this letter. Not a moment is to be lost. Your Royal Highness has promised me. I have spoken as a friend: I speak now as a soldier and Your Royal Highness will only repent it if you do not begin.

To this came the answer before midnight that the crown prince was setting out for Landsberg and that his cavalry was already on the march to take part in the operations of the allied armies.

When day broke on the morning of October 17th, Napoleon's position was already vastly less favourable than it had been on the evening before. Not only was Blücher's victorious army free to begin new operations against him, but, for the allies, reinforcements were approaching from on all sides. All told there would soon be a numerical superiority of no less than 135,000 men. Napoleon has been much blamed for not withdrawing from Leipzig before the final and complete closing in of the allies around him. But, apart from the blow that such a course would have meant to his pride, there was the valid consideration that as his only avenue of escape was to the westward, the allies would quickly have forced him back across the Rhine and this meant the sacrifice of the garrisons in the various fortresses of Germany which numbered no less than 130,000 men.

The 17th of October, save for some insignificant skirmishing of Blücher's army with stray divisions of Marmont and Ney, was a day of rest, a lull before the storm. Both armies stood in battle formation, Napoleon in his old position of Dösen, Wachau, Liebertwolkwitz, Kolmberg.

That Napoleon, by the afternoon of the 17th, had come to consider his own situation desperate may be inferred from the report of one of his prisoners, the Austrian general Merveldt, who was summoned to the emperor's tent at Meusdorf. Napoleon began by fencing. He declared that his own army still numbered more than 200,000 men and Merveldt told him that the allies had more than 350,000, both of which statements were equally exaggerated. Napoleon then burst forth with: "Will this war last forever? It is about time to put an end to it!" proceeding then to unfold his conditions for a peace. He suggested a truce during which he and his army should retire behind the Saale, the Russians and Prussians behind the Elbe while the Austrians should return to Bohemia.

It was *naïve* of him in the extreme to think that the allies at such a juncture would calmly let him walk out of his trap uninjured. Yet he actually despatched Merveldt with a private letter to Emperor Francis, embodying, it must be supposed, this proposal. Merveldt, who did not arrive at the headquarters of the allies until very late at night, found them busily occupied with preparations for the great battle of October 18th, and no notice whatever was taken of Napoleon's communication. He himself, indeed, seems really to have hoped for good results from Merveldt's mission, and he long delayed giving his orders for the fighting of the following day. That night, however, he sent detachments to the Saale and Unstrutt to see to the condition of the bridges, a precaution which he omitted—unfortunately for the French Army—in the case of the Elster and of the many small streams to the south-west of Leipzig.

The allies, for their part, had been glad enough to remain inactive; in fact a council of war held at Güldengossa had voted to postpone operations until the 18th, at eight in the morning; by which time it was hoped, Colloredo's troops, which had arrived in a state of exhaustion, would have had time to rest. There were troops, too, under Bennigsen, that were due to arrive and nothing whatever had been heard from Bernadotte.

The Swedish crown prince really did advance his army to Breiten-feld and one of his corps commanders, Wintzingerode, took part with Blücher in the skirmishes already noted as having occurred on the morning of the 17th, and helped to pursue the French as far as Taucha, which is to the north-east of Leipzig on the little River Partha. In the course of the day came one of Bernadotte's cool demands that drove Blücher to the very verge of exasperation.

Bernadotte wished the actual position of the armies to be reversed, so that as Blücher faced Leipzig to the north of the city the Swedes would form his right instead of his left wing. The ostensible reason for the change was that Bernadotte would thus be enabled to retain his communication with the Elbe bridges by which he had previously been so ready to retreat; but it was very widely believed at the time that Bernadotte's real object was to avoid having his troops placed at the spot where Napoleon was most likely to attempt to break through should he decide instead of retreating to the Rhine to make a dash for the Elbe.

When this demand of Bernadotte's came Blücher had already made his plan to cross the River Partha in junction with the Swedes and swing round on the right of Schwarzenberg who was still facing Wachau. He refused to change this plan. He had reached the point—and who can blame him?—where he was ready to renounce Ber-nadotte and all his works. When the latter invited him to a personal conference he deigned no answer but sent an adjutant to Bülow and Wintzingerode to ask if he could count on them to join in the opera-tions contemplated, and to which Schwarzenberg had expressed his approval, even without Bernadotte's command, Bülow's true-hearted answer was, "that he would not be found wanting where the good of the fatherland was at stake" and that every reliance, too, could be placed on Wintzingerode.

The next developments in the affair with Bernadotte are as credit-able to Blücher as anything that ever happened in his whole career. One notes an utter absence of every selfish consideration, a burning desire to do only what was best for the cause. To state the matter briefly, when he found that Bernadotte's co-operation in the battle could only be secured in that way, he gave up to him the greater part of his own army and thus renounced every opportunity for personal distinction.

In the night of the seventeenth the Swedish crown prince had sent to renew his invitation to a conference, and Blücher had thought best to accept. He had then hurried through the darkness to Breitenfeld, arriving there before dawn to find quite a formal gathering at the prince's headquarters. Prince William of Prussia, the king's brother, and all the military attachés were present. All without exception were in favour of Blücher's project, and had Bernadotte continued to oppose it there is every likelihood that Prince William in the name of the King of Prussia would have cancelled Bernadotte's authority over Bülow.

Bernadotte's strength lay in bringing forward astonishing counter-propositions. He would join in the advance across the Partha and would start at once if Blücher would hand over to him thirty thousand of his men. Blücher seems not to have hesitated even for a moment. The troops were needed in the battle that was imminent; who commanded them was a secondary consideration. The hour appointed for the beginning of the battle was approaching; there had already been too much delay. He gave his consent and hurried off to the scene of the fighting without even waiting for the protocol the weeding of which was as follows:

1. That General von Blücher hands over to the Crown Prince of Sweden 30,000 men of his army comprising infantry, cavalry, and artillery; that these troops, in conjunction with the Northern Army, under command of the crown prince, shall attack the army of the Emperor Napoleon by way of Taucha; that General Blücher with his remaining troops shall continue to hold the position in front of Leipzig and shall in every way attempt to take the city itself so soon as the struggle shall have begun all along the line.

2. It is agreed that, in case the Emperor Napoleon turns with all his forces against the Silesian and Northern Armies, both armies together shall fight until the main army comes to their aid; in which case the crown prince and General von Blücher shall act in accord, and both chief-generals shall confer with each other as to what shall be undertaken.

It is only fair to say that Bernadotte to this day has his defenders who point out that there really was danger, at the post assigned, of Napoleon with his whole force falling on the Swedes, and that it was only the part of wisdom to insist, before taking it, on proper reinforcement. Certainly, the event proved that Bernadotte's premises had been false, for Napoleon was finally to make his escape from Leipzig in the opposite direction. We shall see presently what an effect his long delay on the morning of the 18th, had on the fortunes of the day.

Including Bernadotte's forces, which still had a march before them of several hours prior to coming into action, the allies had now at their disposal 295,000 men and 1,466 cannon. The French forces, on the other hand, deducting the troops which had been despatched to guard and repair the Elster bridges, and also allowing for the severe losses incurred on the 16th, are estimated at only 160,000, with 630 cannon. That, in spite of such disparity of numbers, and with no real ultimate hope of success, the resistance lasted so long, speaks well both for the courage and tenacity of the French and for the excellence of Napoleon's leadership.

Napoleon's aim throughout this battle of the 18th, was to clear a way for the retreat of his army through the defile of Lindenau and to remain on the defensive at all other points. We have here the explanation why, to the south-west, every village and every favourable position—notably Probstheida—was fought for with such utter desperation. As it happened less had been done by the allies in the way of protecting Lindenau than for any other important point in the whole circle, the corps of Gyulai alone, which numbered but 15,000 men being entrusted with its defence.

The attack on Napoleon's position was begun simultaneously and with great vigour from a dozen different directions: from behind Lindenau; from Mark-Kleeberg; from Wachau, Liebertwolkwitz, and Probstheida; from Fuchshain and Seifertshain; from Taucha and from the spot in the rear of the Hallescher Thor where Blücher had drawn up his forces. The French troops were massed closely together to the south and south-east of the city and for the most part at some little distance from it, a few divisions being posted near Lindenau and also along the River Partha to frustrate the flanking movement of Blücher and Bernadotte.

The weather was favourable, for after weeks of almost constant rain the sim had that morning broken through the clouds and was shining brilliantly. Napoleon had been busy all through the night, changing his headquarters to Stötteritz, examining the outposts at Probstheida, which was one of his strongest positions, consulting with Marshal Ney at Reudnitz, then hurrying to inspect his eventual avenue of escape in the direction of Lindenau, and returning to Probstheida, not far from which point, on the Thonberg, he was to remain throughout the greater part of the day.

It would be futile for us to attempt to enter in detail into the operations of each of the attacking columns; the limitations of historical bi-

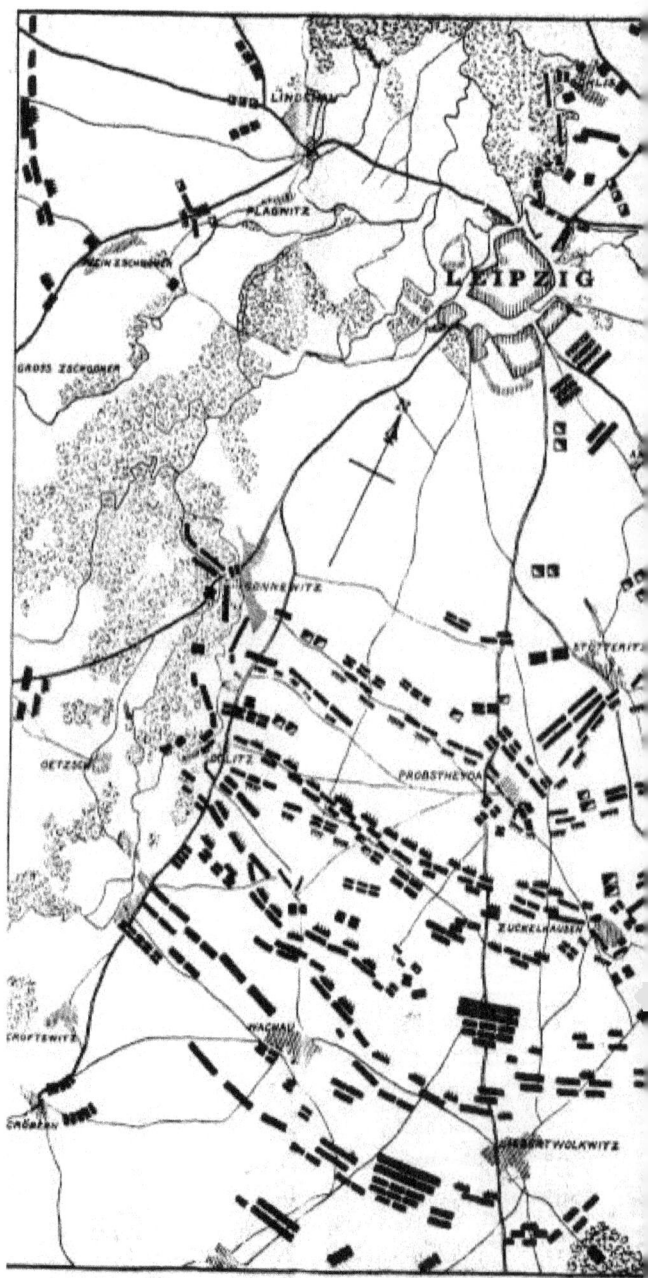

PLAN OF THE
BATTLE
OF
LEIPZIG
OCT. 18 · 1813

FRENCH · ALLIES
INFANTRY INFANTRY
CAVALRY CAVALRY
ARTILLERY ARTILLERY

MOCKAU
PLÖSEN
PLAUSSIG
PAUNSDORF
STÜNTZ
MELKAU
ZWEYNAUNDORF
ENGELSDORF
BAALSDORF
SOMMERFELD
ALTHEN
KLEIN-PÖSSNAU

ography make it not only pardonable but necessary to dwell more particularly on the episodes in which Blücher was directly concerned. In general, it may be said, that by two o'clock in the afternoon the French had lost many of their outlying posts but had not been dislodged from their main positions; while they for their part had succeeded in brushing aside Gyulai and making free the road to Weissenfels.

Bernadotte was extraordinarily late in arriving on the field, and it was four o'clock in the afternoon before his Swedes crossed the Partha. In the interval Blücher, who had taken up his position on a hill near the latter river, directed the operations of Langeron's corps which was the one he had elected to place under the crown prince's orders. An officer of Blücher's staff has vividly described the scene that first unfolded itself before them:

> Here we enjoyed an astonishing spectacle. Along the distant ridge we witnessed the march into position of Schwarzenberg's army. The columns, appearing on the extreme south-eastern horizon, soon occupied the whole ridge and moved quietly on, all the different categories of soldiers, either together or in succession, being represented. Here and there the weapons glistened in the morning sun. The distance was sufficiently great to make the whole army seem like a passing vision, and one could follow the whole endless procession until it sank from sight in the extreme west. Ever fresh hordes kept coming from the east, ever those in front kept vanishing in the west in a steady unbroken stream. One seemed to be looking at a whole people in migration. So must the Teutonic tribes inundating the German plains at the time of the wandering of the nations have appeared. All of us were most strongly affected by the sight.

Blücher's own numbers were too few to ramble him to succeed in breaking through the French lines and he fought for hours without gaining an inch of ground. Towards evening, then, in obedience to a request from the headquarters of the main army, he despatched Yorck's corps on a night march to the River Saale, with instructions to occupy the bridges at Halle and Merseburg in order to cut off Napoleon's retreat, which by this time was confidently anticipated. The latter made, indeed, a wonderful resistance throughout the whole day and, when darkness fell, had lost none of his main positions and was still master of the line of retreat.

A dramatic incident of the day to which French historians have always ascribed great importance as being the real cause of Napoleon's defeat was the defection of the Saxon contingent in the very midst of the fighting. They turned, shouldered arms, formed in a column with the artillery in front, and went bodily over to the enemy.

That the allies made, on the whole, so poor a showing in this gigantic combat of the 18th, is largely due to Bernadotte's delays and to his want of energy in general. Had he made an earlier start from Breitenfeld he might, already before noon, have joined Blücher on the Partha, where no less than 90,000 men would then have been opposed to Ney's force of less than half that number. The benefit would have been twofold; for not only would Napoleon have been forced to send to the River Partha reserves which did him excellent service elsewhere, but Bennigsen, who had been commanded to hold the gap Bernadotte's troops were intends to fill, was prevented from making a flank attack against Probstheida which was the key to Napoleon's whole position.

Late as it was, finally, when Bernadotte appeared on the scene, he might still have accomplished much had he been more enterprising. His artillery alone came into action! How successfully he spared his men may be gathered from the almost incredible fact that while the losses of the Austrians, according to a most careful computation were 420 officers and 14,538 men, those of the Prussians 498 officers and 15,535 men, and those of the Russians 865 officers and 21,740 men, Bernadotte's whole sacrifice was 9 officers and 160 men! Surely the suspicion is justified that, throughout, he had spared his troops from the fear that if he returned to Sweden with a greatly weakened army his own position there would be untenable.

Marvellous as had been the resistance opposed by Napoleon's forces the French emperor knew only too well that he would never be able to face another awful day like the 18th. His retreat was as masterly as his defence had been. It was already daylight on the 19th, before the allies became aware that, under cover of the darkness and of the misty dawn, he had withdrawn his forces from Probstheida, Stötteritz, and Connewitz leaving detachments to tend the delusive camp-fires and ward off premature attacks.

He had, moreover, done what he could to put Leipzig itself in a condition to ward off as long as possible a storm of the enemy. Barricades, palisades, and earthworks had everywhere been thrown up, batteries had been advanced to exposed positions, and a force of 30,000 men had been detailed off for the last desperate defence. Leipzig had been formerly a walled town but the old fortifications had been in great part removed. The outlying gardens, however, were protected by walls and ditches and the three main gates of the city, the Grimmischer Hallischer, and Petersthor, offered strong points for resistance; while the more substantially built houses themselves, in many instances, served as forts and buttresses.

Through a fourth gate, the Rannstädter Thor the French Army had been streaming throughout the whole night, at first in almost total darkness but later aided by the light of the moon. Awful had been the crowding and confusion but there was no panic, no mere hasty flight. The cavalry, the artillery, and the baggage waggons which led the way had left behind them a trail of fallen horses; and broken vehicles and trains of captives, and even herds of cattle, blocked the way. Napoleon himself, who did not leave Leipzig until the next morning when the storming of the city was fully under way, reached the Rannstädter Thor with the utmost difficulty. He was still fully master of himself; his face, so one who saw him pass assures us, did not betray the least sign of fear or anxiety.

It was nearly nine on the morning of the 19th, before the French wholly abandoned the suburbs of Leipzig; by ten all the various forces of the allies had advanced for the last storm on the city itself. There was a short lull, for word was passed round that the Tsar Alexander had granted a general cessation of hostilities for half an hour, having received a deputation from the King of Saxony recommending the city to the mercy of the besiegers. The Saxon king's emissary, Colonel von Ryssel, offered to surrender Leipzig on condition that the troops be allowed to withdraw; and, armed with authority to spare this city should the French soldiers retire and the Saxons lay down their arms, General Toll and Colonel von Natzmer were despatched to confer personally with King Frederick Augustus.

It would be impossible to conceive of a more ridiculous role than that played by His Majesty of Saxony at this most critical juncture. When Toll and Natzmer appeared at his quarters, they were met with the surprising announcement that His Majesty was busy and could not see them. Insisting on an audience they found the king carefully arrayed in his full-dress uniform, but not by any means for their benefit. After despatching von Ryssel with the offer to surrender he had received word that Napoleon, before leaving the city, desired a farewell interview, which had then taken place. The king now told the emissaries of the allies—as if no such suggestion had ever come from himself at all—that the matter of the sparing of the city must be discussed with the French governor, and that even his own troops could not be ordered to lay down their arms because they were responsible not to him but to the French emperor.

The explanation of the whole matter was, that in his last interview. Napoleon, with consummate audacity, had fooled the Saxon king to the top of his bent. The latter finally confessed to Toll that, when he had despatched von Ryssel with the offer to surrender, he had done so in the belief that his august ally, the emperor, considered that all was lost. Napoleon in person, however, had just informed him that he was leaving Leipzig merely for the purpose of manoeuvring in the open field, and would return in a day or two and relieve the city!

Toll and Natzmer seem really to have made the attempt to find the French governor; but long before he could be reached, the storm on the city had begun and the outer defences had crumbled. Blücher had had one of the hardest tasks, a bridge by which he was obliged to pass being strongly guarded. A Leipzig citizen, (Hussell), has recorded that the greater number of the bombs that actually fell in the city came from the direction of the Hallescher Thor.

The fighting was proceeding vigorously, and a detachment of Blücher's troops had made its way round to the right until already in contact with Napoleon's line of retreat, when suddenly, above all the cannonading and musketry was heard the sound of a terrific explosion—a worthy climax to the greatest battle that had ever taken place between nations.

The Elster bridge, Napoleon's only chance of retreat, had been utterly wrecked in the very path of some 20,000 of the French who still remained on the Leipzig side. A whole barge full of gunpowder had, sometime previously, been placed under one of the arches; at the moment of the appearance of the detachment just mentioned as having been sent round to the right by Blücher a subaltern was in command with orders "to blow up the bridge when the enemy should appear for the purpose of taking it." A more responsible officer would doubtless have found means to hold in check Blücher's small detachment until the remnant of the French could have crossed; but only too literally did the subaltern obey his orders.

The scene that now ensued was one of the cruellest, most horrible, and most dramatic that has ever occurred in the course of all history. Those of the retreating army who were further in front were struck by the debris of the wrecked bridge and upon them rained the sundered limbs and the torn flesh of men and horses. Hundreds of those behind sprang into the water from the bridge, hundreds more dashed in from the river's slimy bank. Among them was Prince Poniatowski, who had commanded a regiment of Poles and had committed deeds of valour worthy of heroes of antiquity.

Scales like these at the Elster bridge make one wonder if humanity will never grow wise, will never learn to settle its disputes by some method that does not mean the greatest conceivable suffering to the greatest number. Here in the Elster were sights of unspeakable horror: human dead piled so high that heaps of them projected above the surface of the water with heads, legs, and arms inextricably mingled. And within a circumference of nearly ten miles there was scarcely a spot from which a corpse could not be seen. In and around Leipzig some ninety thousand men had fallen, dead or wounded; and of the wounded an enormous proportion were to die. Bodies, stripped bare by marauders, lay in great naked heaps, pecked at and gnawed at by beast and bird.

It was long before progress could be made with the work of burial, for the inhabitants of the outlying districts had fled in all directions, the army was obliged to march on, and the inhabitants of Leipzig itself, at first at least, seemed as though in a lethargy. Rapidly, as may be imagined the very air grew pestilential. In order to facilitate matters great carts went through the streets of Leipzig and were soon filled high with the harvest of those who had died in the houses. From the windows above corpses were thrown down; and it was too much to expect that in all cases the last breath should be awaited. But if, in the sickening mass, arms or legs were seen to move there was usually someone sufficiently merciful to club them into quietude.

Practically no preparations at all had been made to succour the wounded. A surgeon who had hastened from Berlin writes:

> The wildest imagination, could not picture the misery in stronger colours than I found it to be here in truth. The surrounding villages having been burned and abandoned there were no shelter, no covering, no means of bandaging, no food.

Surgical methods were at best but primitive; add to this that water was not everywhere obtainable for cleansing purposes and that surface drainage was the rale, and one can believe the assertion that from some of the houses where the injured had been brought together, a steady stream of mingled filth and blood flowed down the steps into the street. The germs of disease held high carnival!

The wounded were occasionally altogether forgotten, not merely individually but even collectively. A cotemporary, (Hussell), referring more especially to Blücher's encounter at Möckern writes:

> More than ten days after the murderous battle, I saw in a barn at Maisdorf one hundred and seventy-four French soldiers who had been carried there wounded and lay dead of starvation. A solitary cat wandered tranquilly among the half-decomposed corpses.

All this of course was the seamy side of the victory. In certain parts of the city all was gay as in Paradise. An eye-witness, (Friccius), writes:

> Greater contrast of exultation and mourning, of joy and sorrow, has never been seen.

After the fighting was over, the Tsar Alexander, Frederick William, and Schwarzenberg rode to the marketplace where they were joined by Bernadotte and Blücher, the Austrian emperor reaching the city soon afterwards. No *fête* could have been more lively than the scene in the market-place. The troops formed in lines, the bands played, every window was filled with spectators, and cheer upon cheer arose. One is surprised to see what credit was already given to Blücher for his services in the cause; the English colonel attached to his staff, Sir Hudson Lowe, declares that no one was greeted more enthusiastically than the hoary warrior whose achievements had contributed so signally to the success of the day; and Blücher himself wrote to his wife:

> The Tsar of Russia publicly kissed me in the market-place and called me the liberator of Germany. The Emperor of Austria, too, heaped praises on me; while my own king thanked me with tears in his eyes.

Frederick William, a few days later, sent to him this note:

> By repeated victories you roll up your services to the state more quickly than I can follow them with proofs of my gratitude. Accept a new evidence of this in the appointment as field-marshal general, and long may you grace this position to the joy of the fatherland and as a model to the army which you have so often led to fame and victory.

Blücher himself was intent only on shedding more blood. We shall see again and again how strong was his belief that a pursuing army should spend its strength "to the last breath and to the last horse" in order so to weaken the retreating enemy that no further battles would be necessary. Gneisenau, it is to be feared, was actuated more by real enjoyment of the chase. He frankly admitted that "the highest satisfaction in life is to wreak vengeance on an arrogant enemy."

Blücher was beside himself with vexation at the laxness of Schwarzenberg in this matter of following up the victory. It is true, already on the 18th of October, Schwarzenberg had provided for despatching no less than 60,000 men to different points on the line by which it was expected that Napoleon would retreat, but had changed his arrangements on the ground that the enemy's plans had not been sufficiently ascertained; and on the 19th, he even recalled troops that were already on the march. His general conduct and his real motives and intentions have been the subject of as lively speculation as those of Bernadotte. It may have been timidity that held him back now.

Napoleon's forces were still formidable; might he not turn at bay and change this glorious victory into a defeat? It is equally likely indeed that Schwarzenberg, with whom political considerations always weighed heavily, wished to spare the son-in-law of his emperor from utter ruin and thought that he had already been sufficiently punished.

Blücher, as usual, was the active element in the coalition. Even before going to the Leipzig market-place to pay his respects to the monarchs and receive the acclamations of the crowd, he had despatched his cavalry to Skeudnitz with directions to cross the Elster and come into touch with those forces, under Yorck, which had been sent to the Saale on the evening before. Schwarzenberg, on the other hand, with the exception of sending ahead one single corps, that of Gyulai, did not move from Leipzig until the 20th. Bernadotte was as contrary as ever. On the 19th, he invited the monarchs to a full-dress parade of his soldiers; but he refused to move until he should have ascertained that a French corps under Davoust, that had been operating in Northern Germany, was safely out of the way. It was the 22nd, before he broke camp.

Blücher himself left Leipzig on the 20th, at the head of his remaining troops. He had resumed command over Langeron's corps, for his agreement with Bernadotte had expired. By the 22nd, he had joined Yorck and four days later his cavalry had come into contact with Napoleon's retreating columns near Eisenach. But bitter disappointments were in store for him. He was furious with everyone: with

Yorck for the failure of an attempt to cut off Bertrand's corps, on which occasion Gneisenau maintained that Yorck objected as usual to the continual marching and "wasted his time in cursing headquarters while Bertrand escaped"; with Schwarzenberg, for sending orders to change the direction of his march and leave the further pursuit of the enemy to the vanguard of the main army; with his own cavalry, which had failed to inflict any considerable harm on the enemy. Blücher is quoted as saying to Langeron:

> General! I have often told you that your cavalry was bad. I can say the same of my own—yes, it is even worse than yours.

Regarding Schwarzenberg's change of orders Blücher wrote to a friend:

> I was closely following the French emperor along the *chaussée* and was daily coming to the quarters he had just left. Had I been allowed to continue I should have reached the enemy and have attacked him in the rear while Wrede was engaging him in front.

Wrede coming from the south had appeared with a fresh Austro-Bavarian corps and had placed himself in the way at Hanau, but had greatly needed the assistance Blücher had thus been prevented from offering. Wrede had indeed inflicted terrific losses on Napoleon—9,000 in killed and wounded and 10,000 who were taken prisoners—but had been unable to prevent his breaking through and reaching the Rhine.

Blücher, by this time far in the rear, had been able to capture 5,000 stragglers and 18 cannon; and Napoleon, when he finally crossed the Rhine, did so with but 40,000 men—but one-tenth of the enormous forces he had employed in the campaign. Yet Blücher was not satisfied, he wrote later:

> It is true we accomplished much, but not nearly what we might have done. Napoleon by rights ought not to have come through, and God pardon those whose tardiness and laziness were to blame. But the devil is ever at work and envy is not idle!

God pardon them, indeed! Had Napoleon's forces been annihilated here there would have been no need of the awful campaign in France, no need of Waterloo!

CHAPTER 8

The Beginning of the Campaign of 1814 in France

All that Blücher had experienced during the campaign of 1813, was but child's play compared with what he was to endure in the campaign of the ensuing year. He was to learn the bitterness of defeat, to see his army all but annihilated, to suffer from the lukewarmness of Schwarzenberg and the disobedience of Yorck, at moments when it was no longer a question of inflicting more or less damage on Napoleon but of actual self-preservation. Yet on the whole, here in France, he was more the hero than even at Leipzig or at Waterloo; for his indomitable will carried him to the limit of human endurance, and, although at the last he was a mere physical wreck, brought him to the goal he had persistently striven for—the hurling of Napoleon from his throne.

After the Battle of Leipzig and the pursuit to the Rhine the prospects seemed very bright for the allies. Napoleon had no troops left to send to the aid of the isolated French garrisons in the fortresses along the Elbe, Oder, and Vistula; and it was evident that it could only be a matter of time before these would be forced to surrender. There were sixteen fortresses from which the French flag still waved—Zamoscz, Danzig, Modlin, Stettin, Custrin, Glogau, Dresden, Torgau, Wittenberg, Magdeburg and Hamburg, Würzbturg and Erfurt, Kehl, Castel, and Wesel—and the total strength of their garrisons has been variously estimated at from 140,000 to 190,000 men.

It has often been asked why no effort was made to break through the lines, unite as many as possible of these troops in one body, and come to Napoleon's assistance; and St. Cyr, who commanded the 30,000 men left in Dresden, has been blamed for not taking the initiative. Torgau garrisoned by 16,000 men, was but a two days' march from Dresden; and here, already, would have been the nucleus for a not inconsiderable army. As it was, Dresden capitulated on the 11th of November, and St. Cyr promised on his honour that neither officers nor soldiers should serve again against the allies, unless exchanged for their own captives. Torgau, after the garrison had suffered terrible privations and hardships, surrendered on December 26th; and when at last the men were permitted to march out, nearly 3,500 were in the hospitals, too ill to be moved.

Wittenberg held out until taken by storm on January 13, 1814, and Magdeburg was still unconquered in May, when Louis XVIII. ordered it delivered over to the allies. When one sees such long and brave resistance under every disadvantage imaginable, one is inclined to wonder all the more that these strong positions should have fallen so easily into Napoleon's hands in 1806.

By the end of May the last of the fortresses, Hamburg, had surrendered, and although few of the soldiers, if any, took part in the campaign of 1814, they did in the following year flock in numbers to Napoleon's standard and formed the best element in the army that fought at Waterloo.

Blücher meanwhile had been thoroughly exasperated at the slowness and at the indecision of the allies. He himself was for hurrying on into France; and Gneisenau drew up a detailed plan of campaign, which, however, met with no favour at the headquarters of the main army. Yet Napoleon had practically no army left with which to oppose an advance; the few troops that he had brought back into safety would not even have sufficed properly to garrison the small forts with which France was studded. Just before the Battle of Leipzig he had, it is true, called for a levy of 280,000 men and, on November 15th, he summoned 300,000 more to arms; but, even if the response were to be enthusiastic, much time would necessarily elapse before the forces could become available. These were the golden hours that Blücher was burning to utilise.

Instead, as he desired, of being allowed to head an invasion he was given a much more humble task, that of blockading Mainz. He wrote later to his friend Bonin:

God knows what they were thinking about . . . .neither I nor
the army under my command are in the very least suited either
for a blockading corps or for a corps of observation. But envy,

145

the all-destroyer, has a hand in the affair. . . . There is now gathered together in Frankfort a swarm of monarchs and of princes, and an assemblage like that spoils everything. The war is no longer conducted with any energy and I am afraid that through procrastination much will be sacrificed. . . . It is perfectly certain that had we all, without delay, crossed the Rhine, Napoleon would by this time have been suing for peace.

Again, Blücher writes, full of disgust for the task which, doubtless, had been imposed upon him more for the purpose of keeping him busy and out of harm's way than from any military necessity:

I have a great deal to do just now with this damned fortress of Mainz. I have already effected the investment from this side so that my outposts are within firing distance of the fortress. . . If, as I am urging and hoping, we cross the Rhine we shall also do it from the other side.

Blücher chafed so violently at not being allowed to carry out his wishes with regard to the pursuit of Napoleon that he grew fierce and irritable beyond measure. We are told that his sharp speeches "made wounds like his own sword"; that he took away reputations and accused of cowardice even those in high places; that he used very plain language calling people "rogues" and declaring that they "deserved the gallows." Knesebeck, who had been responsible for Blücher's remaining before Mainz, wrote later that, although he had borne in silence the harsh things that Field-Marshal Forward—so he called him—had said to him, they had nevertheless "made him ill with vexation and annoyance."

Among the "horde of monarchs and princes" at Frankfort, of which Blücher had spoken so scathingly, purely political considerations had by this time assumed such proportions that they completely overshadowed those of a military nature. Austria, as we already know, had her own particular reasons for not wishing Napoleon's power to be annihilated; Frederick William of Prussia, in addition to having been persuaded by Knesebeck that a long rest was necessary for his troops, had the feeling that further encounters with his formidable enemy might endanger what still remained to him of his possessions; Bernadotte, although not present, for he had gone to fight against the Danes on his own account, wrote letters containing specious arguments against carrying the war into the enemy's country.

Alexander alone, who was anxious to place Napoleon forever be-

Pub.d by R. Ackermann 101 Strand London.

NAPOLEON

THE FIRST, and LAST, by the Wrath of Heaven Emperor of the Jacobins, Protector of the Confederation of Rogues, Mediator of the Hellish League, Grand Cross of the Legion of Horror, Commander in Chief of the Legions of Skeletons left at Moscow, Smolensk, Leipzig, &c. Head Runner of Runaways, Mock High-Priest of the Sanhedrim, Mock Prophet of Mussulmen, Mock Pillar of the Christian Faith, Inventor of the Syrian Method of disposing of his own Sick by sleeping Draughts, or of captured Enemies by the Bayonet; First Grave-Digger for burying alive; Chief Gaoler of the Holy Father and of the King of Spain, Destroyer of Crowns, and Manufacturer of Counts, Dukes, Princes, and Kings; Chief Douanier of the Continental System, Head Butcher of the Parisian and Toulonese Massacres, Murderer of Hoffer, Palm, Wright, nay, of his own Prince, the noble and virtuous Duke of Enghien, and of a thousand others; Kidnapper of Ambassadors, High-Admiral of the Invasion Praams, Cup-Bearer of the Jaffa Poison, Arch-Chancellor of Waste-Paper Treaties, Arch-Treasurer of the Plunder of the World, the sanguinary Coxcomb, Assassin, and Incendiary......to

MAKE PEACE WITH!!!

This Hieroglyphic Portrait of the DESTROYER is faithfully copied from a German Print, with the Parody of his assumed Titles. The *Hat* of the Destroyer represents a discomfited French Eagle, maimed and crouching, after his Conflict with the Eagles of the North. His *Visage* is composed of the Carcases of the Victims of his Folly and Ambition, who perished on the Plains of Russia and Saxony. His Throat is encircled with the *Red Sea*, in Allusion to his drowned Hosts. His Epaulette is a *Hand*, leading the Rhenish Confederation, under the flimsy Symbol of a *Cobweb*. The *Spider* is an Emblem of the Vigilance of the Allies, who have inflicted on that Hand a deadly Sting!.

FAMOUS INTERNATIONAL CARICATURE OF NAPOLEON

yond the power of interfering with his schemes in Poland and, in addition, was ably advised by Stein, was heart and soul for further pursuit. He was chiefly responsible for the eventual decision to invade France.

In the deliberations in Frankfort it was determined to offer peace to Napoleon on the basis of France resuming her natural geographical boundaries, the Alps, the Rhine, and the Pyrenees; of Germany, Holland, and Italy being evacuated, and of a congress being called to determine such questions as should relate to England's colonial possessions. It was an important concession to Alexander that, while the negotiations were in progress, the allies should continue their military operations.

It was on November 10th, that St. Aignan, a French captive, was despatched with the proposals to Napoleon; but on the 24th, came back an answer which showed that the Corsican's pride was still unbroken, the lesson not yet learned. This attitude of Napoleon did more than anything else to silence the arguments of the opponents of invasion. Indeed, it could hardly be called an answer at all. The only definite proposal was that the French garrisons should be allowed to withdraw, with their cannon, arms, and supplies from six of the most untenable fortresses in Germany.

By December 2nd, it had been fully decided to renew the struggle; and in a manifesto designed to win the good will of the French people it was announced most emphatically that the allies were warring against the emperor's person and not against France as a whole.

As usual the plan of campaign was full of absurdities. The main Austrian Army, 250,000 men strong, was to make a great detour and enter France from the direction of Switzerland, and the objective point was to be the high plateau of Langres. The chief reason given for this latter choice was that near Langres several of the larger rivers rise and that it would be more easy to cross them at their sources than lower down—a consideration which, the best critics declare, already belonged to a bygone age of warfare. The main object proposed—and this too was founded on obsolete theories of strategy—was not to strike the enemy wherever he could be found, but to cut his communications and endeavour to outflank him.

As had been the case at the outset of the war, the role assigned to Blücher by this *Areopagus* at Frankfort was to be a secondary one. They evidently feared his boldness and felt that he must be kept in check. He was to act as a sort of shield or buffer, while the main army carried out its complicated manoeuvres.

But once more Blücher felt justified in not taking his commands

THE SCENE OF BLÜCHER'S OPERATIONS IN FRANCE 1814

>>>>>>> SHOWS BLÜCHER'S LINE OF MARCH

too literally; and he wrote to General Rüchel:

> It is my good fortune that I am not circumscribed and can act as I see fit. . . I have a good helper in Gneisenau.

And he wrote to his old friend Stein:

> Forward it shall be, that I promise you!

Yet throughout the month of December, he still had to remain, like a war-horse champing its bit, on the right bank of the Rhine. The detour of Schwarzenberg's army consumed several weeks, during which Blücher himself was not even able to complete the investment of Mainz, as the river was too full of ice to permit of the construction of the necessary bridges. Meanwhile *fêtes* were given in his honour at Frankfort and at Wiesbaden; and lest one should imagine that the thirst for blood filled all his waking thoughts it may be well to state that this man of seventy-two occasionally condescended to dance merrily. He had the honour, too, at this period of receiving a decoration from the King of Sweden in token of His Gracious Majesty's great appreciation of the field-marshal's services. The gift seems to have given him little pleasure; no doubt it reminded him too much of Bernadotte. He writes on December 17th:

> The King of Sweden too, has now sent me his order of the *Seraphim*. (Always weak in the matter of spelling Blücher writes here of the *Sera Pinen orden!*) I look like an old coach-horse with all the stuff, and up to date it has brought me in nothing.

On December 26th, finally, having received news from Schwarzenberg, and having learned that the enemy to all appearances could not dispose of more than 50,000 men in the field, and that these, too, were scattered along the whole Eastern frontier,—Blücher wrote to Yorck, who once more commanded one of his corps:

> I beg humbly to inform Your Excellency that on January 1st, at dawn I shall cross the Rhine with the army. The disposition for the troops will follow tomorrow. In order to keep secret my design I shall, on the 29th of this month, move my headquarters to Frankfort and take measures to make it seem as though I intended to stay there for some time.

At last the borders of the promised land were reached. The secret had been well kept; and the cold, starry New Year's Eve found the few

THE BLÜCHER MONUMENT AT CAUB

French who had been left to guard the left bank with no notion of what was in store for them. In order to throw them off their guard and prevent them from offering a strong resistance it had been arranged that the crossing should take place at three widely distant points, at Caub, at Mannheim and at Coblenz.

At Caub, Blücher himself conducted the operations, having gathered together, here, the main body of his troops; and as the crossing was slow and tedious, the current being swift and the river full of ice-floes, he found time to write several letters. We have one to an old friend, l'Estocq:

> Up to this moment 4,000 of the infantry have gone across; the bridge will be ready towards noon and then I shall follow with the whole corps.

And we have this to his wife, written from the further bank of the river and showing how successful the whole movement had been:

> The early New Year's morning was a joyous one for me, seeing that I crossed the proud Rhine. The banks rang with the cries of joy, and my brave troops were enthusiastic in their reception of me. The enemy offered but little opposition. I shall have the investment of Mainz completed, but personally shall go forward with the army. . . . My brave comrades are making such a noise that I shall have to go and hide myself in order that quiet may be restored.

In a later letter Blücher wrote;

> The whole crossing was at a cost to me of three hundred men. . . . So long as the Rhine has gone by that name no army of 80,000 men ever crossed it so cheaply; for I conquered thirteen cannon into the bargain and made 2,000 prisoners. I had the misfortune, too, to have my bridges carried away by the current while we were passing over them. But when fortune is on one's side everything will turn out for the best.

Blücher entered France by a route that was to be rendered still more famous half a century later, crossing the little River Saar and passing by the fortress of Metz. He met for the moment with practically no opposition. Marmont, whose corps numbered less than 10,000 men, not daring to make a stand on the Saar and Metz being so feebly garrisoned as to excite no fear, although Blücher thought best to detach Yorck's corps to hold it under observation while he himself hurried on to Nancy.

Blücher's letters and reports throughout this campaign in France are of such interest and importance as to remind us of the commentaries of another great conqueror of Gaul written nearly two thousand years before. On January 12th, he writes to Schwarzenberg:

Today I arrived with the Silesian Army before Metz. Saarlouis and Landau are invested, Thionville and Luxemburg blockaded. I can give battle, at the present moment with 74,000 men, or on the 19th, in front of Metz with 90,000, or later still with the number that Your Highness knows.

On the 14th, he writes to Rüchel:

The enemy had his forces all drawn up at Metz; but today I receive the announcement that they have marched away to Verdun. So, we are off for Paris! Unless we do something foolish, we shall carry all before us. Marshal Schwarzenberg is a fine man but he has three monarchs around him. Alexander is cleverer than any of his generals, besides being the noblest of men. He said to me: "Blücher, it would be a good thing if you were twenty years younger; but your good health will doubtless carry you through. The war cannot last much longer and I believe that peace is nearer at hand than people imagine."

Blücher writes, in these days, of Napoleon's great efforts to rouse the whole population of France to action, but imagines that the French emperor will find himself much hampered by the difficulty of procuring weapons in sufficient number. The Prussian field-marshal's own mind is firmly fixed on the one object, the march on Paris. He is only waiting to concentrate his forces before starting; he hopes that Schwarzenberg will make up his mind to join in the expedition:

Should the main army advance far enough to enable us to effect a junction, I believe we shall be quite strong enough to strike an absolutely decisive blow. It is possible that Napoleon will oppose us with a considerable army, but they are men who have been pressed into the service and who are lacking in courage besides being badly armed and equipped. Our troops are in every respect the opposite and are inspired by courage and good will. My 50,000 Russians will follow me to the ends of the earth, and my own men are unsurpassed in bravery. The thing that troubles me most is the lack of officers; I have lost too many of them.

Blücher's march on Paris was by no means to be effected as rapidly as he had hoped. It was like trying to turn Acheron to make Schwarzenberg, whose co-operation was so necessary, listen to arguments in favour of it; while even Frederick William, who for all his fine phrases seems never to have placed implicit confidence in Blücher but rather to have feared the latter's impetuosity, was not to be convinced. In vain Gneisenau wrote to Knesebeck dissecting every argument against, and bringing forward every argument in favour of, the move: France was in a state of inconceivable weakness and disorganisation; her fortresses were but feebly garrisoned; Napoleon's own influence was waning; for the *corps l'égislatif* had just been dissolved for attempting to prescribe reforms, and popular sympathy was with the deputies. Gneisenau concluded:

Now or never, is the time to march to Paris and to dictate a peace such as the tranquillity of the nations and the security of the old reigning dynasties demand.

In the Austrian camp the consideration that it would be better not wholly to overthrow Napoleon by taking his capital, and the antiquated military idea that the object of war was not to strike but to outmanoeuvre the enemy, were crystallising into open antagonism. There was a feeling of superiority to this madcap Prussian field-marshal that comes out most strongly in a private letter of Schwarzenberg's—a letter to his own wife:

Blücher, and still more Gneisenau;—for the old fellow has to lend his name—are urging the march on Paris with such perfectly childish rage that they trample under foot every single rule of warfare. Without placing any considerable force to guard the road from Châlons to Nancy they rush like mad to Brienne. Regardless of their rear and of their flanks they do nothing but plan *parties fines* in the Palais Royal. That is indeed frivolous at such an important moment!

Knesebeck only reflected the timorous views at headquarters when he wrote to Gneisenau that he considered any further advance beyond the plateau of Langres—a few divisions had already been sent ahead to Troyes—to be highly dangerous so long as ignorance prevailed as to Napoleon's point of concentration. He advised entering into negotiations which could be made to drag along for ten days or two weeks, during which time the emperor's whereabouts could be better ascertained!

Those were critical days at Langres; there was danger of the whole coalition falling to pieces, for the *Tsar* remained a faithful ally to those inclined for immediate action. Stein, who had come to Langres, wrote to Gneisenau on the 27th of January:

> I always show your letters to the *Tsar* who alone stands there strong and noble and spurns the counsels of the weak and of the despicable. The kingdom of tyranny shall fall and the cause of righteousness and liberty prevail.

Gneisnau, for his part, with the consciousness that his letters are to be read by Alexander, points them more directly at him and fills them with arguments that he knows will have weight:

> To have come all the way from Moscow only to allow ourselves, when within a few marches of Paris, to be duped by an accursed traitor!

The *Tsar* grew stronger in his demand that peace should be dictated in Paris and nowhere else, and that Napoleon should be deposed and the whole dynasty changed. He even thought for a moment of placing Bernadotte on the French throne; but, because of the general opposition to this plan, finally declared himself in favour of recalling the Bourbons. Austria, on the other hand, was all for delay, for sparing Napoleon, for calling a congress of ministers which should meet at once at Châtillon; and Metternich at last declared roundly that not a step would the Austrian troops advance until his demands should have been granted.

The *Tsar* responded to this last sally that in such a case he was prepared to carry on the war alone; and Frederick William of Prussia, though naturally only too inclined to sympathise with dilatory and half measures, had sufficient loyalty to declare that he would join his troops to those of Alexander.

Great was the tension; but on January 28th, a compromise was effected which materially cleared the situation. It was agreed to hold the conference of ministers at Châtillon, but, at the same time, to continue vigorously the military operations. The main army, 120,000 strong, was to march to Troyes and thence to Paris; while Blücher's army was to proceed in the same direction along the Marne, past Vitry and Châlons.

Blücher already had a surprise in store for Schwarzenberg. The latter had believed him to be much farther to the east, covering the main army's right wing, when suddenly news came that he was at Brienne—forming, as it were, that army's vanguard. Schwarzenberg's first fear was that Napoleon might cut the line of communication with Germany; but Blücher, on the 28th, wrote to reassure him:

> It would be the best thing that could happen to us, for then we could take Paris without striking a blow.

Blücher was at this time as optimistic and also physically as vigorous as a youth of twenty. Count Schwerin, who had been with him the whole time since crossing the Rhine, declares that all who came in contact with the old hero were astonished at his endurance, at his indifference to discomforts, and at his unfailing high spirits. He places "Marshal Forward" on no pedestal, indeed; for he declares that Blücher's language, when they were seated around the camp table, was occasionally so improper that he, Schwerin, "would rather not have heard what was said and least of all could repeat it," which was exactly what the English *attaché*, Sir Hudson Lowe, once asked him to do, much to staid Schwerin's embarrassment.

Blücher's exultation that now at last something decisive was likely to happen breaks out in a letter that he wrote to his wife on this same 28th of January;

> Once more we are in close proximity to the enemy and on the eve of a decisive battle. If we win, of which there is no doubt, we shall be before the walls of Paris within a week from now. . . I must close, as a report has come that Napoleon has arrived at Vitry which is only a short distance from here. So up and to horse! My men are simply longing to meet the tyrant. . . . You may soon expect interesting news.

He wrote at the same time to his friend von Vincke:

> I stand at this moment face to face with the enemy, the announcement having just reached me that Napoleon is at Vitry. The all-decisive hour appears to have come. Napoleon would like to negotiate, but all we right-minded ones wish to fight. Noble Alexander, too. But the diplomats have a hundred other projects. For the good of humanity, we must march on Paris.

There our monarchs can conclude, I may say dictate, a good peace. The tyrant has visited, plundered, and robbed every capital; we won't commit the same crime but our honour demands the satisfaction in retaliation of visiting him in his nest. . . . If they begin negotiating again, I shall quit the army and betake myself to rest.

The report that Napoleon had arrived at Vitry was to prove false. He was, as a matter of fact, even nearer—at Méizières which is in the opposite direction from Brienne, where Blücher's troops were assembled. Nor was the latter's prophecy that a decisive engagement was at hand to be fulfilled. There was merely a rather serious skirmish in which Blücher was worsted, although the operations of his army were only checked for a moment. He lost 3,000 men, but the French losses were equally severe.

Here at Brienne Blücher personally escaped being captured only by the narrowest of margins. It was evening, the fighting had apparently ended, a good part of the town being in flames; and Blücher had ridden back to the *château* which had been his headquarters earlier in the day. He and Gneisenau mounted to an upper storey whence they could count the camp-fires that were beginning to gleam through the darkness and estimate the strength of the enemy. Suddenly bullets began to fall in the courtyard and it was evident that the *château* was being attacked. Blücher was hurried away through a back door by some of his officers and they succeeded in reaching their horses which were fortunately standing in readiness.

The *château* was meanwhile surrounded and occupied by the French troops; it had grown dark and Blücher and his little escort rode almost into the arms of French detachments. But the old field-marshal's chief emotion seems to have been one of vexation that "that fellow"—so he designated Napoleon—should sleep that night in his, Blücher's, bed. He presently ordered an attack on the *château*, which, however, proved fruitless; and in the course of the night, after executing one of the most daring manoeuvres known to military science he drew up his whole army, farther to the south, on the heights above Trannes.

Here Blücher was able to effect his junction with Schwarzenberg; while at the same time Yorck, who it will be remembered had been left behind at Metz but subsequently ordered to the front, had fought successfully with a French division at St. Dizier and was now near enough for eventual co-operation.

Napoleon had commanded his troops to "pursue the enemy as far as Bar-sur-Aube"; but pursuit presupposes flight and Blücher, as we have seen, instead of being in retreat was drawn up on the heights of Trannes. He was in strong battle formation and all that Napoleon could do was to occupy La Rothière, a village on the highroad that runs from Brienne to Trannes and Bar-sur-Aube.

Even without the assistance he hoped for from Yorck, Blücher's forces numbered 125,000 men as against only 45,000 of the enemy. But he was hampered by the fact that, while Schwarzenberg had handed over to him the actual conduct of the battle, that cautious commander had previously determined minutely where each separate corps of the reinforcements that he sent should stand. That seems to have been, for the most part, outside of the line of fire.

A modern military critic, (Janson), writes:

One imagines oneself back in the times of the Trojan War in which single heroes fought each other in view of the onlooking armies. There were available 125,000 men; there were employed only 79,000... Schwarzenberg's conduct becomes more comprehensible when we reflect that the Austrian policy did not call for Napoleon's annihilation, but yet that it was absolutely necessary to make some concession to the progressive element and more particularly to the Tsar of Russia. It was the actual expressed wish of the latter, in accord with the King of Prussia that Blücher should assume the chief command.

This handing over to Blücher of the command at La Rothière was one of those "gifts of the Greeks" that needed to be accepted with caution. Not the least hampering clause of the agreement was seemingly a perfectly innocent one;

When the attack on Brienne shall have succeeded, the army of Field-Marshal Blücher shall turn against Vitry.

But turning against Vitry meant desisting, after the battle, from the pursuit of Napoleon! The Austrian object was attained; the enemy would not be destroyed, as was Blücher's wish, but would simply be "dislodged," to use Schwarzenberg's own expression.

One gains the impression that Schwarzenberg disapproved at heart of the whole plan of fighting a battle at La Rothière; that he was jealous at seeing Blücher act, even temporarily, as commander-in-chief of the combined armies; that he dreaded Blücher's influence over the *Tsar* and Frederick William.

Whatever the motives, and there certainly must have been additional ones, Blücher was informed on the eve of the battle that, so soon as it was over, he would be expected once more to separate his forces from those of the main army, which would continue to Troyes while he, Blücher, was to carry out the original plan and follow the right bank of the Marne past Vitry and Châlons.

The incidents of the Battle of La Rothière itself offer little of interest. There was an almost simultaneous struggle for several different points which were of strategic importance: for the village of La Rothière itself, for the wood known as La Giberie, for Chaumésnil. It was one in the afternoon when the allies began their attack; and the battle was brought to an end by the falling darkness of the short February day, while the fighting was rendered more difficult by the fact that the ground was soft and the cannon could only be moved with difficulty. Repeatedly flurries of snow hid the view and at times entirely prevented the infantry from taking aim. All this, in connection with Schwarzenberg's over-cautious disposition of the troops, explains the relatively insignificant results of the day.

It was a victory, for the enemy was forced to yield the field and even to vacate Brienne, where a final skirmish took place. Blücher, too, had the personal satisfaction of riding up to the *château* from which he had made such an undignified exit and of having his health drunk there in champagne by the monarchs and chief officers. But the results as a whole were far behind what the great disparity in numbers would have led one to expect The losses were about equal—6,000 on either side—and, as Schwarzenberg had ordained, there was practically no pursuit; so that Napoleon came forth from an ordeal that might easily have crushed him, unscathed and far from dispirited. In all his measures and manoeuvres he had shown to the full his old energy and decision, his old ability; he was already planning to renew operations and not to remain any longer merely on the defensive.

Neither Blücher nor the monarchs saw the battle in the perspective in which we can view it today, and they greatly overestimated its importance. "Blücher," the Tsar Alexander said to the commander-in-chief, "today you have set the crown on all your victories; mankind will bless you." Blücher himself wrote in a state of great excitement that Napoleon had received a crushing blow and would never dare to show his face again:

For me it was the happiest day of my life, the day on which, as it were, all has been decided. If Napoleon is to retain his throne, he will have to look upon it as a gift from the hands of our monarchs. I doubt his retaining it, indeed.

The troops were as jubilant as their commanders; and when at dawn the next morning they first caught sight of the old field-marshal, they broke out into such wild cheering—he relates it himself—that the tears rose to his eyes.

Gneisenau was not carried away by the victory to the same extent as his chief. He spoke of routing the "next to the last forces" of the enemy and expressed his firm conviction that the last forces too would soon be annihilated; but he did not hesitate to confess that, through ignorance of the locality, proper use had not been made of the cavalry.

We have the minutes of the council of war, held on February 2nd, in the *château* of Brienne, which decided on the final details for the separation of the Silesian from the main or Bohemian Army:

That the allied forces shall separate anew; that the Silesian Army of Field-Marshal Blücher shall at once march from here to Châlons, unite there with the scattered divisions of Generals von Yorck, von Kleist, and Count Langeron, and then press on along the Marne, past Meaux, to Paris; while the main army turns towards Troyes, and likewise presses on to Paris along both sides of the Seine.

The search for the golden fleece was not to be accompanied with greater difficulties than this endeavour of Blücher's, which had at first seemed so practicable, to reach Paris. At this juncture, indeed, it seemed as if the endeavour must be crowned with success. Here was a great force of 180,000 men that was to sweep on along the Seine and the Marne and unite where the rivers converged in the neighbourhood of the capital. At the starting-points, between the Seine at Troyes and the Marne at Châlons, there was a distance of no less than forty-seven miles, so that effectual co-operation became difficult; but arrangements had been made for mutually rendering assistance in case of need, and Wittgenstein's corps was to be so posted as to maintain direct communication between the two armies.

Almost simultaneously, Blücher gave too much rein to his rashness, and Schwarzenberg, without proper notification, changed the existing arrangements so that the basis of all Blücher's calculations was removed. His left flank which should have been covered by Wittgenstein was exposed in consequence of the latter's being summoned by headquarters to take part in an intended attack on Troyes. Wittgenstein had left a detachment under Seslawin to fill the gap caused by his own withdrawal; but Schwarzenberg, by changing the projected attack on Troyes into one of his favourite flanking movements, had even widened the distance between himself and Blücher and yet at Alexander's suggestion had summoned Seslawin to protect his extreme left wing,

Blücher, although his corps-commander Yorck had for some days been in his vicinity, had not yet effected a junction with him. Yorck, after fighting his way through the enemy's lines at St. Dizier had, on February 3rd, engaged in a skirmish at La Chaussée and, on the 4th, had taken Châlons, driving out Macdonald, his own old commander during the campaign of 1812. Macdonald was known to be retreating in the direction of Paris; and a desire to cut off this retreat caused Blücher to scatter his forces and involved him in a series of almost overwhelming disasters.

In order to understand the ensuing operations a few simple facts must be borne in mind. From Châlons all the way westward to La Ferté-sous-Jouarre there are two highways that at the latter point converge into one, continuing thus to Paris. Between Châlons and La Ferté the roads form a regular oval, the upper outline of which is called the "big Paris road," the lower outline the "little Paris road." The former runs along by the River Marne and passes the towns of Épernay and Château Thierry, while the little Paris road runs through Étoges, Champaubert, and Montmirail.

By February 8th, Macdonald had reached Château Thierry; and Blücher who, but a day or two before, had received news from Schwarzenberg that Napoleon "to an almost complete certainty" was at Troyes with the main body of his forces, and who had every right to expect at least a warning should this news have proved incorrect, had allowed his forces to become widely separated. Yorck was closely following Macdonald to Château Thierry; Sacken was on the lower road at Montmirail with orders to hurry to the junction of the roads at La Ferté-sous-Jouarre and await Macdonald there; while Blücher himself was with the Russian general, Olsufiev, at Étoges, and his remaining forces, under Kleist and Kapzewitsch, were still at Châlons.

Entirely unknown to the main army, the scouting and information service of which was beneath all criticism, Napoleon had branched off from the Seine at Nogent, and, while Schwarzenberg was still preparing in his usual leisurely manner to outflank him, was hurrying north to Suzanne where he concentrated his forces. Suzanne is due south of Champaubert and but a short march from the little Paris road, along which Blücher's troops were scattered.

On the 9th of February, with Napoleon already within pouncing distance, Blücher had so little reason to expect his approach that, when a request came from Schwarzenberg for reinforcements, he prepared to accede to it at once and to despatch not only Kleist's corps, which Schwarzenberg had mentioned by name, but the corps of Kapzewitsch and Olsufiev as well. Schwarzenberg's panic was due to the fact that while at last it had been discovered that Napoleon had some enterprise in hand, his true purpose was so misinterpreted that Schwarzenberg believed he was preparing to give battle to him, Schwarzenberg, at Nogent!

Blücher's present plight was caused by a regular combination of misunderstandings; by Wittgenstein's withdrawal; by the blindness at headquarters, which had not ascertained until two days after the departure of Napoleon that the latter, with the greater part of his troops, had vanished; and now, finally, by a misunderstanding—if indeed we may so call it, and not by a harder name—with Yorck.

Already when despatching the reinforcements to Schwarzenberg it had come home to Blücher that his own positions might be in danger, and that he had better concentrate his remaining forces. He sent word to Yorck to march to Montmirail and join and support Sacken.

Between Yorck and Blücher as we know there did not exist the most ideal relations; and Yorck had more than once taken upon himself to criticise severely the commander-in-chief's measures. We have it on the authority of Yorck's confidant, Count Schack, that the hero of Tauroggen considered the junction with Sacken at Montmirail to be "quite superfluous." If he did not directly disobey Blücher now he altogether disregarded the spirit of the command, advancing but a few miles on the road to Montmirail. It is almost incomprehensible that a second, still more urgent command should have met with the same reception as the first. Blücher had by this time learned that Napoleon in person was nearing Sézanne, and he insisted on the necessity of Yorck's reaching Montmirail as soon as possible.

Yorck "saw the matter in a different light," to quote again his own friend, and clung to a clause in the orders which directed him, in case Napoleon should already have broken through Blücher's lines, to devote himself to repairing a certain bridge over the Marne. As no news could possibly have reached Yorck of the prescribed eventuality having occurred, his conduct looks very much like rank disobedience.

Napoleon then proceeded to devour his enemy piecemeal. On February 10th, he fell upon Olsufiev at Champaubert and drove his little force entirely asunder, taking captive the Russian general himself; on the 11th, he engaged Sacken's corps at Montmirail; and as Sacken retreated in the direction of Château Thierry, Yorck's corps, too, did eventually become involved in the struggle. But one scarcely recognises the hero of so many brave fights in this emergency. He had been near enough to hear the cannon at Montmirail, yet had not rushed to Sacken's assistance; for some unexplained reason he employed now but one fourth of the forces that he had actually at hand. Strange to say he was filled with a grim, unholy wrath against Blücher to whose faulty commands he ascribed all the misfortunes.

Yorck and Sacken, with losses aggregating nearly 3,000 men, retreated past Château Thierry in the direction of Rheims. Napoleon in his bulletins, to be sure, placed the losses much higher; he was seriously endeavouring now to rouse the masses against the invaders, and the general spirit was becoming much more hostile. The allied soldiers, chiefly the Cossacks, could not be altogether restrained, and undoubtedly did commit brutal excesses which all seem to have been charged to the credit of the Prussians. They were *plus chiens que les rustres et les autre chiens*, ran the popular witticism.

Once more, as in the dispute with Yorck, Blücher's voice was to be that of one calling in the wilderness. He had sent to ask Schwarzenberg to give him breathing-space, by operating in Napoleon's rear; and Schwarzenberg put him off with platitudes; the enemy was doubtless merely manoeuvring in order to gain time; Blücher would probably find himself quite able to concentrate his forces in season to ward off an attack; it would be very inconvenient for him, Schwarzenberg, to come to his aid—the roads were bad and there would be a scarcity of supplies. The truth seems to be that the turn things were taking just at that time at the congress of Châtillon made it Austria's aim to end the war as soon as possible.

Meanwhile the very life-blood was being drawn from Blücher. He had succeeded in recalling the troops that he had despatched to aid Schwarzenberg and disposed of a force of about 15,000 men. (Unger places the numbers at more than 19,000.) But he was thrown off his guard by a ruse of war. Near his camp at Étoges the pickets captured a Frenchman, who gave himself out for a legitimist and an enemy of Napoleon and announced that the latter, together with his guards, was already returning to Paris by way of La Ferté-sous-Jouarre. As the news received some slight corroboration, Blücher began to look at things in a more hopeful light. He wrote to his wife:

I have had three bitter days; three times in the three days Napoleon attacked me with all his forces including his guards; but he has not attained his purpose and today is retreating to Paris. Tomorrow I pursue him; then both of our armies unite and a battle before Paris will decide everything. Don't fear that we shall be beaten; that is out of the question unless unheard of mistakes are made.

At the very moment Blücher himself was guilty of an "unheard-of-mistake." The French legitimist and enemy of Napoleon was almost certainly a spy; and Blücher, as he marched his forces in the direction of Montmirail where he had determined to concentrate them, fell into a regular ambush. Attacked by Napoleon with a greatly superior force of cavalry, they fought their way back to Étoges with terrific loss. We have it on the authority of one who accompanied him that Blücher himself looked "desperately grim."

And well he might. In less than a fortnight, in mere skirmishes, he had lost 14,000 men, and now his reputation as a general was in jeopardy. He exposed himself so recklessly to the fire of the enemy that one imagines he longed for a bullet to strike him.

Yet his conduct of the retreat was masterly beyond description. Sir Hudson Lowe writes:

I lack words to express my admiration of the intrepidity and discipline of the troops. The example of Field-marshal Blücher himself, who was everywhere and in the most exposed situations, of Generals Kleist and Kapzewitsch, of General Gneisenau who directed the movements on the Chaussée, of General Zieten and Prince Augustus of Prussia, always at the head of his brigade, animating it to the most heroic efforts, could not fail to inspire the soldiers with a resolution that must even have struck the enemy with admiration and surprise.

Blücher and Gneisenau adopted the settled policy of making light of their disasters:

We tried to act as though we had not been beaten.

Gneisenau confessed later. Blücher reported to the *Tsar* and Frederick William that:

> Napoleon, in three bloody skirmishes in which he led his old guard against the Silesian Army, did not succeed in striking any decisive blows.

And to Hardenberg he wrote, not without a side-thrust at Schwarzenberg:

> My three corps, Yorck's, Sacken's, and Kleist's have all three fought separately with Napoleon. Many have fallen; but I have accomplished my purpose and detained the emperor here for five days. If, during this time while it was practically unopposed, the main army has accomplished nothing then it is a matter for regret. The hour has struck; a decisive battle must take place as soon as possible. If we stand still and wait we exhaust our supplies and render the people here desperate; they will rise *en masse* against us. . . . On the 19th, I make straight for the enemy, on that you can pin your faith. But the main army must go forward or things may turn out badly. Use your utmost endeavours to bring matters to a conclusion. If we defeat the emperor, we shall have won the nation entirely; but the emperor wins it if we delay.

Against Yorck, Blücher showed no animosity, but, on the contrary, when Yorck asked to be allowed to lay down his command, Blücher pleaded with him to remain and finally brought him to consent. He himself was admirably cool and self-controlled now that the worst had happened. He was serene, even gay; and declared that although the dinner in the Palais Royal to which he had invited his friends would have to be postponed, it was only for a short time.

Schwarzenberg was as sneering and as condescending about Blücher as ever, he wrote:

> My old Blücher feels once more so strongly drawn to the Palais Royal that he is again preparing to run ahead like mad.

There certainly was a contrast in the rapidity of movement of the two men!

CHAPTER 9

Napoleon's First Overthrow

Napoleon's victories at Champaubert, Montmirail, and Étoges, had quite changed for the moment the tide of his fortunes. He returned to Schwarzenberg's neighbourhood lustily blowing his own trumpet, and spreading the report that Blücher's army had been annihilated. His attitude at the Congress of Châtillon was very different now from what it had been a fortnight previously, after the defeat at La Rothière. Then he had allowed the Duc de Bassano to write to his plenipotentiary, Caulaincourt:

> His Majesty bids me tell you that he gives you *carte blanche* to end the negotiations favourably, save the capital, and avoid a battle which would be the last hope of the nation.

Now on the contrary it was he who delayed the negotiations for peace, much to the disgust of Schwarzenberg. All Napoleon's old prestige seemed to have been regained; and the town of Troyes, which had received him coldly enough on his previous visit, now outdid itself in making him welcome. A Frenchman (Houssaye), writes:

> Never, not even after the triumphant returns from Austerlitz and Jena, had the acclamations been more full, more sincere, more ardent. Scarcely could the emperor make his way through the crowd; people struggled to hug his boots and to kiss his hands.

And when in Paris, the trains of prisoners from Blücher's army, thousands at a time, were marched down the Rue de la Paix and through the Place Vendôme amid cries of "Long live the Emperor!" it must indeed have seemed as though the good old days had returned.

Schwarzenberg trembled. Upheld by the Tsar Alexander he sent an urgent demand to Blücher to join his forces to those of the main army; and Blücher, with only two days of rest after his terrible experiences, was already on the march by the 18th of February. On the 19th, Schwarzenberg sent to inform him that two days later, on the 21st, a battle would be fought at Troyes—news which was more than welcomed at the headquarters of the Silesian Army.

Meanwhile, in order to gain time, Schwarzenberg resorted to a ruse of war that did none too much honour to his intelligence, although the monarchs in his camp, too, lent it their approval. He sent to Napoleon's headquarters to say that he had ceased all hostilities having received a despatch, dated already the day before, to the effect that peace was on the very point of being signed at Châtillon. He is addressing Berthier:

> I hear, prince, that your hostilities continue, and I propose your doing as we have done in order to stop the bloodshed; else I should have no alternative but to continue the operations that the expectation of seeing the preliminary treaty concluded induced me to cease.

Napoleon deigned no answer, but his scornful comment to his brother Joseph was:

> At the first stroke of misfortune these poor wretches fall on their knees!

He had defeated one of Schwarzenberg's generals at Montereau a day or two before.

By the 20th of February, Blücher was already at Arcis-sur-Aube, and he sent Grolman and Gneisenau to Schwarzenberg's camp to arrange for the expected battle. But Schwarzenberg's courage was already weakening; and news that came that night from Spain, from the south of France, and from Geneva, in all of which places events more or less favourable to Napoleon had occurred, completely turned him from his purpose. Although he commanded, now, 150,000 men against less than half that number of the enemy, although he knew that he should meet with the bitterest opposition from Alexander, from Frederick William, and from Blücher, he made up his mind to retreat, and once more to take up his position on that plateau of Langres where he had already idled away so many weeks.

On the 21st, the day of the expected battle, Blücher was sent on a reconnoitring expedition; on the 22nd, Schwarzenberg came out openly with his plan in the presence of his own emperor, of Frederick William, and of Alexander. The deliberations were full of dramatic incident; over them hung a vague uneasiness as to what great plot Napoleon was hatching. Lord Castlereagh, the English envoy, arrived from Châtillon and urged peace with Napoleon as speedily as possible. Then came a letter from the French emperor himself, addressed to his "very dear father-in-law," in which he alluded to "the battle which had ended with the ruin of Blücher's army," hinted that his own army now outnumbered that of the Austrians in every respect and stated the terms, which he alluded to as his "ultimatum," on which he was willing to make peace.

Alexander and Frederick William had not yielded when, later in the day, a Cossack general brought to Schwarzenberg the report, as the culmination of all the disquieting news, that Napoleon was preparing to give battle with 180,000 men. On his own responsibility, then, Schwarzenberg gave the order to begin the retreat to Langres.

With a presentiment that matters would take some such turn Blücher already on the 21st, had ordered Grolman to go to headquarters, to declare that the Silesian Army would bear the whole brunt of it if only they would announce a battle and have the main army act as a reserve; to propose, finally, should all his other efforts fail that there should take place a renewed separation of the armies. Blücher's army in itself was now too small to accomplish anything, but there were two corps that had been operating in Belgium and that were already on their way south: one under Wintzingerode had reached Rheims; the other, under Bülow, was nearing Laon. Grolman was to suggest Blücher's returning to the River Marne, joining Bülow and Wintzingerode and then, at the head of 100,000 men realising his old dream and descending upon Paris.

On the 23rd, Schwarzenberg vacated Troyes, but not before it had come to a skirmish between his rear-guard and Napoleon's advancing army. On that same day Blücher seems to have received formal permission to carry out his enterprise, for he writes to the *Tsar* and the king, thanking them in the warmest terms. Like a child who fears the revoking of his privileges he made all haste to be gone and that very night was under way. And not a moment too soon.

Schwarzenberg still cherished the hope of concluding a truce with Napoleon and feared lest his efforts in that direction might he frustrated through Blücher's impetuosity. He first tried to hold the latter a little longer in his neighbourhood, and sweetened his proposals by the prospect of a battle on the heights of Colombey-les-deux-Églises. When these proposals produced no effect Schwarzenberg stormed the king and Alexander with representations and finally sent positive orders to Blücher accompanied by the following missive from Frederick William:

> As negotiations for a truce with the Emperor Napoleon are in progress, and this truce will very likely soon be effected, the case is altered with regard to the order to assume the offensive which the army under your command received; and you will now be obliged to change the direction of your march from Arcis to Dienville. Prince Schwarzenberg will already have informed you of this orally; but I hereby, and in order to dispel any uncertainty, repeat the directions in writing.

That evening Schwarzenberg wrote that the anticipated truce had not become a reality, but that there was all the more necessity for speedily rejoining the main army and that he was confident Blücher would already have marched in the direction of Dienville.

But Blücher had taken the bit in his teeth and was not to be restrained. He wrote to Schwarzenberg:

> In the course of last night I received Your Grace's honoured communications of the morning and evening of the 24th, and perceive to my regret that there must be a misunderstanding or that a despatch has been lost. I have acted entirely according to the oral agreement which Colonel von Grolman brought me. Yesterday my vanguard drove the enemy as far as La Ferté Gaucher and is drawn up in face of that position. Were I to turn back I could under no circumstances effect my junction with Your Grace within the stated time and should expose the army to the gravest perils. By moving on Paris, on the other hand, and operating in the rear of the Emperor Napoleon I hope to secure for Your Grace the most effectual relief.

In reckoning up Blücher's services to the cause, his firmness and determination in a case like this might not be forgotten. He was braving not only Schwarzenberg but his own king and the *Tsar* as well. He doubtless knew, however, just how far to go; and, sure enough, Frederick William wrote on the 25th:

> The expected truce has not come to pass. Accordingly, my orders to you of yesterday lose their validity. It has now been

decided that Prince Schwarzenberg's army . . . shall continue its retreat. Henceforward the outcome of this campaign depends on you.

The *Tsar* wrote in very similar terms, declaring that Blücher was now in a position to "conduct very energetic offensive operations against the left wing of the French Army." Even Schwarzenberg changes his tone and seems more anxious to explain the reasons for his own retreat than to dictate further operations to Blücher; he has to go to meet his reserves, he writes, and to oppose a French force that is threatening his outposts on the Swiss frontier. Whenever Blücher needs him, however, he will run to his assistance.

After a skirmish on the Marne, where Kleist lost a thousand men, Blücher marched northward to the River Aisne, as usual not sparing his troops, which at the time of the junction with Bülow were in such a plight as to call forth the latter's unsparing criticism, he wrote:

The army is nearly starved, all discipline and order are dissolved, and I confess to our shame that it looks not unlike a band of robbers.

Bülow's criticism may or may not have been just—it must be remembered that little over a fortnight had elapsed since the severe fighting at Étoges and that the troops had been obliged since then to march very long distances—but it marks the unfortunate tone that was to prevail at Blücher's headquarters from the moment that Bülow joined it. Bülow's own troops had been tenderly nurtured, and he had little sympathy for the spirit that led Blücher to neglect such matters in order the quicker to attain his goal.

It was at Soissons, which Bülow and Wintzingerode had already forced to surrender, that Blücher crossed the Aisne and, with all the different corps united, he now disposed of an army of 113,000 men. Meanwhile Schwarzenberg's army in its retreat had run upon Oudinot's corps at Bar-sur-Aube. Frederick William III, had insisted upon his giving battle, and with his two young sons, the future Frederick William IV. and the future Emperor William I., had been most active throughout the day. It must be said of Schwarzenberg, too, that he conducted himself bravely, winning the victory and inflicting losses on Oudinot doubly as great as those suffered by the Austrians.

But the little flare of military ardour soon died down; the pursuit was lax, and the opportunity to crush a much weaker antagonist was allowed to escape. All the same the result of the day at Bar-sur-Aube

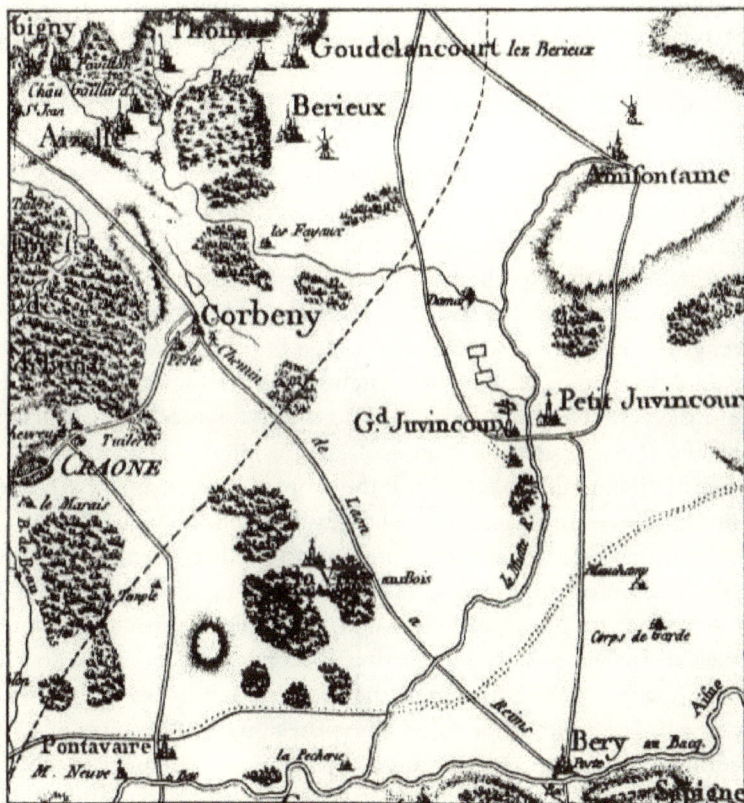

A SECTION OF CASSINI'S MAP

(Used by Napoleon)

was deemed so encouraging that the three allied monarchs, joined by England's representative, formed a new alliance to last for the long term of twenty years, and providing that should France not accept the conditions already proposed to her at Frankfort the war should be carried on with energy until a general peace could be secured. Each of the four powers was to furnish 150,000 men exclusive of garrisons, and England, besides, was to pay the enormous sum of five million pounds yearly by way of subsidy. All measures were to be concerted in common and no separate treaties or truces to be permitted. The success at Bar-sur-Aube, too, emboldened Schwarzenberg to retake Troyes, and the Austrians held a formal entry into the city.

Napoleon by this time was in pursuit of Blücher, crossing the Aisne at Berry au Bac on the fifth of March and establishing himself at Craonne. He had formed the general plan of marching to release the garrisons from the fortresses of the Moselle and of the Ardennes and forming with them a new field army; this done he would leave the pursuit of Blücher to the new army and himself turn back to deal with Schwarzenberg. He had, unfortunately, underestimated Blücher's strength, a mistake for which he was soon to pay dearly.

As Napoleon was about to march along the highroad that leads from the River Aisne at Berry au Bac to the town of Laon, Blücher sent the Russian general, Woronzoff, to occupy the heights at Craonne, intending him to descend at the proper moment and give battle. Almost at the same time, for valid reasons, Blücher and Napoleon changed their plans, the French mounting the heights to give battle there, and Woronzoff not descending but awaiting their attack.

Rising like a great promontory from the plain north of Craonne a plateau runs in a westerly direction almost as far as Soissons. To the north it slopes to the Ailette; to the south, rough banks, crisscrossed by streams, descend to the Aisne. The plateau itself is very irregular in width harrowing near the farm of Hurtebise to a mere ridge which is lower in the middle than at the two extremities. Along the whole length of the plateau runs the road known as the Route des Dames, having been constructed in order that Louis XV.'s daughters might more readily visit Narbonne's *château* at La Bove.

The isthmus, if one may so call it, of Hurtebise was as evil a place in which to fight a battle as the imagination could well have invented,—the banks on the Ailette side descending precipitously to the ravine known as the Trou des Demoiselles, on the Aisne side to the Trou d'Enfer, which its name alone sufficiently characterises.

Blücher had planned a magnificent manoeuvre. The night before the battle he had sent Wintzingerode across the Ailette and round by Fétieux, to fall upon the enemy in the rear while Woronzoff was engaging them in front on the plateau itself. Kleist and Langeron were to cut off the retreat. But Wintzingerode, for reasons known only to himself, had advanced but a few miles and then camped for the night; while Blücher, not finding him at hand at the appointed hour, abandoned the command on the plateau to Sacken and wandered in search of Wintzingerode until two in the afternoon, when the whole project of a flank attack had to be abandoned.

All the more desperate had been the fighting on the ridge, for Sacken had been momentarily expecting the co-operation of Wintzingerode. He despatched word to Blücher that the enemy were bringing all their forces to bear:

> I accordingly beg most urgently that Your Excellency hasten the operation against the right wing. . . . The enemy has drawn up all his artillery against us.

All that Blücher could do was to order a retreat.

And such a retreat as it was! Woronzoff who had held out for five hours considered it less perilous to continue fighting than to retire and only yielded to Sacken's positive commands. At one point the way was so narrow that the cavalry had to halt under fire while the infantry filed by. Yet the Russians yielded only step by step, we are told, and "as if on the parade-ground." When night put an end to the terrible ordeal, the whole plateau was in French hands and once more, as at Brienne, Napoleon occupied what had been Blücher's headquarters the night before. Strange to say the losses of the French were even greater than those of Blücher, although Napoleon, for effect, declared in the *Moniteur* that he had inflicted enormous damage and won an almost decisive victory. He ordered it to be everywhere proclaimed that he "had beaten what remained of the Russian Army."

Napoleon could not know that only a relatively small part of Blücher's forces had fought at Craonne; that Bülow and his whole corps had previously been despatched to Laon and ordered to take up a strong position there; and that Wintzingerode with his ten thousand cavalry, after failing to support Woronzoff, had been ordered to the same place. It was to Laon, too, that Woronzoff himself withdrew after his bloody retreat along the Route des Dames; so that Blücher had here united, in spite of his recent losses, a force of at least 100,000

A SECTION OF CASSINI'S MAP
(Used by Napoleon)

men.

Laon itself, although not well fortified, occupied a very strong natural position on a hill that rose abruptly at an angle of forty-five degrees. It had numerous projecting points that served as bastions; while the approach to it was through suburbs that would have to be taken before the hill itself could be stormed. A little to the north-east was the town of Athies, which was to be the scene of the most dramatic incident of the battle. Near it was posted the corps of Yorck, who with Kleist formed the left wing of Blücher's battle array; Bülow, Sacken, and Langeron being in the centre and Wintzingerode on the right.

The first day of the battle ended without special incident, but after furious fighting for the possession of the suburbs. Marmont's corps had taken Athies. His soldiers, young, inexperienced, and many of them for the first time under fire, were wearied to death after marching for eight hours and fighting for four, and bivouacked where they had fought without stopping to take even the ordinary precautions: A Frenchman, (Houssaye), writes:

> Overcome by fatigue, stiff with cold, weak with hunger, they slept around their campfires like a drove of sheep huddled together.

An emissary from Yorck to Blücher, and one from Blücher to Yorck met half way with the same proposal, a night attack on Athies. Yorck himself undertook the operation. Silently the Prussians glided forth in four columns. Yorck had issued the written order:

> Not a shot shall be fired; the attack is to be made with bayonets alone.

Zieten, meanwhile, had been despatched with the cavalry to fall at the proper moment on the rear of Marmont's corps, and extinguish as rapidly as possible the light of life and intelligence in this heap of young humanity.

The attack was a complete success. Hundreds of these poor boys awoke to find themselves transfixed by bayonets while hundreds more were trampled by the horses. The silence of the night gave way to wild uproar. A participant, (Yorck's friend, von Schack), writes:

> All at once all the division's trumpets, horns, and other instruments were sounded; one hurrah after another rent the air, and panic and confusion spread throughout the hostile army.

Marshal Marmont reported to Napoleon at two the next morning:

> We have not been able to restore order to the different bodies of troops, which are all mingled together and in no condition to carry out any evolution or perform any service.

He had lost more than three thousand men, the greater part of whom had been captured, indeed and not killed.

Blücher was extravagant in his praise of Yorck and his men. He wrote:

> Your Excellency has once more shown what clearness of mind combined with decision can accomplish.

He was heard to remark that the heavens would fall were Yorck, this pillar of support, to be removed. At midnight he gave his directions for the following day: Yorck's corps and Kleist's corps were to pursue the enemy and outflank Marmont's right wing.

This praise of Yorck was to be Blücher's last burst of enthusiasm for many a long day. All through the day's fighting he had struggled with fever, and his eyes had become painfully swollen. Save for the attack on Athies, for which only half of the credit was his, his measures had shown unwonted timidity and hesitation. He had announced a general attack but never gave the order for it, being possessed all day by the fear that a French column might appear from some unexpected quarter. He gave credence to a French captive who placed Napoleon's numbers at a much larger figure than was actually the case. On the second day of Laon, Blücher was in such a state of bodily and mental collapse that he could scarcely sign his name.

Gneisenau was thrown into the most difficult position by Blücher's illness. Together they had planned the campaign; but were Blücher to be totally incapacitated, Langeron or Yorck, who had been longer in the service than Gneisenau, would take command. The matter therefore was hushed up as much as possible; but Gneisenau so felt the responsibility that, on the second day of the battle, learning that Napoleon was planning an attack, he went to the very extreme of caution, first modifying the command that Blücher had given to Yorck, and finally imperatively ordering the latter to return to Laon. Napoleon had meanwhile retired after making fierce attempts to take the suburbs of Laon.

It was a lamentable condition of things that now prevailed at headquarters; one of Yorck's officers, (Brandenburg), writes that the indecision, hesitation, and general slackness beggar description. Sacken, who was usually Blücher's warmest adherent said:

> Listen, General, I have always heretofore respected the decisions of the field-marshal, but since four days he has lost his head. Why did he change this disposition that would have enabled him to give Napoleon his *coup de grâce?*

The wildest rumours were circulated about Blücher's health; he was declared by some to be utterly unconscious of what was passing around him; rumours of plots and of intrigues were rife. Yet not only Gneisenau, not only Blücher's own *aide-de-camp*, Nostitz, considered it indispensable for him to remain in command lest the whole Silesian Army should fall to pieces, but even Langeron who would have been next in command once cried out:

> For God's sake let us carry this corpse along with us.

Nostitz, who was with him day and night, has given the following description of Blücher's malady:

> His extremely inflamed and thickly swollen eyes made it absolutely necessary for him to wear a bandage, since every ray of light caused violent pains. Confined to his room on a strict diet, unable to take his usual exercise, and with his heart full of vexation at seeing himself doomed to inactivity just as the last decisive blow was on the point of being struck: all this taken together had not alone undermined his health but had also most strongly affected his temper and put him in a condition of mind that was apt to go with his bodily sufferings.
> To see him thus, constantly thinking with fear and anxiety of death, bearing pain with anything but fortitude, torturing his mind by always imagining he had found new symptoms, thinking of himself alone, indifferent to all that went on around him, even to the greatest and most important events—but then again, so soon as he recovered, surpassing all around him in strength of character, endurance of hardships and heroic scorn of every danger—one could not but be amazed at the great power his physical condition exercised over his mental faculties. This was the condition of moral lassitude and complete indifference to external affairs into which he had now fallen. The field-marshal's one idea was to resign his command and quit the army. Every announcement, every report, no matter from

whom or about what, was disgusting and loathsome to him.

In the midst of all the trouble and anxiety came an episode with Yorck that threatened to precipitate the disruption of the army which Gneisenau and the rest had dreaded.

Yorck could not forget the withdrawal of the order that had been given him to pursue Marmont; rightly or wrongly he believed that with one blow an end might have been put to the war. He was still further irritated by a command that came from Schwarzenberg to detach some of his cavalry as an escort for provision waggons; he believed that he was the victim of an intrigue, and seems also to have credited the rumour that Gneisenau was usurping functions that did not pertain to him, and that Blücher was not in his right mind.

Yorck finally sent General von Schack to headquarters to say that on account of his health, he was laying down his command and re-tiring to Brussels. His travelling coach was made ready, his baggage loaded on it—which was the first intimation given of his intention—and, after taking leave of his officers, he gave the signal and was off. One who was present writes:

> As the coach drove away, we stood as if paralysed; we began to realise that this was a deadly blow for the corps and for the Silesian Army.

In great excitement three of Yorck's officers hurried to Laon and announced themselves to Blücher. Refused admittance to headquarters on the ground that Blücher, Gneisenau, and Müffling were all three ill they at last, through Count Nostitz, had their mission explained to Blücher and received a note from him that they were to deliver to Yorck. The field-marshal's eyes were so swollen that he could only write in large coarse letters, the note ran:

> Old comrade, history should not have to relate such things of us! Be sensible and come back!

The brother of the king, too, Prince William of Prussia, wrote and urged Yorck not to abandon the fatherland at a critical moment like this, when there was more need than ever of clear-headed leaders:

> As your fellow citizen, as general under you, as grandson, son and brother of your kings, I implore you not to lay down your command! Your true friend, William Prince of Prussia.

Yorck yielded. Nostitz maintained that the mere sight of Blücher's handwriting, proving as it did that the latter could think and act for himself, had made him relent; and he answered in terms as frank and affectionate as those employed by his old commander:

Your Excellency's personal letter is the expression of your upright heart which I always did and always will esteem. This very uprightness, indeed, must tell you how painful it is to a man who feels his worth and is conscious of no wrong to have received a slight. I have returned to my post. I will continue to fight as long as there is need but then will gladly give way to the arrogant and the theorists. From the bottom of my heart and with sincere sympathy I wish you a speedy restoration to health.

In spite of the fact that, two days later, Napoleon took revenge by falling on St. Priest at Rheims and inflicting heavy losses, the battle of Laon was really a turning point in his fortunes. His operations in Spain and in Southern France were proving unsuccessful; and his own brother Joseph Bonaparte, the ex-King of Spain, urged him to make peace with the allies:

Good or bad we must have peace; in the present state of affairs any peace would be of advantage.

The most important effect of Laon was that the news of the victory gained by Blücher galvanised the main army, which had remained inert since the Battle of Bar-sur-Aube, into new life and activity. Shortly before, in his usual state of trepidation, Schwarzenberg had written:

I have no news and I confess that I tremble. If Blücher suffers a defeat haw can I myself give battle? For if I am conquered what a triumph for Napoleon! And what a humiliation for the sovereigns to recross the Rhine at the head of a beaten army!

Almost immediately after the reception of the news of Blücher's victory Schwarzenberg began to assume a menacing attitude towards Macdonald who wrote to the French Minister of War:

My left is outflanked and I am forced to evacuate Provins in order to cover Nangis. I shall defend the ground every inch of the way but am in urgent need of assistance.

The news that Napoleon was approaching, the fear that the Gorgon's head might once more turn those who looked on it into stone, brought a return of the old wavering on Schwarzenberg's part and the Prince of Thurn and Taxis wrote on March 18th:

> It would be vain to try to depict the uncertainty that reigned at headquarters from the moment of the first announcement until the next morning. Project followed project. Finally, following the old principle, it was determined to retreat.

But the hesitation was but momentary. Already on the 20th, Napoleon was attacked at Arcis-sur-Aube, the fact that the Congress of Châtillon had closed without the least result having acted as an additional spur. Since nothing more was to be gained by negotiation the only alternative, even for Austria, was to crush him by force of arms.

The Battle of Arcis-sur-Aube, which lasted for two days, did much to dispel the old dread of Napoleon. Discovering on the second day that he was greatly outnumbered, the tottering demi-god of France saved himself from utter annihilation by a timely retreat. There was no credit to Schwarzenberg in this, but the power of mere numbers was distinctly beginning to tell.

Blücher's army, now, was treated to what Nostitz called a moral mustard plaster. On the 22nd, when within but a day's march of Schwarzenberg's army, news of the Battle of Arcis was received while, at the same time, an intercepted letter disclosed Napoleon's intention to march hastily to the rear of the main army, cut its communications at St. Dizier, and save Paris by making Schwarzenberg turn and give him battle. The news dispelled Blücher's long apathy. Nostitz writes:

> From that moment, there was no further thought of laying down the command, although the inflammation of the eyes continued as violent as ever.

With the knowledge that there was something to be done immediately all the old feeling of responsibility, all the old love of action revived in full force. Blücher hastened with his three Russian corps to Rheims and thence to Châlons. Too ill to mount a horse he lay back in an open carriage, offering a spectacle that may well have raised a smile. For on his head, in order to shade his eyes was a woman's green poke-bonnet!

Napoleon, as Blücher learned at Châlons, was now in retreat—not towards Paris as one might have expected but, as the Cossack scouts quaintly announced, "towards Moscow." The outposts of the main army, as Blücher also now found, were close to his own, for Schwarzenberg had followed Napoleon in the direction of St. Dizier.

It was indeed time for the eternal aimless evolutions to stop. How often had Blücher, how often had Schwarzenberg marched and countermarched along the French roads! Blücher and Gneisenau were now more eager than ever to play the final act of the drama and have the march of the combined armies on Paris begin. Great was their joy at receiving a despatch from Schwarzenberg couched in the most resolute terms:

> The enemy has marched by way of Vitry and St. Dizier to cut our communications, *therefore* it has been decided to march on Paris with the full force of all the armies by the shortest route. I shall consequently, with all my troops, be on the 25th, in Ferre Champenoise, on the 26th, in Treffaux, the 27th, in Coulommiers, the 28th, in Meaux or Lagny where I reckon positively on Your Excellency's joining me with your entire forces.

For Schwarzenberg to write that he was marching on Paris, for the very reason that Napoleon was hastening to cut his communications and attack him in the rear, betokened an entire change of heart in the commander of the main army; and Nostitz wrote:

> This coinciding of the decisions at main headquarters with what he himself considered wisest made the field-marshal very happy; all the more as it was the first time in the course of the two campaigns that such harmony had existed.

Before dawn on the morning of the 25th of March, the advance was begun, the two armies proceeding at a distance from each other of about ten miles in order that there might be a wider stretch of territory from which to draw supplies. Schwarzenberg's route was that which he had announced, while Blücher's led through the very districts where he had suffered his worst defeats: from Montmirail to La Ferté-sous-Jouarre. At Ferre Champenoise Schwarzenberg came on the only considerable body of troops, save Napoleon's own, that was still in the field—the combined corps of Marmont and Mortier, variously estimated at from 16,500 to 18,000 men. With great spirit this little army resisted throughout the whole day the ever-increasing Austrian forces; but between four and five in the afternoon was already in retreat, when cannonading was heard in the distance and the cry was raised that Napoleon was coming to the rescue. In point of fact the cannonading came from a detachment of Blücher's army.

Earlier in the day, near Villeseneux, Nostitz, descending from Blücher's carriage to enquire more fully into an indistinct report brought by a Cossack, had found that a hostile column was ahead. It was under Pacthod and Arney and was escorting a long train of waggons bearing rations and ammunition. It was the cannon of General Korf, whom Blücher had sent in pursuit of Pacthod, that was heard at Ferre Champenoise. Korf had driven his prey into the very jaws of Schwarzenberg's batteries and a terrible slaughter ensued. The defence was heroic but so vain that Alexander and Frederick William, who had just come on the scene, sent members of their suite to conjure Pacthod to surrender. He did so at last although not until his divisions were almost annihilated and he himself was wounded; and to his firm resistance it was largely due that Marmont and Mortier were able to save the remnant of their forces. As it was, the losses of the French that day are estimated at 10,000 men.

Blücher, when he heard of Napoleon's intention to cut the Austrian communications at St. Dizier had despatched Wintzingerode's corps to that point; and here Napoleon chronicled his last success in the campaign, inflicting a loss on Wintzingerode that is estimated by French authorities at between 2,500 and 3,000 men, by German, at less than 1,000. Even the greater estimate would have counted for but little, so low had the scale of Napoleon's fortunes now sunk.

He would gladly have reopened the negotiations for peace, and have accepted terms that he would not hear of while the Congress of Châtillon was still in progress. On the 28th of March, Caulaincourt, his plenipotentiary at that congress, wrote to Count Hauterive:

> His Majesty seems determined to make the necessary sacrifices.
> A few days earlier all might have been saved.

On the very day after Caulaincourt wrote thus, on the 29th of March, the allies were so near to Napoleon's capital that their cannon could be heard by the trembling inhabitants. The goal Blücher had been following over so many battlefields strewn with the dead—like a mirage in the desert that leads men to their destruction—was at last to be attained. He sent his own son to parley with General Vincent, who commanded the French outposts, and to propose that he issue the following proclamation to the Parisians:

> It rests with the city of Paris, under the actual circumstances,
> to hasten the peace of the world. Its resolve is awaited with an
> interest proportionate to so great a result: let it speak, and from

that instant the army before its walls will become the upholder of its decisions.

Vincent refused the overtures; the outposts gave fight and then retreated, hard pressed by the enemy.

That night was spent by the *Tsar*, Frederick William and Schwarzenberg in the *château* of Bondy, whence they could see the lights of Paris; Blücher had chosen Villepinte for his headquarters. All the way from the Bois de Vincennes to St. Denis, St. Ouen, and Neuilly extended the great half circle formed by the invading troops. Blücher might easily have taken the city before Schwarzenberg's army arrived in position but had been ordered to wait. The *Tsar*, it is generally believed, wished for himself the satisfaction of riding in at the head of his guards and dictating the terms of peace; he dreaded, too, the violence of these Prussians and feared lest in their thirst for revenge they should defeat his own more pacific intentions. But the delay was most unfortunate; for it gave time for the troops that had been defeated at Ferre Champenoise to reach Paris, where Marmont and Mortier hastily organised a resistance.

On the morning of the 30th, an army of 42,000 men, composed indeed of the most promiscuous elements—of national guards, students, and veterans—was drawn up outside of the city walls; and a battle, consisting mainly of numerous small separate combats, raged until late in the afternoon, when the *Tsar's* proposal to negotiate was accepted. This battle before Paris, although the result was a foregone conclusion, proved one of the bloodiest of the whole war, the allies losing 8,000, the French more than 9,000 men.

Blücher, still suffering and with his eyes swollen and inflamed, had witnessed the greater part of the battle from his carriage and then, unable longer to refrain, had mounted his horse and directed an attack on the hill of Montmartre, which was finally occupied by his troops. Finding that the negotiations for the surrender of the city were not progressing as he wished, he had the heaviest guns dragged up the hill and all preparations made for the bombardment of Paris should such a step become necessary. By two o'clock in the morning, however, the last conditions had been made and accepted.

It was agreed that at seven Marmont and Mortier should retire from the city, and not until two hours after their departure might hostilities with them be renewed. The national guards and the municipal *gendarmes* were to be disbanded should the allies so desire; and the wounded and stragglers who remained in the city were to be treated as prisoners of war. Technically Paris was at the mercy of the allies; it was "recommended to their generosity" by the treaty; but Alexander's emissary had promised, in his master's name, that it should suffer no violence.

Napoleon received the news of the intended surrender at La-cour-de-France, halfway between Fontainebleau and Paris. He had hurried from St. Dizier, leaving his troops behind him. He kept on his way to the capital declaring that he purposed having the bells rung and the city illumined and that he would call on every inhabitant to rise in arms. Of all the sleepless nights that he had passed in the pursuit of his trade of war, doubtless this was the most anxious and despairing.

Shortly after dawn on the 31st, he learned that the capitulation had been actually signed, and that the allies were to make their entry into the city that very morning. A letter from Marmont told him that no hope could be placed in the loyalty of the people. While Alexander and Frederick William were being frantically acclaimed by the Parisians, the former idol, once all but master of the European world, was returning bowed and broken along the road to Fontainebleau.

The allied monarchs themselves were thoroughly astonished at their welcome. To this fickle populace, that saw nothing now but the breaking of the dawn of peace, they were not enemies, they were deliverers. It is Madame de Staël who relates that Frederick William expressed his astonishment at the pleasure these people seemed to take in being conquered. A cotemporary writes:

> An innumerable crowd had gathered in the side-streets; it was difficult to make room for the victors. All the windows of the splendid apartments were filled with shouting spectators, the ladies in their most elegant costumes. White handkerchiefs fluttered in the windows; a rain of lilies fell from every story on the victorious enemies. In the streets all well-dressed gentlemen appeared with white cockades. One would have thought a victorious French Army had annihilated a dangerous enemy and was making its triumphal entry into the city.

Blücher, who had done so much to render it possible did not share this triumph. He was once more in the condition in which Nostitz described him to be just after the Battle of Laon, we are told:

> Everyone rode up to him, and urged him to march in with the troops. But it was impossible to make this seem desirable. In vain Gneisenau expended all his eloquence on him; he would

184

FRENCH CARICATURE OF THE TIME ENTITLED '' THE AMIABLE PRUSSIAN ''

like at least to show him to the Parisians: "what have I to do with the Parisians? What is Paris to me?" And so, he remained quietly in Montmartre.

Countess Schwerin', the wife of the king's adjutant, who gives these details, tells a story of Frederick William, in connection with the brilliant review in Paris, that is not to the king's credit. He severely criticised the appearance and bearing of the troops that had so bravely fought for him. It was suggested to him that there was some excuse for them: "I cannot see it," was the answer, "the one thing does not exclude the other,"

Blücher's own son wrote:

> We did look heavenly, there was not one whole garment on our bodies—no stockings, no shoes, our feet wrapped in rags. A fine way to parade about in Paris!

Alexander's guards and Frederick William's were in splendid array. "Have you seen my guards?" the king is said to have asked of Yorck.

And Yorck answered, pointing to the ragged regiments which had fought with Blücher: "Your Majesty, *those* are your guards!"

Napoleon's fate is well known. On April 1st, a provisional government under Talleyrand's presidency was established; on April 3rd, the emperor was deposed; on the 4th and 5th, he still thought of war and actually reviewed troops; on the 6th, after learning of the, defection of Marmont, he agreed to abdicate and the senate proclaimed Louis XVIII. King; on the 11th, the formal act of abdication was signed at Fontainebleau. On the 4th of May, Napoleon landed from the *Undaunted* on the shores of his new little kingdom of Elba, and showed his appreciation of the name of the ship that had borne him, and the application of the lesson to himself, by immediately mounting his horse and proceeding to the inspection of the island's fortifications!

CHAPTER 10

The Renewal of the War

Although he had taken no part in the formal entry of the troops
Blücher moved to Paris on April 1st; and what happened to him on
the 2nd, is best described in his own words. He wrote to his friend,
von Bonin, exactly four weeks later;

> That day a deadly illness fell upon me and, already on the third,
> they feared for my eyesight, and for my life. For six days I lay
> blinded, but my nature rose above it all and I am fully restored
> to health. The king and the *Tsar* came to see me. I laid the com-
> mand of the army at the king's feet and asked to retire. He would
> not hear of it, but finally said: "Well in God's name rest and take
> care of yourself. You may choose your own place of residence."

We have another account of Blücher's illness from his physician,
Bietzke, who wrote later that his patient had not in the least been
easy to manage, and who gives details which bear out the assertions of
Nostitz as to the wonderful contrast between Blücher well and Blücher ill. Bietzke declares that the old field-marshal would sit crouched
in a corner brooding over his condition and fearing that he had now
dropsy, now heart-disease, now tumour, now cancer. Death was ever
before his eyes and more than once he begged Nostitz and Bietzke to
stay with him to the end which, he declared, must surely come before
morning.

As soon as he was able Blücher wrote to the king:

> On the point of availing myself of Your Royal Majesty's gra-
> ciously accorded permission and parting from an army the
> bravery and unshakable courage of which has alone enabled
> me, in a long succession of almost invariably victorious bat-

tles and skirmishes, to lead it from the banks of the Oder to the walls of Paris—I have to thank this army for the happiest and brightest moments of my life,—there is but one heartfelt wish the realisation of which will complete the happiness that Providence has so freely showered upon my grey hairs. Your Majesty cannot fail to find this wish justifiable and natural, since it is none other than to see properly rewarded, at this moment of peace won by bloody sacrifice, those of my brave comrades who earned the right to claim your exalted favour on so many glorious and decisive days. My great age, my health, ruined by the fatigues of war, will probably leave me but little time for the enjoyment of this period of glorious achievement. But I regard the army as if it were my family, and it would pain me to feel that I had to leave it for ever without seeing it in possession of that inheritance the obtaining for it of which I regard as my holy duty.

Blücher had decided to leave Paris for Berlin when a letter from the Prince Regent of England, the future George Fourth, changed all his plans. Blücher writes:

I went with the letter to the king, he said: "Blücher, you must take the journey; it is something that cannot be refused. But wait a week, still."

The letter spoke of Blücher's renown, which would go down to posterity, and expressed the conviction that to him should be attributed a great part of the credit for the final result of the campaign. Then came a pressing invitation to visit England in order that the prince regent might show his admiration, his gratitude, and his sincere esteem.

It was finally arranged that the visit to England should take place early in June and that it should be made in the august company of the *Tsar* and of Frederick William himself. Hardenberg, Alexander von Humboldt, and other distinguished personages were to be of the party, and it would be interesting to know if any of the Austrian and Russian commanders were included in the invitation.

In the intervening weeks Blücher celebrated his restoration to health by entering heartily into the gaieties of Paris. His old passion for gambling revived; and he might have been seen daily risking large sums at the resorts in the Palais Royal. It is told on credible authority that he eventually carried away with him winnings to the amount of 19,000 gold *thalers*.

Altogether, material rewards for his great exertions in the field were not lacking. He was overwhelmed with gifts—many of them perfectly useless—as tokens of appreciation. He wrote on April 28th:

> The city of London has awarded me a sword of honour which is to be presented to me there. The sword I receive from the Tsar Alexander is estimated by the jeweller here to be worth 20,000 *thalers*; another sabre like it is coming from St. Petersburg. What the devil shall I do with all the bejewelled weapons?

From every quarter justice was done to his achievements. On May 6th, he writes:

> The new King of France is now here and has said publicly while thanking me that I was the prime cause of his regaining his throne.

Among those with whom Blücher was now thrown was the Duke of Wellington and they are said to have been inspired with a mutual liking and admiration.

By the 3rd of June, Blücher was already in Boulogne whence he writes to his wife:

> At last, at last, I am out of Paris and have reached the sea, but must wait two days still until the king arrives so that I can cross with him to England. Yesterday I dined with the Duke of Clarence on the ship of the line *Impregnable*. I am still deaf from all the thundering of the cannon and well-nigh beside myself with all the great doings in my honour. If that sort of thing continues, I shall go crazy in England. In London I am to be forced like the devil to stay with the prince regent but shall do my best to get out of it. . . .
> The English flock here by hundreds to see me; I have to shake hands with each and every one, and the ladies make regular love to me. They are the craziest people I know! I am bringing along a sword and a sabre on which are 40,000 *thalers* worth of jewels, and the city of London too has given me a sword. I have been taken into the London Clubs without being put up and voted for; and in Scotland they have made me an honorary member of the learned society of Edinburgh. If I don't go mad it is a wonder. What will happen to me in Holland God only knows!

The *Impregnable*, on board which Blücher had dined with the Duke

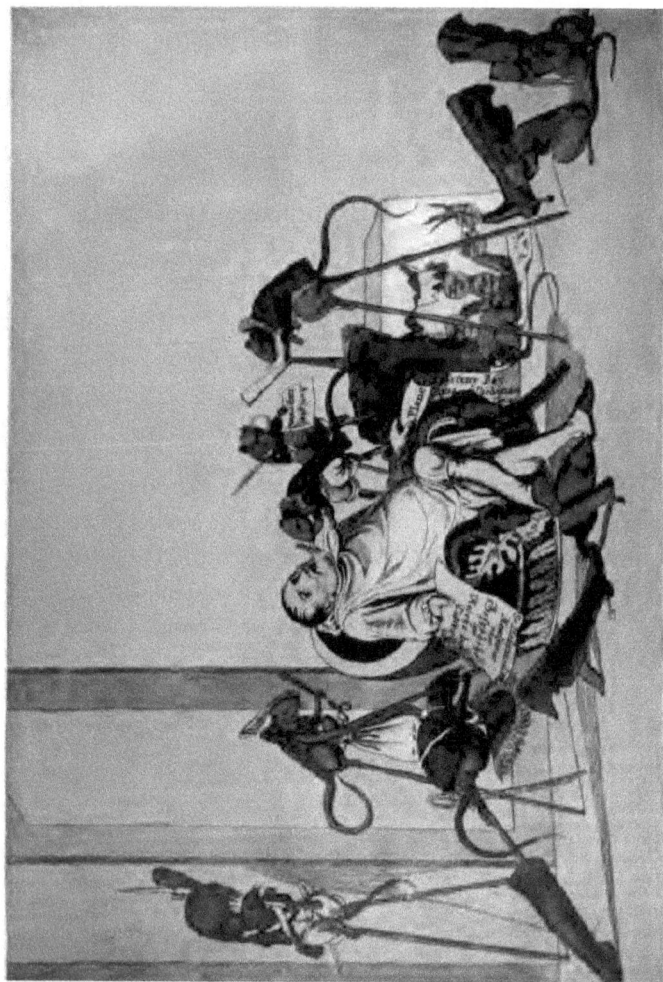

NAPOLEON'S LITTLE COURT AT ELBA

of Clarence, was the admiral's flagship, sent to bring the distinguished party to England. Only one sea-going steamship, and that in America, had as yet been constructed. As they landed at Dover on June 6th there were never-ending cries of "Blücher forever!"

The English newspapers had been full of his praises, had called him "Blücher the Immortal," and had appealed to the whole nation to celebrate properly the coming of "this noble veteran"; "it is worthy of England and of Blücher that a heroic nation should honour a hero!"

It is not unprofitable to dwell on this triumphal progress of Blücher in England. We at a distance both of time and of place can only calculate his achievements mathematically, as it were, by the number of his battles and the length of his marches. But here we see, amid a people not noted for its appreciation of Germans, an enthusiasm for Blücher's great deeds that was wide-spread and that amounted almost to frenzy. At Dover he was actually seized, shaken, embraced, and kissed and was implored to tear his coat in pieces that all might have mementoes. People, and especially ladies, we are told, cried for a lock of his hair, but he could only show them his half-bald pate and pray them to be merciful.

In London, when his carriage drove up to the regent's palace, such a crowd of horsemen and of others rushed to catch sight of him that the guards were trampled underfoot. Beneath the open colonnade he knelt and kissed the hand of the prince regent, who decorated him with an order. No crowned head was ever received with greater demonstrations. On the evening of June 9th, when he entered the opera-house, the singing was forgotten and the whole house rose and uttered thundering "hurrahs!" (Keller, *Fürst Blücher*, 1863.) He wrote from London on June 30th:

> The French could not succeed in killing me; but the regent and the English are in a fair way to do it with all their kindness.

It became the fashion to relate the most incredible stories about his social triumphs: that lords impersonated servants so as to have the honour of waiting upon him; that he was besieged by ladies who refused to leave him until he should have kissed each and every one of them; that his servant sold the plumes from his helm, and countless plumes that were not from his helm, until he had grown quite rich; that for the hand which was shaken to the limit of endurance there was substituted, finally, a stuffed hand at the end of a false arm.

The University of Oxford conferred upon Blücher the degree of

Doctor of Laws; which caused him to smile and to say: "If I am to be a doctor they should at least make Gneisenau an apothecary, for we go together"—a fine pendant to his other tribute: "*Gneisenau lenkt und ich geke vorwärts!*" He wrote to Gneisenau immediately after his return to Germany:

I have come out of England alive, but worn and weary. Words fail to express how they treated me; no one could have had shown to him greater kindness or goodwill. . . . As far as concerns drinking in England, I had great fears; but they did not force me. I had declared from the beginning that I drank no other wine than Bordeaux and I kept to it.

His own countrymen honoured Blücher no less enthusiastically than the English. Already before leaving France Frederick William offered to make him prince. Blücher accepted only conditionally, and the matter was not pressed. But in July he wrote:

In spite of all my opposition they have made me prince. I was obliged to consent because they insisted that I must do so for the sake of the nation. Yet it was as 'Blücher' that the nation had cried its approval to me.

To his cousin he wrote:

I was expected to change my name to Wahlstadt, but this I positively refused to do; so now I am to be called "Prince Blücher von Wahlstadt." Everything will depend on the sort of principality I am to receive in Silesia. Under no circumstances will I consent to add one more to the horde of sickly, hungry princes.

Blücher's progress through Germany when he returned from England was one continued triumph. Bietzke writes:

In every town), yes in every village, almost, the prince was most heartily greeted and was adorned with flowers by the most beautiful girls. . . . The prince was wont to answer the addresses that were made to him in a religious strain, regarding himself merely as the instrument with which a higher Being had freed the land from sore oppression and to whom alone thanks and praises were due.

The University of Berlin conferred upon him the degree of Doctor of Philosophy. He was banqueted and toasted and took every occasion to acknowledge in his responses the debt that he owed to others. Once he took occasion to apostrophise Scharnhorst in warm, stirring words:

Art thou present, spirit of my friend, my Scharnhorst? Then be thyself my witness that without thee I could have accomplished nothing!

He made a hasty visit to his Silesian estates and then returned to Berlin. The political situation disquieted him greatly; for he was not satisfied with the peace of Paris, believing that those who concluded it had shown a lack of intelligence and too little firmness. He wrote to Bülow:

Whether or not the future holds another struggle for us Heaven only knows. I feel no confidence in the matter. They neglected their opportunities in Paris. France's tone is growing too assured; they should more effectually have clipped her wings.

He had written while still in Paris:

Napoleon continues to have followers here, I have no faith in what the French may do when our armies shall have marched away.

And he more than once characterised the situation by saying:

We are but having a day of rest.

The Congress of Vienna—that Congress of which the witty Prince de Ligne said that it danced but did not walk—met in September, 1814, and its deliberations lasted through the winter. Blücher felt it as a personal slight that, while the Duke of Wellington and the Bavarian general von Wrede were allowed to take part in the deliberations, no notice was taken of himself. He was more than vexed at the role Prussia played in the whole proceedings. She had expected to be reinstated in all the possessions she had lost in consequence of her wars with Napoleon, or at the very least to receive a compensation commensurate with those losses.

The *Tsar* complicated matters at Vienna by announcing his intention of reviving the kingdom of Poland as a constitutional monarchy of which he, as Emperor of Russia, should be the head. It was clear that Russia had earned the right to some reward by her great sacrifice of men and money in the war; yet none of Napoleon's other con-

NAPOLEON

quests appealed to her. Nor had Prussia any great, affection for the provinces ceded to her in the partitions of 1793, and 1795. They had never been assimilated like the province of West Prussia which had fallen to her in the partition of 1772.

The *Tsar's* proposition was to secure to Prussia only such parts of the Polish provinces as were needed to round off her boundaries, and, in return for the rest, to have her annex Saxony. Saxony's king, it will be remembered, had fought on the side of Napoleon and it seemed not unfair that he should lose his territory. The plan appealed to Frederick William, but was bitterly opposed by England, Austria, and the Netherlands; and the strangest complications resulted from the new conflict of interests. It was considered too great an aggrandisement for Prussia; moreover, her boundaries would now touch those of Austria and the balance of power would be imperilled.

The victors quarrelled over the spoils until it came to the very verge of a new European war; and a military commission appointed by England, Austria, and the Netherlands actually drew up a plan of campaign against Prussia and Russia. One of the strangest results was the renewed political influence these dissensions gave to France which sided with the powers opposed to the cession of Saxony. Talleyrand, the great turncoat who had sailed with every wind that blew since, as high priest of the Revolution, he performed mass on the Champ de Mars, was allowed to rise and declare pompously that it was Napoleonic not legitimistic for Prussia to wish to overthrow the Saxon king.

The *Tsar* had promised Frederick William that Saxony should be his, but had given no definite guarantees, and in the final settlement Prussia came out less well than many of the patriots, including Blücher, had anticipated. She was given only a part of Saxony, to which was added a strip of territory on the left bank of the Rhine including Aix-la-Chapelle and Cologne, and the *Tsar* renounced Thorn and Danzig in her favour. On the other hand, she had to renounce her old provinces of East Frisia and Ansbach-Baireuth.

When these results became known, as they did in February, 1815, Blücher was furious and at once handed in a request for honourable discharge from the service. He had long since, as we know, laid down the chief command. He wrote bitterly to Gneisenau:

It honours and rejoices me to have shared in the war that is ended; but my chief satisfaction is in not having shared in the peace that has been concluded.

TALLEYRAND

He wrote scathingly to Rüchel of:

> Our brilliant reward for the sacrifices and hardships which the nation had so dutifully endured.

The loss of Ansbach–Baireuth and of East Frisia was what rankled most in his mind. Blücher could not believe, so he wrote, that three hundred thousand Poles and as many Saxons, who detested the Prussians, would ever be so faithful and self-sacrificing as these old comrades in arms:

> O ye politicians! Little do you know of humanity! The good Vienna Congress is like a fair in a small town to which each man drives in his own cattle to sell or exchange. We drove in a fine bull and have got in return a shabby ox, as the Berliner says. I for my part at once determined to leave, and have asked for my discharge. I am daily awaiting the answer and then shall retire for the rest of my days to Silesia and never see Berlin or the court again. It is unheard-of the way they treat us military.

The request for discharge from the service was respectfully, even humbly, worded. Perhaps Blücher remembered in his old age the long years of sorrow that had come from the arrogant wording of his similar request to Frederick the Great, nearly half a century before. Blücher's letter to Frederick William began:

> Since peace is entirely concluded, I hope and pray that Your Royal Majesty will have no further conflicts to wage. The years have so rolled up upon me that I no longer deem myself competent for a campaign. Therefore, I must fulfil my long-cherished determination of serving only so long as my inner consciousness tells me that I can do justice to all my obligations. So, I humbly ask for my discharge.

He was mentally in an evil turmoil in these days. Rightly or wrongly he felt that the two toilsome campaigns had been in vain. He took to gaming more fiercely than ever; but did not win as in the happier Palais Royal days. On the contrary his friend Eisenhart, whose memoirs have only recently, (1911), been published, records that he lost large sums of money. He told Eisenhart that he did not care; that he was gambling only out of desperation; that the "gentlemen of the pen" were to blame for everything and were ruining all that the sword had achieved. But should Heaven help him to reach Paris once more, there should be a great change in the method of procedure! The French would have to bleed in quite another fashion; he would rake out at least a hundred millions for the king!

Blücher was greatly in advance of his age in insisting on such an indemnity, but also far behind the present. What would he have said to the five billions that Bismarck required from France and that were to give to the development of Germany so wonderful an impetus?

Blücher's request for honourable discharge from the army was still under consideration by Frederick William, when Europe was startled by the greatest "bolt from the blue" that had fallen upon it since Frederick the Great invaded Silesia.

In the middle of the night of the 8th of March, Gneisenau came to Blücher's bedside, and waked him to say that his old enemy, the dreaded Corsican, had escaped from Elba and landed in France. The old warrior, still smarting over what he considered Prussia's wrongs, was in ecstasies, he cried:

> It is the greatest piece of good luck that could have happened to Prussia! Now the war will begin again, and the armies will make good all the faults committed in Vienna!

He showed all the fiery zeal of a crusader. His old uniform had been laid aside doubtless from disgust; but it came out now from its hiding-place. He declared without the least hesitation that he would once more take the field; and to General Kalckreuth who did his best to dissuade him he cried more forcibly than politely: "What silly nonsense are you talking?" Nostitz assures us that the old warrior had awakened to new life, that he thought of nothing, spoke of nothing but the great events that were about to take place.

The developments in France that caused and enabled Napoleon to leave Elba do not concern us here. It is enough, for our purpose, to know that the oppressor of Europe was again free; that the nightmare that had caused the nations to groan and writhe was once more upon them. On the first of March, Napoleon landed at Antibes and spread abroad his flaming proclamations among his old soldiers; on the sixth occurred the wonderfully dramatic scene near Grenoble where the outcast who was fighting to regain his throne threw open his coat within pistol shot of the opposing troops and cried: "If there be one soldier among you who wishes to kill his emperor, let him do so now"; and where every voice joined in the ringing shout of "Long live the Emperor!" Napoleon himself declared later:

LOUIS XVIII.

As far as Grenoble, I was the adventurer; in it I was the sovereign!

On the 10th of March, Lyons opened its gates; in the next three days no less than six regiments changed their allegiance; on the 14th Marshal Ney abandoned Louis XVIII., having declared, it is said, that he could not hold back the waves of an ocean with his hands; on the 20th, Louis XVIII. fled his capital and the next day one might have read the following announcement in the *Moniteur*:

> Yesterday evening at eight o'clock, His Majesty the Emperor returned to his palace of the Tuileries. He entered Paris at the head of the troops which, in the morning, had been sent against him to oppose his return.

Blücher had a worthy enemy with whom to cope. By granting constitutional liberties Napoleon was able to secure zealous co-operation in the matter of raising an army, and he soon had 200,000 men in the field. He organised them with consummate skill and rapidity and proclaimed, besides, the *levée en masse* which called out the whole able-bodied male population of France.

On the 13th of March, the eight powers represented at the Congress of Vienna signed a formal document declaring that Napoleon by his return had destroyed the only lawful grounds for his existence; that he was to be looked upon as outlawed, beyond the pale of the civil and social order, an enemy of the public peace; that as such he had exposed himself to the public vengeance, *il s'est livré à la vindicte publique*.

This declaration of the powers rivalled in the force of its language some of the old bulls by which the mediaeval church called down upon the head of him who had braved it all the wrath of Heaven and the fires of hell. Napoleon's enterprise is spoken of as a "criminal delirium."

One clause of the declaration was important. The powers expressed their willingness to give France *and its king* every aid and support in restoring tranquillity. Many were to wish later that that clause had been omitted. Among such was to be Blücher.

On March 15th, Frederick William answered the letter in which Blücher had tendered his resignation from the army:

> I have not been able to grant your request to be discharged. Inasmuch as Bonaparte's appearance in France makes it posable, at least, that he must once more be opposed by the allied armies I should like to feel sure that, in such an eventual struggle, I

can rely on you as I did last year when I placed the fate of the fatherland in your hands.

This was followed only two days later by the formal bestowal of the supreme command over the whole Prussian Army upon Blücher, who was, however, to remain in Berlin until further developments, while Gneisenau, who was once more appointed to be his chief of staff, was despatched to the Rhine to assemble and organise the forces that were to take the field.

Gneisenau at this time was a disappointed man, and his heart was full of bitterness; for he had expected to be given a separate command, Hardenberg wrote to console him in terms tending to show that Blücher had been chosen more because of his popularity than from any expectation of great achievements:

Once more you are not in a very agreeable position. The credit for what you accomplish will be claimed by another. But how can it be helped? The king adheres to the system of advancement by age; otherwise it is you who would command the army. At present you actually do command; but old Blücher gives his name. Few will be deceived about that matter.

Müffling, too, once wrote of Blücher:

All Europe knew that the old prince, who was past seventy, understood nothing at all about leading an army—so little, indeed, that when a plan was laid before him for his approval, even If it had only to do with some minor operation, it conveyed no clear meaning to him and he could form no judgment whether it was good or bad.

The truth seems to be that Blücher really was ignorant of many of the technicalities of his trade, but that he was, all the same, an inspired commander. Müffling maintains that he was:

Merely the bravest in battle, the most tireless in bearing fatigue, the one who set the example and who through his fiery addresses understood how to rouse enthusiasm.

Marwitz, who also criticises Blücher, states this still more clearly and relieves our minds of the fear that perhaps, after all, Blücher was in a position that he was not competent to fill:

What was it then that attracted the soldiers to him so mightily?

GNEISENAU

The boldness that flashed from his eyes; his heroic personality; his grey hairs; his voice as he uttered a few laughing words in passing; the certainty that he would be on hand the moment he was needed and that in the most desperate situation he would never fail one, that he would always take advantage of a turn of fortune.

Müffling adds to the picture:

You can reckon on it that if the prince has given his word to engage in a common operation that word will be kept even if the whole Prussian Army be annihilated in the process.

Surely this is much; and the thought obtrudes itself that those who lay too much stress on Blücher's shortcomings are lacking in the imagination that enables one to appreciate the superiority of genius over mere routine. The immediate future was to prove that the *vox populi* had a truer ring than the voice of the critics.

The four great powers—England, Russia, Austria, and Prussia—agreed each to furnish a contingent of 150,000 men. Added to what the smaller powers provided, the sum total of soldiers called out to crush Napoleon came to nearly 900,000—a fine tribute to the outlaw's greatness. The army that we shall, for the sake of convenience, call the English Army in spite of the fact that it contained more Germans and Netherlanders than Englishmen, was under the command of the Duke of Wellington. He had already won undying laurels in Spain, where the popular uprising had served as an inspiration if not as a model to the Prussians. Wellington was now the first of the commanders to take the field, concentrating his forces on the Belgian frontier.

The Austrian and the Russian armies were to be respectively under Schwarzenberg and the *Tsar* but were so behindhand with their preparations that a council of war ordered the postponement of operations first until June 1st, and eventually until June 27th, by which time the fate of the campaign had been decided.

Blücher, meanwhile, who on April 19th, had joined his army at Liège—Wellington had requested that the Germans should protect his left flank—found himself involved in a difficulty that might have had very serious consequences had Napoleon hastened his attack. It had been decided at Vienna, as we have seen, that a part and not the whole of Saxony should fall to Prussia as indemnity. Although the arrangement had not actually been ratified and put into force it was thought best, as the campaign was commencing, to segregate those Saxon soldiers who were soon to become Prussian subjects from the rest; a proceeding which outraged the soldiers, who were sore enough already over their political prospects.

They objected, not so much to serving under the Prussians as to having their whole military organisation torn asunder—all the more as their own king had not yet released them from their allegiance. The Prussian standpoint was that, by deserting to the allies in the midst of the Battle of Leipzig, whereas Frederick Augustus had remained true to Napoleon until taken prisoner, they had themselves severed the bond with their king. They had taken an actual oath of obedience to the allied sovereigns, and, in addition, the Saxon king's reinstatement in even a part of his domains had been made under the condition that he should liberate these soldiers from their oath.

All the same it was known at Prussian headquarters that there was likely to be difficulty with the Saxon contingent and the conversation is recorded that took place between Blücher and Gneisenau when the king's order to segregate the Prussian from the Saxon subjects arrived. It was on the first of May.

"What will happen," asked Blücher, "if we try to carry out the cabinet order?"

"There will be a revolt," was the answer.

"Well, what is to be done?"

"Obey," declared Gneisenau; "we must carry it through, come what may."

It was Gneisenau who addressed the Saxon commanders on the 2nd of May, announcing that the separation was to take place and that no interference of any kind would be permitted. He declared:

Rather than permit in our midst a corps that plots in secret I will command, sirs, that the way to France be opened to you and let you share the fate of Bonaparte. For I should prefer to see you drawn up against us as open enemies to having you in our midst as false friends.

Even as Gneisenau was speaking a mob of soldiers in citizen dress was gathering round Blücher's quarters with cries of "Long live King Frederick Augustus!" and "We won't be separated!" The Saxon commanders, hurrying from the conference with Gneisenau were able to restore order for the moment; but as darkness gathered the demonstrations were renewed. Stones were thrown at members of Blücher's staff

SAXON SOLDIERS

and swords were drawn. The mutineers, a number of whom were intoxicated, could with difficulty be prevented by the guard from forcing their way into the house; and, as it was, they broke in the windows of the very room in which Blücher was standing.

The old field-marshal who, in the whole course of his life, had never had to cope with a situation like this, flew into such a rage that he could with difficulty be prevented from using his sabre. At last—and one can imagine what a blow it was to his pride—he was obliged literally to run away and escape by the back door. Naturally it was not only his person but the dignity of the commander-in-chief of the Prussian Army that had been outraged; moreover further violence was employed when, now, he gave the order to replace by Prussians some of the Saxon regiments and battalions that he had purposely kept in his neighbourhood, to show his confidence.

This episode with the Saxons is important as showing all the grimness and determination of Blücher when his rightful authority was assailed. There is no talk of an investigation, none of a court-martial for the offenders. Blücher reports to the king the line of conduct he means to employ towards the mutineers:

> I shall surround them, disarm them, and then have them commanded to deliver up their ringleaders. If they do so, I shall have the latter shot dead; if they refuse, I shall take every tenth man and have a number of them shot. I shall then dismiss these battalions from the army as unworthy to fight.

These intentions were carried out and four men were shot as an example; while one battalion was condemned to the disgrace of having its standard publicly burned. This last order resulted in a fresh act of insubordination—this time on the part of a Prussian corps-commander, Borstel. Borstel had felt great sympathy for the battalion condemned to lose its standard—it was a battalion of the Saxon bodyguards, and the Saxon queen had embroidered the banner with her own hands. Borstel first interceded with Blücher, then flatly refused to carry out the order on the ground that he had given his word of honour that the standard would not be destroyed.

It was the first time in any of the campaigns that one so high in rank as Borstel had been subjected to discipline; but Blücher did not falter. The banner was burned as he had previously directed; and Borstel himself was suspended from his command, not allowed to take any further part in the campaign, and, finally, after being brought before a court-martial, was imprisoned in a fortress.

Almost as monarch to monarch Blücher wrote at this time—on the very day indeed of the military executions—to the King of Saxony:

> Through your earlier measures Your Royal Majesty plunged your subjects, a worthy German people, into the deepest misery; your later measures resulted in covering the people with shame.
>
> The rebellion in the army, organised in Friedrichsfelda and Pressburg, has broken out just as all Germany is marching against the common enemy. The criminals have openly proclaimed Bonaparte their protector and have compelled me, who in my fifty-five years of service have been in the fortunate position of being called upon to shed no blood save that of my enemies, to order, for the first time, executions in my own army. From the enclosure, (an appeal to the Saxon troops), Your Majesty will see how, up to this very moment, I have striven to save the honour of the Saxon name. But it is for the last time. If my words are not heeded, then not without sorrow but with a good conscience and with the assurance of duty fulfilled, I shall restore order by force even though I be compelled to shoot down the entire Saxon Army. Before the judgment-seat of God the blood thus shed will fall on him who alone is guilty. And, before God's omniscience *giving* and *permitting* commands will be regarded as one and the same thing. Your Royal Majesty knows that an old man of seventy-three can have no other earthly aim or object than that the voice of truth prevail and that justice be done.

None of the Saxons, eventually, save a few of the cavalry, were found sufficiently reliable to serve in the Prussian Army; so that Blücher, at the outset of the campaign and after the troops had already assembled at the chosen seat of war, lost 14,000 men.

All the same, by the 24th of May, Blücher's army numbered 120,000, while 75,000 more were on the way from the more distant provinces. The providing for all these troops, indeed, was not so easy. Funds grew so scarce that Blücher and Gneisenau had to pledge their personal credit to English merchants to the extent of 50,000 pounds.

A report of Blücher's to his king, on June 4th, shows how impatient he was growing at the long delays:

> The enemy grows in strength relatively far more rapidly than

A SECTION OF CAPITAINE'S MAP

(Used by Napoleon)

we, and Napoleon gains time to thoroughly re-establish his power in the interior of France. Prince Wrede is quite of my opinion; and inasmuch as here, because of the faulty arrangements of the Netherland authorities, provisions grow scarcer and the burden on the country grows heavier day by day, I must humbly ask Your Majesty to hasten the beginning of hostilities as much as possible.

It was Napoleon himself who put an end to all Blücher's anxiety; and, in the days between the 15th and the 19th of June, inclusive, the Prussian commander-in-chief was to have no reason to complain of not being quite sufficiently occupied. For Napoleon was upon him almost with the suddenness of a hurricane. Forced not so much by military as by political considerations to strike, and to strike at once; fearing his own people more than he did the enemy should the sacred soil of France be once more invaded; knowing that one of his old dazzling achievements would call forth the old frantic enthusiasm; the French emperor had determined on the desperate manoeuvre of thrusting himself in between the great armies of Blücher and Wellington.

He would drive these two enemies asunder crippling the one or the other, or both, and then swiftly turn and meet the oncoming Austrians and Prussians. The manner in which, without his manoeuvre being detected, Napoleon massed forces to the number of 120,000 within half a day's march of Charleroi—the River Sambre, it is true, ran between—is one of the most notable achievements in all military history. It must be remembered, however, that the French boundary was nearer to Charleroi than it is at present, and that a number of small fortresses masked the movements of Napoleon. Blücher's scouting system, too, partly from lack of funds, was very imperfect.

For some days there had been disquieting reports at Blücher's headquarters; but in each case they had been contradicted. On June 9th, Gneisenau wrote:

The enemy will not attack us but will retire as far as to the Aisne, Somme, and Marne in order to concentrate his forces.

And again, on the 12th:

The danger of an attack has almost vanished.

Still on the 13th, Wellington writes to Lord Lynedoch that Napoleon is reported to have joined his army and to be on the point of giving battle; but that, in all probability, it will be some days yet before the emperor leaves Paris. So little fear was felt by either the English or the German commanders, that the forces of both were widely scattered—a measure that had been rendered necessary by the increasing difficulty of obtaining provisions.

By midday of the 14th, however, Blücher had heard news enough to make him begin to draw together those divisions of his troops that were posted at the more distant points; and late that night Gneisenau received such distinct information of the imminence of a French advance that, without waking Blücher, he gave orders on his own responsibility for a general concentration of the Prussian forces. Less than four hours later Napoleon's army was crossing the Belgian frontier and had encountered the Prussian outposts!

CHAPTER 11

The Battles of Ligny and Waterloo

In order to understand the operations that culminated in the Battle of Waterloo one must bear in mind the relative positions of the points at which fighting occurred. From Charleroi near the Belgian frontier, two roads diverge, the one running northward all the way to Brussels, and passing first through Quatre Bras, then through Genappe, Belle Alliance, La Haye Sainte, Mont St. Jean, and Waterloo; the other running north-eastward through Fleurus, then passing close to St. Amand and Ligny, and finally joining almost at right angles the highway that runs in a general easterly and westerly direction from Nivelles through Quatre Bras and Sombreffe to Namur and Liège.

The Charleroi-Brussels road formed the line of communication for Wellington's, the Charleroi-Liège road that for Blücher's army; along them reinforcements came and also ammunition and supplies; and in case of retreat they would naturally be chosen by preference. Should the armies be forced back each along its own line they could still communicate with each other until after passing the Quatre Bras-Sombreffe road. In other words, Charleroi was the apex of a triangle of which the line between Quatre Bras and a point a little east of Sombreffe formed the base.

Napoleon, in descending upon Charleroi, had counted on the secrecy and on the swiftness of his own movements to counterbalance the danger that the English and German commanders would here unite all their forces to oppose him. It was a fine piece of strategy to attack not the weakest but the strongest point of his adversaries: far more easily might he have won a victory had he appeared for instance, as Wellington fully expected would be the case, on the extreme right wing of the English Army and attempted to round it and cut it off from the sea.

PLAN
OF THE OPERATIONS
of the
CAMPAIGN
in the
NETHERLANDS.
June 1815.

Anderlecht   BRUSSELS
St Gilles
Fort Monterey
Vert Chasseur   les 3 Fontaines
Petite Espinette   Nd de la Bose
Oversssche
G Thirielle   Strelenbergh   Tombeek
FOREST OF SOIGNES
Waterloo   Ter la haye
Chain
Les Vieux Amis   R
Mocke Braine   St Lambert
Mont St Jean   Frischmont
Braine la Leude   Limale
Smouhen   Genappe corps
La Belle Alliance   Wavres
Plancheheit
Lillois   Mont St Guibert
Observatory
Genappe   N
NIVELLES   Quatre Bras
Tilly
Frasnes   L
Ney   Sombref
Gosslies   Gembloux
Fleurus   Grouchy
Centre of the French   Templeux
CHARLEROI   NAMUR
Chatellet   Sambre Riv.
Marchiennes
-au-Pont
Sambre Riv.
Lobbes
Thuin

Infantry	English
Cavalry	Belgians & Hanov.
Artillery	Prussians
	French

But an isolated victory would have availed him little. His whole plan, his whole desire was to thrust himself in like a wedge between the two armies and drive them back beyond the cross-road by which alone they could readily communicate. His great mistake, the mistake of his life one may say, was to imagine that under no circumstances would Blücher, if beaten and retreating, abandon his line of communication with Germany.

Charleroi was in the hands of Napoleon almost before Blücher, who had his headquarters at Namur, even knew of his approach. At half-past four on the morning of June 15th, Zieten, who, with the first Prussian Army corps, was in command in that neighbourhood, heard the sound of the first French cannon. He at once sent to inform Blücher in Namur and the Duke of Wellington in Brussels; and, later in the day, despatched the information to Blücher that, according to a French deserter, General Bourmont, Napoleon's forces numbered 120,000 men. Zieten abandoned Charleroi without a struggle; and Blücher ordered him to retreat along the highway, expressing the hope, however, that he would not need to retire beyond Fleurus:

> For tomorrow I expect to concentrate the army in the neighbourhood of Sombreffe.

The order for the Prussian Army to concentrate, given by Gneisenau on the night of the 14th, while Blücher still slept, had, unfortunately, only in part been obeyed. Bülow, with the whole fourth army corps, was not to be at hand when the critical moment came. The reason is a strange one and shows what small circumstances may influence the fate of nations; Gneisenau between whom and Bülow there was a certain amount of friction, had worded his despatch too politely, and therefore less peremptorily than in the case of the other generals. Of this there is not the slightest doubt, for the despatch is still preserved and it reads literally;

> I have the honour humbly to request Your Excellency to be kind enough to concentrate the fourth army-corps under your command tomorrow, the 15th, at Hannut in close cantonment. Information received makes it more and more probable that the French Army has concentrated against us and that we must expect from it an immediate change to the offensive. . . . Your Excellency had doubtless better make Hannut your headquarters.

Bülow had already made other arrangements in consequence of

earlier orders; to obey Gneisenau at once would have necessitated a night march and the soldiers were fatigued. Habitually distrusting Gneisenau, he believed that the latter was now exaggerating the danger; even as it was, the orders did not sound particularly alarming. So Bülow sent word to headquarters that, in view of all the circumstances, he had taken the responsibility of postponing the required concentration in close cantonment at Hannut until the next day! The next day took place the Battle of Ligny, in which, for want of Bülow's support, Blücher was defeated.

On the very morning of the battle, Bülow was still at Liège, and of course had not received the much more urgent orders despatched to Hannut in the full expectation of finding him there. The same adjutant who had ridden to Hannut had then dashed like mad through the whole night to Liège. When told that Blücher was on the very point of giving battle at Sombreffe: "My God, why was I not informed of that before?" was Bülow's cry. He started at once on a forced march, but it was too late. The Battle of Ligny was over before he even arrived in the neighbourhood.

Through a despatch sent from Hannut Blücher already knew, on the morning of the 16th, that he could not count on the assistance of Bülow's corps; but from another direction he had every reason to hope for efficient aid.

On the previous evening at seven o'clock Müffling, a member of Blücher's staff, deputed to act as his representative at Wellington's headquarters, had written from Brussels that the news of Napoleon's attack on General Zieten at Charleroi had just arrived, and that the duke had determined to assemble all his troops "at the rendezvous." Müffling continued:

> So soon as the moon rises, the reserves will begin their march, and if the enemy do not straightway attack Nivelles the duke will be in the neighbourhood of Nivelles tomorrow to support Your Highness; or should the enemy have already attacked Your Highness, to fall on his flank or on his rear as shall have been agreed. I imagine Your Highness will be pleased with this explanation and with the duke's activity.

Shortly after Müffling penned these words he received a despatch from Blücher himself, announcing his intention to give battle at Sombreffe and asking to be speedily informed when and where the duke was concentrating and what his general intentions were. Wellington

Wellington   Blücher

materially modified his orders in consequence of this despatch, sent only 21,600 men, instead of his whole army to Nivelles and—strange to say—seems to have failed to notify Blücher of the fact. The duke made another incomprehensible omission that night. He failed to occupy Quatre Bras, and left a gap in the defence that might have had serious consequences had not General Perponcher seen the danger and on his own responsibility sent 7,000 men from Nivelles. It was on Quatre Bras that Marshal Ney, on the following day, made his attack!

On the evening of the 15th, the duke remained in Brussels, and at a time when, it would seem, his presence was very much needed elsewhere, attended the ball of the Duchess of Richmond, which has become so famous in history. One fails to see what was to be gained by seeming to regard Napoleon's advance with indifference, at a moment when one corps of the duke's ally was actually in conflict with him and Blücher himself was preparing to make a desperate stand on the following day. It was, after all, at Wellington's request that Blücher had come to Belgium, and they had promised each other mutual support.

The duke had noble qualities, which some appear to think should make him immune from criticism; but his appearance with his officers at that ball in Brussels seems to have been prompted by mere vanity. He might well have spent the time in informing himself of the true position of his troops, for the report on the subject that he sent to Blücher the next morning was so full of inaccuracies that few German historians can be made to believe that he did not purposely make false statements.

It is scarcely necessary to review the dramatic incidents of the ball. Towards one in the morning, as the duke sat at supper with his hostess and with his own corps-commander the Prince of Orange—who was bitterly chagrined at being far from his corps at that moment—word was brought that the enemy had appeared at Quatre Bras. The duke rose, gave a few commands to his adjutant, then reseated himself at the feast, calming the fears of all around him. He told the Prince of Orange that he could not believe the news. The dancing was renewed and the duke and his officers slipped away unobserved. At five the army was on the march.

At half-past ten, from the heights behind Frasnes, the duke sent a glowing account to Blücher of the number of troops that he had at hand. No one denies the falseness of his assertions, but English writers maintain that he himself was deceived. He announced troops as already at points which they would be unable to reach for many hours, and thus gave a totally wrong impression of the amount of aid on which Blücher might rely. It was stated, for instance, that a whole division of the army was at Quatre Bras, and that the entire reserves, 29,000 men, would, by midday, reach Genappe. It has been estimated that had all Wellington's statements proved correct no less than 68,000 men could, by four o'clock, have effected a junction with Blücher's right wing. Gneisenau wrote at the time in this connection:

> On the 16th of June, in the morning, the Duke of Wellington promised to be at Quatre Bras at ten o'clock with 20,000 men with his cavalry in Nivelles. On the strength of these arrangements and promises we decided to fight the battle (at Ligny).

Blücher, too, in his report, speaks of the duke's failure to concentrate his forces in time to be of aid as "contrary to expectation and agreement."

The explanation of Wellington's conduct given by German historians like Delbrück and Lettow-Vorbeck, and even by the unbiassed Italian General, Pollio, is that the duke feared lest Blücher, if he were to learn the real state of affairs, would refrain from giving battle at Sombreffe; that the war would not be concluded before the Russians and Austrians reached the scene, and that the *Tsar* would frustrate the plan of English statesmen to replace Louis XVIII. on the throne.

In all probability the truth lies between extremes. The duke had every interest in making it appear that his army would furnish efficient aid. He overstated his case; he boasted just a little of what he could accomplish. He certainly never meant to lure Blücher on to defeat. The supposition that he really miscalculated the distances and the time that his different detachments would require for their marches seems the most untenable of all. He was no novice; he had had years of experience in leading armies.

At midday on the 16th, Wellington rode over from Quatre Bras and met Blücher near the mill of Bussy. The mill was situated on a height between Sombreffe and Brye and overlooked the position that Blücher had chosen for a battlefield. This was nearer now to Ligny than to Sombreffe, for Blücher had changed his original dispositions in view of the expected English aid. Just what agreements were made in the course of the famous interview it is impossible now to establish, for the reason that the accounts of those who were present—all written as it happens after the lapse of years—differ even in essential particulars. All agree that much was said about the aid that Wellington was to furnish in the battle; but Müffling states that as they parted the duke said to Blücher:

All right, I shall come, provided I am not attacked myself.

The interview must have been very friendly, for Dörnberg, who escorted Wellington on his return, writes:

As we rode away good Blücher accompanied us a part of the way; and, as he turned back, the duke said to me: "What a fine fellow he is!"

Among the reports that cannot be verified is one to the effect that after looking over Blücher's dispositions for the battle Wellington said:

If they stay here, they will be damnably mauled.

Wellington was attacked, as we know, at Quatre Bras and had on hand, not the great forces he had proclaimed to Blücher, but only the seven thousand men that had been withdrawn from Nivelles the night before without his orders. As the day wore on reinforcements came up, but even at nightfall he had but about 30,000, with which, indeed, he easily repulsed the 21,000 of Ney. There was nothing to spare for Blücher, for Wellington could not know to what extent Napoleon would reinforce Ney.

It was fortunate for the allies that Napoleon was guided by a number of singularly false impressions. He believed that Wellington's and Blücher's armies were both retreating, each along its own line of communication. It must have strengthened this view that, on the 15th, so small a force was to be found at Quatre Bras. Zieten, as we know, had retreated from Charleroi to Fleurus, but Napoleon was ignorant of the fact that Blücher meant to make a stand against him at Sombreffe. The French emperor's instructions to his marshals, Ney and Grouchy, show clearly that he meant to make short work of what he considered to be merely Blücher's rear-guard, and then proceed in force to Brussels. He expected no great opposition, even from Wellington, during this march; but hoped to isolate the English Army, and so to speak, drive it into a corner.

There are signs to show that, in spite of the successes in Spain, Napoleon had a poor opinion of Wellington as a general, and a still poorer one of Blücher. With the latter he had more than once had to do in the previous campaign at moments when untoward circumstances seemed to argue great inefficiency on the part of the commander— notably at Montmirail, Champaubert, and Étoges, where the ultimate fault lay with Schwarzenberg, and at Laon where Blücher had been laid low by illness. That Blücher had, all along, been the animating spirit of the allies, that his troops were ready to die for him to a man, that he could bear defeat and the worst possible fatigues but would cling to his purpose with the tenacity of iron was entirely undreamed of by Napoleon.

So certain was the latter now of the success of his new plan that he carried with him a proclamation printed probably in Charleroi but dated from Schloss Laeken near Brussels, which was addressed to the Belgians and to the inhabitants of the provinces on the left bank of the Rhine. We have the wording of it; the old sonorous periods roll forth once more, and for the last time:

> The momentary successes of my enemies had detached you for a brief space from My Empire. In my exile on a rock in the sea I heard your laments. The God of weapons has determined the fate of your fine provinces. Napoleon is in your midst! You are worthy to be Frenchmen! Rise in a body! Join my invincible *phalanxes* to annihilate the remnants of the barbarians who are your enemies as well as mine! They have taken to flight with rage and despair in their hearts.

Surely greater pride never went before a fall!

On the morning of the 16th, while Ney attacked Quatre Bras, Grouchy was ordered to take Sombreffe where Napoleon expected that he would find at most but one corps of the Prussian Army, but where, as we know, three corps were in reality assembled. Grouchy made his attack from the south sending word to Ney who, as he imagined, would soon have completed the capture of Quatre Bras, to fall on the Prussians in the rear. The battle began at half-past two and the forces stood 86,000 to 78,000 in favour of the Prussians; but the lay of the land and the fact that in anticipation of the aid of the English too large a force had been sent to guard the line of communication with Namur, prevented nearly a whole corps from being available as a reserve.

Not until after eight o'clock in the evening was the hope finally abandoned that the English might still come. The battle resolved itself into one long continuous struggle for the same two villages, Ligny and St. Amand, which were taken and retaken a number of times. Then came an awful climax. At a moment when, partly through the error of one of Blücher's generals, the reserves were massed only behind the wings Napoleon burst through the weakened centre with his guards—like a veritable god of war, for a dense black thundercloud, combined with the dusk which was already falling, almost hid him from view. Hastily collecting what cavalry he could from the right wing Blücher placed himself at its head and, brandishing his sword, rushed into the breach.

In vain; and it was only by a miracle that the old field-marshal himself escaped death or capture. Struck by a ball his horse fell under him and rolled over partly upon him. He was dazed for a moment, then found himself unable to rise or even to draw his leg from underneath the horse. Yet the French were almost upon him and groups had already dashed by. Nostitz could not release him alone; but help finally came; he was lifted on to the horse of an under officer and reached the Prussian lines in safety.

Ligny was a serious and a bloody defeat; but it would have been more serious and more bloody still had not a French corps of 20,000 men under D'Erlon first marched to near Quatre Bras and then been ordered to return hastily to Ligny, proving of no assistance at either point. Blücher's losses are estimated at the large total of 12,000 men, and the Prussian Army seemed to the French, at least, to be utterly demoralised. The French official report signalised the victory as a complete one and declared that:

> He (Napoleon) drove asunder the hostile lines. Lord Wellington and Blücher have scarcely been able to save themselves. It was like a change of scene in the theatre; in an instant the enemy fled, routed, in all directions. We have several thousand prisoners and forty guns.

Even the next day Soult wrote to Ney that the Prussians were routed and that it was hardly likely that the English would offer further opposition.

Napoleon this time was not boasting, not lying for effect. He really believed that Blücher's army was *hors de combat*, that it was retreating in confusion along the Sombreffe-Namur road. His pursuit lasted but half an hour and he then allowed his weary troops to rest.

Blücher and his staff—not Gneisenau alone as has often been stated—had meanwhile swiftly formed the courageous decision to order the retreat instead of along the road that formed the line of communication with Germany, as Napoleon had so confidently anticipated, by a narrower road that led almost north to Wavre, which is on a line with, and to the east of, Waterloo. Here, or rather at the neighbouring Mont St. Jean, Wellington had decided to take up his position; so that the two armies were only a very few miles further apart than they had been at Quatre Bras and Sombreffe.

It is incomprehensible, but Napoleon, still firm in the idea that Blücher's army had been routed, completely lost sight of the Prussians and knew neither where they were, nor that they were once more in fighting trim and had been joined by the uninjured corps that Bülow led from Liège, until they actually gripped him in the flank on the afternoon of Waterloo.

The retreat through the night from Ligny had been orderly considering the circumstances. Blücher and Gneisenau had met unexpectedly in a little village along the route and had laid all their plans. They had had hourly reports from Ligny as to the position of the French, and had at last learned that the corps of Marshal Grouchy had been sent in search of them, and that they might have to stand an attack from him the next day. By the morning of the seventeenth all four corps of the army were safely encamped around Wavre, and, like a gift of the gods, a long train of ammunition waggons arrived from another direction to help them in their wonderful rehabilitation.

That same morning of the seventeenth, messengers crossed each other between Wellington's and Blücher's camps bearing similar proposals—a common attack on Napoleon. Wellington declared that he would give battle that very day if one single Prussian corps would join him. To this Blücher demurred. His own condition was such, after his fall and the night march, that he remained recumbent the whole of the seventeenth; but he declared that on the morrow he would be present not with a part but with the whole of his army—"with the fresh corps and with the others" was his literal expression.

When he made this promise scarcely twelve hours had elapsed since his troops had suffered one of the great defeats in history, and the horrible harvest of dead and wounded had not yet been gathered in. His courage, his decision, his optimism all showed that his choice as commander-in-chief had been fully justified. What was needed now was a man and not a strategist or a tactician; Scharnhorst, in recommending him in 1813, had not praised his knowledge or his cleverness but had declared with warmth that he was the only general not afraid of Napoleon. Even during the wild turmoil at the beginning of the retreat Blücher is said to have remarked:

We have had a blow and now we must straighten out the dent.

While still stretched on his couch at Wavre on the 17th he wrote letters in the most courageous strain:

> If Napoleon fights a few more battles like this he and his army are done for!

And again:

> My troops fought like lions, but we were too weak; for two of my corps were not with me. Now I have drawn them all together.

Nostitz relates that although suffering in body Blücher was clear and bright in mind; that he had declared with great emphasis that "no matter what his condition he would rather have himself tied on his horse than resign the command of the army," and that "a thirst for bloody vengeance had taken possession of his will and of his intelligence." Blücher's order of the day to his troops concluded with the stirring words:

> I shall once more lead you against the enemy; we shall defeat him *for we must!*

Whether he himself survived or perished in the operation was indifferent to him. When on the morning of the fateful 18th of June, Bietzke the physician proposed to rub ointment on the bruises he had incurred in his fall, he refused, saying that it was indifferent to him whether he went *balsamirt* or *nicht balsamirt*, anointed or unanointed, into eternity, he concluded:

> But if things go well today, we shall soon all be washing and bathing in Paris!

The march from Wavre to Waterloo would have been no remarkable achievement under ordinary circumstances; and Blücher, when he gave his promise to be present with his whole army, had not the slightest doubt of being able to be on hand at the beginning of the battle. But the circumstances were not ordinary, for everything conspired to make the march as toilsome as possible; and nature lent Napoleon every aid in this his greatest and last struggle.

The previous day had been hot but at night the rain had fallen in perfect torrents. The Prussian soldiers—wearied by the long fitting at Ligny and by the subsequent night march—had lain down on the bare ground seeking by preference the hollows and the furrows. They awoke in the morning wet to the skin and covered with a thick slime. They were hungry and could not be fed because, for the most part, the supplies had gone astray. The mud made it difficult for the horses to drag the cannon and ammunition, so that at every rising of the ground the infantry had to put their shoulders to the wheels. Bülow's corps, which being the freshest, was despatched first to the scene of the fighting, happened to be stationed the furthest away and was obliged to march past the other corps which already occasioned some delay.

To complete the gloom of the situation, before the third and last corps had left Wavre it was fallen upon by Grouchy with 33,000 against 18,000 men. Twice that day the commander of the corps, General Thielmann, was to send word to Blücher that he could not hold his own against such frightful odds; but Blücher's answers were worthy of a Spartan commander. Thielmann must manage as best he could; he must hold fast Grouchy as long as possible and then, if need be, retire; but no troops could be spared from the battle with Napoleon. It would already be a great achievement if these 18,000 Prussians could hold back 33,000 Frenchmen from joining in the combat at Waterloo.

By midday, after the battle had already begun, the corps of Bülow which Blücher himself had joined, had only reached St. Lambert, scarcely more than half way between Wavre and Waterloo. Had the forest known as the Bois de Paris, which now lay directly in the path of the Prussians, been occupied by only a small detachment of the French, Blücher's whole manoeuvre might have been frustrated. To his joy and surprise, he found that the forest was completely undefended, and that from the village of Couture, on his left, there was no danger of a flank attack.

The march, which had been interrupted for the double purpose of reconnoitring and of awaiting the columns behind, was renewed with redoubled courage. The steep hill that rose from the bed of the little River Lasne proved the most frightful natural obstacle of the whole march; and it seemed like the labour of Sisyphus to advance the cannon up the steep slope. Here Blücher accomplished what it is doubtful if any other general in the Prussian Army could have done. He threw his whole soul into this last effort, and none could resist the sight of those grey hairs and the pleading of that beloved voice. The men were spurred on to incredible efforts, he cried:

Forward, boys! Some I hear say it cannot be done, *but it must be done!* I have promised my brother Wellington. You would not make me a perjurer?

The best modern military authority for this period, (Von Lettow-Vorbeck), writes:

Without the example and the encouraging words of the old hero, the troops needed to bring about the decision at Plancenoit could scarcely have arrived in time.

In the meanwhile, on the field of Waterloo, such a cannonading was in progress as had never been known since artillery came in use. Wellington's position, in a line more than two and a half miles long, with his back to Brussels, was on a low ridge—a mere swelling of the ground—which runs from near Braine l'Alleud on the extreme west to La Haye and Papelotte on the east. His headquarters was in front of Mont St. Jean, at the point where the main Charleroi-Brussels road intersects with one that runs from Braine l'Alleud to Smohain. As natural bastions Wellington had the *château* of Hougomont on his extreme right, the farms of Papelotte and La Haye on his left, and that of La Haye Sainte in the centre.

The village of Waterloo itself is far in the rear of Mont St. Jean, from which it was hidden by the Forêt de Soigne. There was no fighting whatever in its vicinity, and there was no reason for giving its name to the battle except that Wellington had his sleeping quarters there, and from there dated his despatches. His actual numbers were 69,000 as opposed to 73,300 of the French. Such at least is the most recent German computation. (See Lettow-Vorbeck, i.) The French returning from Ligny had passed Quatre Bras, where, it is recorded, they saw their own dead lying in naked heaps, despoiled by marauders.

They had then taken up their position facing the English; with Frischermont on their right, Mon Plaisir, south-west of Hougomont, on their left, and the farm of Belle Alliance as their centre. To the south-east of Belle Alliance lies the not inconsiderable village of Plancenoit which was to be the chief scene of operations for Bülow's corps. The distance between the two armies was less than it would be in a modern battle where cannon have a much longer range, and nowhere exceeded three-quarters of a mile.

It was well for the Prussians that Napoleon was in no haste that day to begin the battle. He had not the least suspicion that they were straining every nerve to reach him, and believed them as we have said, to be *hors de combat*. As for the English his one fear was that they might in some way escape him. He is reported to have said:

> We shall be most fortunate if they stand and face us.

At one o'clock at night, in the pouring rain, he had visited his outposts to make sure that his intended prey was still there. The next morning, he had taken time for a comfortable breakfast and then, possibly to impose upon his enemies and flaunt his superiority in their faces, had held a review of his troops as if on a parade-ground. The music played *Partant pour la Syrie*, the banners were lowered before him, and the men cried "*Vive l'Empereur*," doubtless for the last time. He himself wrote later of this display:

> The earth seemed proud to carry so many brave men.

Not until half-past eleven—at which time indeed, as we have already seen, the Prussians were but nearing St. Lambert—did the battle begin with the French attack upon Hougomont; which was to be fiercely fought for throughout the day, the gains being made only inch by inch. Not until after one did the carefully planned attack upon Wellington's centre take place. Just as the signal for the cannonading here was about to be given, Napoleon, scanning the horizon with his glasses saw a sight that must have chilled his blood—the Prussians swarming on the heights near St. Lambert. A letter that had been captured from a Prussian hussar, and that was now brought to the emperor, left no doubt that this was Bülow's corps appearing on his right flank.

Orders had just been written, but not yet despatched, to Grouchy telling him to draw nearer to Waterloo in order to cover this same right flank; and an urgent postscript was now added:

> A letter just intercepted announces that General Bülow is about to attack our flank. We believe that already we perceive this corps on the heists near St. Lambert. Lose not a single moment therefore in nearing and rejoining us in order to annihilate Bülow, whom you will take in the very act.

Had Grouchy been near enough to obey these orders the day of Waterloo might have had a different ending!

It was to be hours still before the Prussians could reach the field of battle. Not until three o'clock did they begin their progress through the Forêt de Paris. But their coming was nevertheless of immedi-

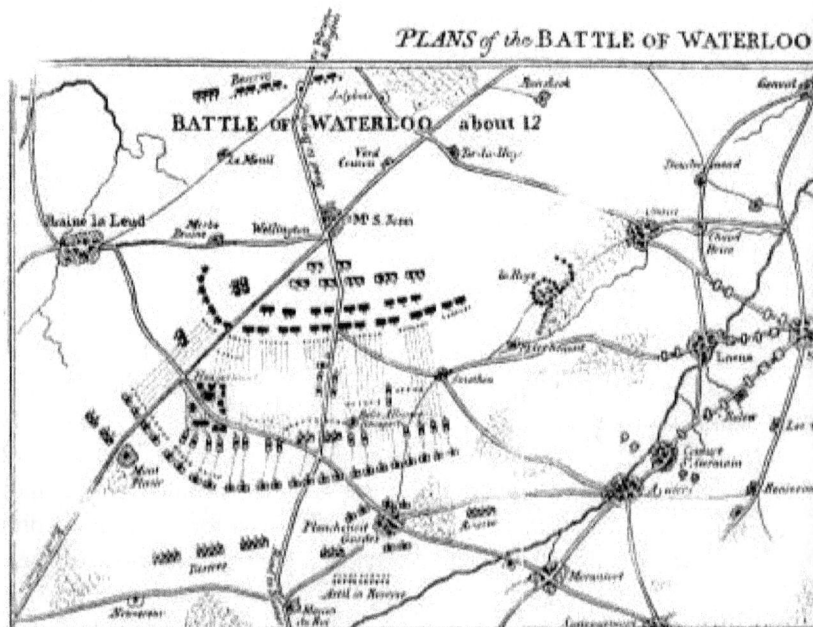

BATTLE OF WATERLOO about 12

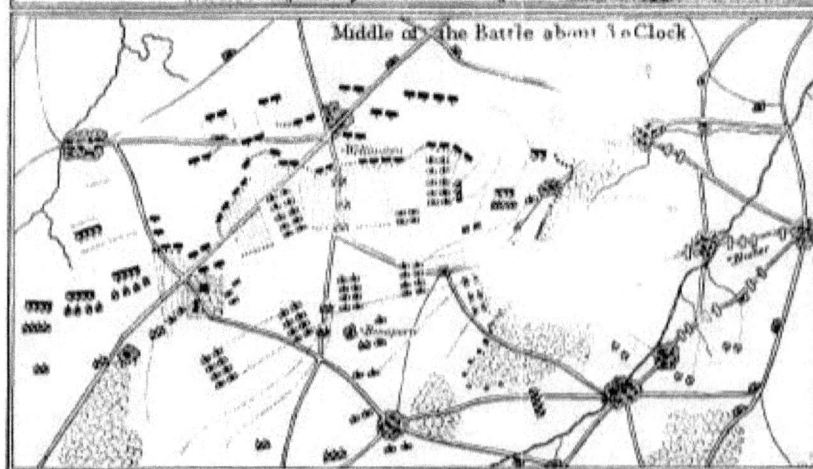

Middle of the Battle about 3 oClock

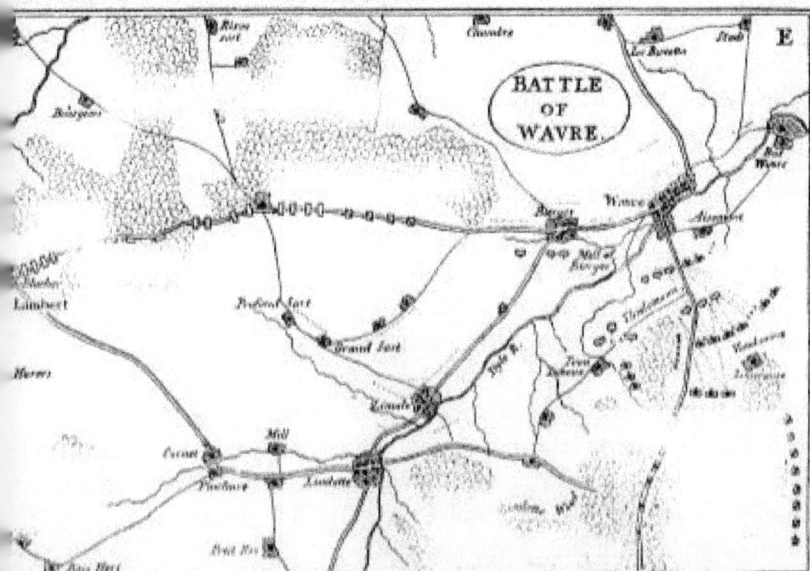

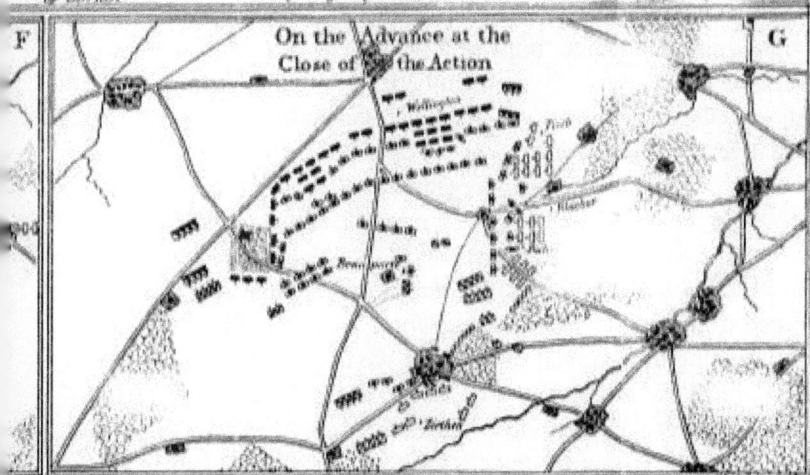

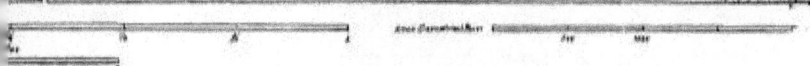

ate advantage; for at a time when he most needed all his forces to hurl them against the enemy's centre Napoleon was forced to detach 10,000 soldiers—2,300 cavalry under Doman and 7,000 infantry under Lobau—to guard at least the exits from the forest. Nor was this all. Later in the afternoon, knowing that within an hour or two Bülow would be upon him and that his forces would be needed in another direction, Napoleon countenanced a too hasty advance of Ney's cavalry; not supporting it with infantry to the extent that he would otherwise have done. The attack, although fierce and bloody to the last degree, was repulsed by the impact of the British infantry and by the coolness of the Iron Duke.

To return to the oncoming corps of Bülow, we have that general's own account of what happened after passing through the forest. Unobserved the troops had already been ranged in battle order and at half-past four, although only two brigades were as yet at hand, the head of the column emerged from the woods at Frischermont and the cannonading began. As an objective point the farm of Belle Alliance had been designated and towards it a regular and steady advance was made. The enemy retreated at first, but finally made a stand at the village of Plancenoit where, and on the heights beyond, Lobau had stationed his brigades. Blücher now commanded in person.

Napoleon had already perceived that were Plancenoit to be lost the Prussians would be directly in the rear of his reserves at Belle Alliance, and that the danger must be averted at all costs. More and more troops therefore were diverted from the attack on Wellington: first eight battalions of the young, then two battalions of the old guard. The latter drove the Prussians out of Plancenoit, a position which they were to find it very difficult to regain.

For the French emperor it was the most favourable moment of the day. For the fourth time the intrepid Ney, with what fresh troops he could muster, had returned to the attack on Wellington and had even wrested from him La Haye Sainte, where a battery was installed that raked the English centre at short range. We have it on the authority of a staff officer, Kennedy, that at no time was the "result so precarious." It was Kennedy who first informed Wellington that a regular gap had been made in his line of defence by the almost total destruction of Ompteda's, and the great weakening of Kielmansegge's, brigades. But the duke, strong in the knowledge that more Prussians, commanded by Zieten, were actually joining his left wing, drew forces from that direction to restore and strengthen his centre.

Zieten had been met by Müffling and implored to direct his march towards Wellington's left wing rather than join, as he had been ordered to do, with the force which attacked the French at Plancenoit. There was an unfortunate moment when Zieten, taking some of the duke's own Nassau soldiers for the enemy, fired into their midst and drove them from the village of Smohain in such a panic that they had gone a quarter of a mile before the error could be explained. Zieten's advance from this unexpected quarter—he finally effected his junction with Bülow and advanced with him against Belle Alliance—was the last straw that broke Napoleon's resistance. It came on top of a last bright flare of hope that left nothing but the ashes of despair when it died down.

Napoleon had rallied his troops to one supreme effort, advancing himself at the head of his guards. Just then the sound of cannon was heard far to the right in the direction of Papelotte; and the one thought of all was: Grouchy is coming! Deliverance is at hand! If Napoleon himself had any suspicion of the true state of the case he let no one remark it, but sent his adjutants down the lines to spread the glorious news. No tonic, no draught of burning spirits, could have been more effective. The final attack was made with the wildest fury of enthusiasm, and seemed about to be crowned with success, for a number of Wellington's soldiers took to flight. The duke himself, however, rallied the fugitives and repulsed the attack.

A very short time after this, the whole French Army was in confusion. Just what brought about this result is a matter of everlasting controversy between English and German writers, a controversy that began with the reports sent from the field and that has lost nothing of its bitterness in the intervening century. Gneisenau in the official report to which Blücher signed his name says:

At this moment (it was about 7.30 p.m.) the first columns of the corps of General Zieten arrived on the points of attack near the village of Smohain, on the enemy's right flank, and instantly charged. *This moment decided the defeat of the enemy.* His right wing was broken in three places; he abandoned his positions. Our troops rushed forward at the *pas de charge*, and attacked him on all sides, *while, at the same time, the whole English line advanced.*

The question at issue of course is: Did the attack of Zieten decide the defeat and flight of the French? An account not often cited, that published by the Austrian Government, (see Booth's *Battle of Waterloo*

10th edition, 1817), reads as follows:

> When the enemy saw himself taken in the rear, a flight com-
> menced, which soon became a total rout, when the two allied
> armies charged the enemy on all sides.

This agrees with the Prussian report, though apparently independent of it. Zieten's attack in the rear caused a flight which became a
rout when Wellington charged.

Wellington's own official report, in two successive clauses, grants
the full credit for the victory to Blücher's assistance and then entirely
takes that credit away:

> I should not do justice to my own feelings, or to Marshal Blüch-
> er and the Prussian Army, if I did not attribute the successful
> result of this arduous day to the cordial and timely assistance,
> I received from them. The operation of General Bülow upon
> the enemy's flank was a most decisive one, and, *even if I had not
> found myself in a situation to make the attack which produced the final
> result*, it would have forced the enemy to retire if his attacks
> should have failed, and would have prevented him from taking
> advantage of them if they should have unfortunately succeeded.

Wellington is wrong. He may have thought that he "made the attack that produced the final result," but the Prussians, who had their
faces, turned towards him while his back was to them, were in a better
position than he to see where the flight began. There is no need to
suspect dishonest intent. It is a matter in which Wellington might easily have been deceived.

A very reputable German historian, (Von Lettow-Vorbeck), infers
that the reports of the division commanders would have told a different story from that of their chief, and relates that Wellington, in
consequence, locked up all these reports in his private archives in
Apsley House and refused to let anyone see them; that he advised Sir
Walter Scott not to write an account of the battle, because even those
concerned were apt not to remember things in their exact order and
importance; and that to another person who asked for material the
duke said in so many words:

> You have my published report, is not that enough?

It must not be inferred that at the time of the battle at least Blücher's relations with Wellington were of any but the most cordial kind.

Blücher's son, during the pursuit to Genappe, wrote as a postscript to a letter of the field-marshal:

> Father Blücher embraced Wellington in such a hearty manner that everybody who was present said it was the most affecting scene that could be imagined.

It was at Belle Alliance that the meeting between the two commanders took place, and it must have been an unforgettable moment for both. A great hymn of victory was pouring from the throats of thousands of the German soldiers. The French were in a rushing, panicky flight. It was a *sauve qui peut!* Many believed that Zieten's coming in Grouchy's stead was part of a plot, and shouted wildly, "We are betrayed! We are betrayed!"

Blücher believed, as we already know, in following up a victory with the utmost emphasis; that failure to do so might necessitate another battle.

He persuaded Wellington now—whose troops were exhausted, though why more so than Blücher's, which had had the terrible march from Wavre, it is not altogether easy to see—to leave the pursuit in his hands. He personally rode after his victim that night as far as Genappe. Gneisenau called the pursuit a mad chase, *die reine Klapperjagd*, and declared later "it was the most glorious night of my life!"

Blücher himself found time, before he finally retired to rest, to write to his wife:

> You well remember what I promised you, and I have kept my word. The enemy's superiority of numbers obliged me to give way on the 17th; but on the 18th, in conjunction with my friend Wellington, I put an end to Napoleon's dancing. His army is completely routed, and the whole of his artillery, baggage, caissons, and equipages are in my hands. The insignia of all the different orders he had won have just been brought to me, having been found in his carriage in a casket. I had two horses killed under me yesterday. It will soon be all over with Bonaparte.

In an official letter written the next day Blücher has fresh details to add:

> The victory is the most complete that ever was gained. Napoleon escaped in the night without either hat or sword. I send both sword and hat today to the king. His most magnificently

embroidered state-mantle and his carriage are in my hands, as also his perspective glass with which he observed us during the battle. His jewels and all his valuables are the booty of our troops. . . .

A Prussian officer writes on the 24th, of Napoleon's seal ring which "now blazes on the hand of the hero, Gneisenau," and also of the great number of diamonds found:

The fusiliers sold four or five diamonds as large as a pea, or even larger, for a few *francs*.

Not only one carriage, but eight were taken and the accounts of what they contained make one think of the Arabian nights. One of the coaches, we are told, had been destined for the grand entry that Napoleon had intended to make into Brussels, and was to have been drawn by eight cream-coloured stallions. (From letter in Booth, i.)

The pursuit was kept up until Napoleon's army was dispersed in all directions. It had simply ceased to exist. There only remained Grouchy, who indeed, managed to bring back his corps in safety to France. Napoleon himself, as everyone knows, having returned to Paris and found the ministers as well as the deputies hostile to him abdicated the throne. Not so well known is the fact that he expressed his intention of crossing to North America and devoting his life to scientific work and to travel. Who knows what might have been the result? One thing seems certain that he would have been tempted upon the lecture platform, and would have earned unprecedented sums at a minimum cost for advertising.

Would he have been welcomed with open arms? It is difficult to say. But there is one bit of hitherto unpublished history that is interesting in this connection. The inhabitants of the island of St. Helena, off the Carolina coast—negroes for the greater part—were seized with such a panic when they first heard the name of Napoleon's destined place of banishment that they wrote a formal protest to the British Government.

Blücher, indeed, had views greatly at variance with the pleasant life Napoleon had mapped out for himself. He wrote on June 24th, while his own army and that of Wellington were still on the march to Paris:

Bonaparte has been deposed by the *corps législatif*, and General Morand has asked me to cease hostilities. You can readily understand that I would not hear of it, and I answered that Bonaparte dead or his surrender to me, and, at the same time the surrender of all the forts on the Maas and the Sambre, were the only conditions on which I would cease hostilities; that I was marching without a halt straight on Paris and if the Parisians did not kill or give up Napoleon they should feel my wrath as perjurers; that they had better remember Moscow.

Blücher came forward with other demands, too: the surrender of Paris, besides Laon, Soissons, and other fortresses; and also, the return of all the works of art Napoleon had stolen from different countries. Already after the first peace of Paris the great car of Victory with her four splendid steeds that Napoleon had lowered from the Brandenburg gate had been sent back to Berlin forming a load so heavy that it took twenty horses to draw it. But there were, besides, countless statues and paintings; one or two of the largest of which, indeed, still grace the Louvre Gallery.

The two armies, like fate, marched relentlessly on Paris. On June 28th, Blücher writes to his wife that he expects within three days to have entered the city, and adds:

> It is possible and highly probable that Bonaparte will be surrendered to me and Lord Wellington. My wisest course will doubtless be to have him shot. It will be rendering a service to mankind.

We have Blücher's directions to Müffling, who, it will be remembered, was his military *attaché* in Wellington's camp and concerted all measures with the duke:

> Bonaparte was placed under the ban by the declaration of the allied powers. The Duke of Wellington might, for parliamentary reasons, have scruples about carrying out the sentence. You will therefore direct the negotiations in this matter towards having Bonaparte surrendered to us so that he may be executed. Such is the requirement of everlasting justice, such the intent of the declaration of March 13th. Thus, will the blood of our soldiers, slain and mutilated on the 16th and 18th, be avenged.

A spirit of opposition, not on this one point alone but on others too, was developing between Blücher and. Wellington. The former was not at all pleased with the latter's designation of the battle as the "Battle of Waterloo." In the official report Gneisenau gave his reasons for wishing another name:

In the middle of the position occupied by the French Army, and exactly upon the height, is a farm called La Belle Alliance. The march of all the Prussian columns was directed towards this farm, which was visible from every side. It was there that Napoleon was during the battle; it was thence that he gave his orders, that he flattered himself with the hopes of victory; and it was there that his ruin was decided. There, too, it was, that, by a happy chance, Field-Marshal Blücher and Lord Wellington met in the dark and mutually saluted each other as victors. In commemoration of the alliance which now subsists between the English and Prussian nations, of the union of the two armies, and their reciprocal confidence, the field-marshal desired, that this battle should bear the name of La Belle Alliance.

That Wellington chose and adhered to the name of Waterloo—the Prussians, as we know, still adhere to the name of Belle Alliance—can only be taken as a sign that he wished the preponderance of credit for the victory to be on the English side.

In the matter of handing over Napoleon to the tender mercies of Blücher, Wellington was equally unyielding. Blücher gave way reluctantly, and Gneisenau wrote to Müffling:

The field-marshal also commissions me to have you inform the Duke of Wellington that it had been the field-marshal's intention to have Bonaparte executed on the same spot where the Duke of Enghien was shot, but that out of regard for the duke's wishes he would omit the execution; but that the duke must bear the responsibility of said omission.

Gneisenau had been as eager as Blücher to execute Napoleon, he wrote:

Should we not regard ourselves as the instruments of Providence, which had given us such a victory to the end that we should exercise eternal justice? Does not the death of the Duke of Enghien alone demand such vengeance? Shall we not expose ourselves to the reproaches of the Prussian, Russian, Spanish, and Portuguese peoples if we neglect to do justice?" Wellington's argument, on the other hand, was a strong one: that it was not for the generals but for the sovereigns to deal with so important a matter.

Neither Napoleon nor Paris was as yet so completely in Blücher's

BLÜCHER AND WELLINGTON AT BELLE ALLIANCE

hands as he had imagined. It is true, still on the 29th, he wrote to his wife:

> I stand before Paris. Wellington dined with me and we took counsel as to how to end the whole matter. Last night I had sent your brother to capture Bonaparte who was in Malmaison. The bridge had been burned or the *coup* would have succeeded.

Finally, simultaneously from opposite directions; and, in the endeavour, which failed, there was more bloodshed. But on July 3rd, just as Blücher was about to storm the city, Paris surrendered. Blücher wrote to his wife:

> In my last letter I said that your next letter should be from Paris. You see that I keep my word. But yesterday and today I have again lost nearly 3,000 men. I hope to God that they are the last in this war. I am heartily sick of the murdering.

It was agreed by the terms of the capitulation that the French garrisons should retire behind the Loire, and that the allies should once more make a formal entry into the city. To this last provision Wellington had objected heartily, but it was Blücher's turn to remain firm; he declared it to be a point of honour to "enjoy the same distinction that the French had enjoyed in Berlin, in Vienna, and in Moscow." And he gained his point. He wrote in connection with the surrender of Paris to his wife:

> I owe it all to the indescribable bravery and unexampled endurance of the troops as well as to my iron will. . . . God be thanked, the bloodshed will cease!

And to Knesebeck he wrote:

> Now, friend, my day's work is done!

Blücher had now a few days of glory in which he was practically ruler of Paris. He laid on the city a contribution of 100,000,000 *francs*—that sum it will be remembered had been fixed in his mind many months before—and demanded in addition that his troops be thoroughly re-equipped, even to the furnishing of fresh horses where needed. Each soldier was to be given a *douceur* equal to two months' pay. He was like Rhadamanthus in his severity. When the commander of the *château* of Vincennes refused to hand out munitions of war, the fortress was immediately invested. Blücher determined to blow up the

CELEBRATION OF NAPOLEON'S BIRTHDAY ON THE ISLAND OF ST. HELENA

Pont de Jena as a shameful monument of Prussia's humiliation. (See anonymous article in the *Allgemeine Militärzeitung, 7ter Jahrgang*; 1895.)

The bridge was immensely solid, being built of great blocks of stone. By July 6th, preparations for the explosion were already under way. On the 7th, Count Goltz, in Talleyrand's name, urged Blücher to desist, but the latter answered:

> The bridge shall be blown up and I should be pleased if Mr. Talleyrand would previously seat himself upon it! How can this despicable man call the bridge a precious monument? Our honour demands the destruction of this memorial erected to our shame!

On the 10th, some blasting was done, but on the 11th after Beugnot had promised in Louis XVIII.'s name that the bridge should receive another appellation, the attempt was abandoned.

Already Blücher's brief orgy of authority was over; for the monarchs, including Louis XVIII., entered Paris. A Prussian nobleman, (Marwitz), writes:

> Now Louis *dix huit*—whom the French called mockingly Louis *tout de suite* and Louis *biscuit* because he followed directly, and because he was baked over, as it were—came waddling into Paris behind the English Army and met there the three monarchs of Prussia, Austria, and Russia. Things at once assumed the appearance as though the whole war had been waged solely for his benefit and he once more took possession of France.

The further proceedings were one long series of vexations for Blücher. In the wake of the monarchs came the ministers and in the course of their deliberations every one of the measures that Blücher had taken, except that about the return of the works of art, was revoked. At a royal banquet the old commander-in-chief had eased his mind and had expressed "the pious wish that the diplomats would not for the second time destroy what the army had victoriously achieved with its blood." Yet that was exactly what happened. He was driven to express another pious wish, that "you gentlemen of the pen might come just for once under sharp fire to learn what the correction of your errors means." In vain he pleaded for the indemnity:

> Such an opportunity will not recur. Our finances need some such penalty, and we must not again leave France under the reproach of having been tricked by this rotten people. Talleyrand

NAPOLEON ON ST. HELENA

could threaten us in Vienna; here in Paris let him now pay. As far as our army is concerned I myself promised it that if Paris were conquered I would have it equipped anew and that they should receive two months' pay as a *douceur*. They deserved this and I must keep my word.

When he heard that his measures had definitely been revoked, he handed in his resignation. The king, he said had both orally and in writing approved his conduct, and now he was exposed to the reproaches of the whole French people:

I cannot and will not remain here any longer.

He was induced to remain by the consideration that the war had not, as he had anticipated, ended with the capitulation of Paris. There were still garrisons in numerous small French forts, and these were to hold out for several months. Eleven of them had been conquered by the Prussians alone before the end of September. On the 4th of October, Blücher himself writes that peace is as good as concluded though not yet publicly announced.

He is still very sore about the negotiations. He refused a renewed invitation of the prince regent to come to England, and, as he did so, expressed his mind very plainly:

Gracious Sir, it is regrettable that such unity is never to be found among ministers as has existed so beneficially in these last wars among companions in arms. When I learned of the divergence of views among the diplomats I left Paris so as not to have to witness how the French, who had sinned so grievously against God and man, were openly taken under the protection of some of the allies; and although I had sacrificed 26,000 brave Prussians no regard was paid to that at all, and everything that I had ordered for the general good was reversed because, according to the opinion of the bookworms it had not been done according to the rules. Heir Talleyrand and Fouché more readily obtained a hearing; and, on this occasion, too, have preserved the French from their just merited castigation.

******

It is better for us to leave Blücher here at the point where his life-work was completed than to enter into the trivial details of his last years. Strange to say, the great fatigues, even of the Waterloo campaign, had not permanently injured his health. Once before leaving Paris

THE CHARIOT OF VICTORY ON THE BRANDENBURG GATE

he rode out to the races and met with an accident which might have left a serious impression on a man much younger in years. His horse while in full gallop caught its foot in a rope barrier and Blücher fell, dislocating his shoulder. Yet he seems to have been disabled only for a short time. He lived to be seventy-seven years of age passing his winters in Berlin, in a palace, near the Brandenburg Gate, that had been bestowed upon him, and his summers on his Silesian estates.

Here he hunted, gamed, attended banquets, and improved his land until the end. When he met an Englishman, he took pleasure in speaking of the Battle of "Belle Alliance" and grew angry when one mentioned "Waterloo." We have the authority of his old *aide-de-camp* Nostitz for it that when his last great enemy came, when death stalked up to him and refused to be brushed from his path as Napoleon had been, he turned and faced him with "the calmness of soul of a really great man."

www.ingramcontent.com/pod-product-compliance
Lightning Source LLC
Chambersburg PA
CBHW032043080426
42733CB00006B/182